Cases and Materials on The Law of the European Union

Authors

Daryll Bewick

Chris Garside

Alex Lawson

Karl Sharp

Editors

Glenn Robinson

Karl Sharp

First edition July 2010

Fifth edition July 2015

Published ISBN 9781 4727 3343 6

Previous ISBN 9781 4727 2121 1

British Library Cataloguing-in-Publication Data
A catalogue record for this book is available
from the British Library

Published by
BPP Learning Media Ltd
BPP House, Aldine Place
London W12 8AA
www.bpp.com/learningmedia

Printed in the United Kingdom by
Charlesworth Press

Flanshaw Way
Flanshaw Lane
Wakefield
WF2 9LP

Extracts from the Law Reports, the Weekly Law
Reports and the Industrial Cases Reports are
reproduced by permission of:

The Incorporated Council of Law Reporting for
England and Wales, Megarry House,
119 Chancery Lane, London WC2A 1PP

Extracts from the All England Reports, and other
LexisNexis titles are reproduced by permission of
LexisNexis which is a trading name of,
Reed Elsevier (UK) Limited, Registered office, 1-3
Strand, London WC2N 5JR

Extracts from Westlaw publications (including
journal articles) are reproduced with permission of
Thomson Reuters (Legal) Limited, Registered Office,
100 Avenue Road, London NW3 3PF

Extracts from the Office of Fair Trading are
reproduced under the terms of the Open
Government Licence:
http://reference.data.gov.uk/id/open-
government-licence

Contents

Index of Cases

A

B

C

D

E

F

G

H

O

P

R

S

T

U

V

W

Introduction

When reading this case book, it is important to recognise that the current legal framework governing the European Union is the culmination of a series of treaties which have established and transformed the framework over several decades. These can be traced back to the **Treaty Establishing the European Coal and Steel Community 1951 ('ECSC')** which established the first European community. Two further communities were established a few years later by the **Treaty Establishing the European Atomic Energy Community 1957 ('EUROATOM')** and the **Treaty Establishing European Economic Community 1957 ('EEC')**. The latter is more commonly known as the Treaty of Rome. Further treaties provided for various reforms as well as the accession of new Member States including the United Kingdom in1973. It was not until 1993 that the European Union was born under the **Treaty on European Union 1992 ('TEU')**. This is more commonly known as the Maastricht Treaty. It provided for the European Economic Community to be retained as one pillar of the European Union but for it to be renamed the European Community. The EEC Treaty was accordingly renamed the **Treaty Establishing the European Community ('EC')**. Further amendments were made over the next two decades by the Treaty of Amsterdam 1997 and the Treaty of Nice 2003. The Lisbon Treaty of 2007 has now established the current legal framework based on two treaties. One is the TEU. The other is the EC Treaty which has been renamed the **Treaty on the Functioning of the European Union ('TFEU')**.

One of the consequences of all of this is that the designation of treaty articles, such as their number, in cases that pre-date the changes in the Lisbon Treaty will almost invariable differ from that in the current governing treaties. Articles referred to in an earlier case may have been renumbered over subsequent years, possibly more than once. The treaty may have been renamed or an article moved to a different treaty. An article may have been repealed in whole or part. In particular, this fate befell a number of articles in the original EEC Treaty which made provision for a transitional period. Some articles which have been repealed now have their function performed by completely different provisions. Others do not. One of the challenges in reading EU law cases is to navigate these changes. This case book addresses this issue by referring not only to the designation of the relevant treaty article used in the case but, where possible, also to the corresponding designation in the current treaties. An example of this is "Article 48 EEC (now Article 45 TFEU)". Some caution should be exercised nevertheless. There may be some instances in which, due to amendment, the wording of the current provision does not retain exactly the same wording as the provision being addressed in the earlier case.

The acronyms used in this case book to identify the treaties reflect those used by the courts of the European Union and the other institutions.

1

Enforcent In National Courts

Topic List

Introduction

The finding of individual remedies under an international treaty originally conceived as commercial and enforceable by States or EU institutions required a change of thinking on the part of the Court of Justice. This involved a move from the international law norm to one based upon the concept that as this is a 'new legal order' it needed new legal remedies. Such thinking inevitably engaged with fundamental and emotive issues such as state sovereignty. It was not usual for an international court to specify the way a state should absorb international rules and the need for case law was inevitable. This departure from the traditional international law approach allowed individuals to challenge both EU law and its implementation by the Member States in a way not possible without it. As a result any EU measures, not just those that were directly applicable (and so part of the national law) were opened up to challenge.

1.1 Direct Effect

It is perhaps difficult to perceive the radical nature of the decision in the 1963 case of *NV Algemene Transporten Expeditie Onderneming van Gend en Loos v Nederlandse Administratie der Berlingen* (Case 26/62) [1963] CMLR 105 after it has been around for so many years. During those years its basic message has been added to and pushed and pulled in different directions. It perhaps just seems as if it ought to be have been there from the start. Radical though it may have been, *van Gend en Loos* has quickly spawned a small family of remedies designed to address the issue of individual losses resulting from the interplay of State and EU legislation. This family is the subject of the present chapter and, dysfunctional though it undoubtedly is, serves to illustrate some imaginative attempts to grapple with the legal problems presented by a developing Community.

NV Algemene Transporten Expeditie Onderneming van Gend en Loos v Nederlandse Administratie der Berlingen (Case 26/62) [1963] CMLR 105

Panel: Donner P, Delvaux, Rossi, Riese, Hammes, Trabucchi and Lecourt, JJ, Herr Karl Roemer, Advocate-General

Legislation: Article 12 EEC Treaty ('the Treaty of Rome 1957'). This was a predecessor to Article 30 TFEU.

In the excerpts: Articles 169, 170, 177, 187, 189, 191 and 192 EEC are now Articles 258, 259, 267, 280, 288, 297(1) and 298 TFEU respectively

Facts: In 1960 van Gend en Loos (a Dutch company) imported a quantity of the chemical emulsion ureaformaldehyde from Germany into the Netherlands. Due to a recent change in the classification of this substance the Dutch tariff charged upon its import had risen from 3% to 8%. As a result van Gend en Loos appealed to the national Dutch Inspector of Import and Excise Duties and then to an internal tribunal (the Nederlandse Tariefcommissie) that the imposition of this increase after the entry into force of the EEC Treaty violated Article 12 of the EEC Treaty. The Tariefcommissie duly referred two questions to the Court of Justice:

(a)   Whether Article 12 EEC could be applied within a Member State by the citizens of that Member State enforcing individual rights which could be protected by the national courts.

(b)   If this were so whether the increase of the duty to 8% was an illegal increase within the meaning of Article 12 or simply a reasonable alteration that was not so prohibited.

ADVOCATE-GENERAL ROEMER

He who is familiar with the law of the Community knows that in fact it is not restricted to the contractual relations between a number of States viewed as subjects of the law of nations. The Community has its own institutions, independent of the member-States, endowed with the power to take administrative action and to issue legal rules which directly create rights and obligations not only for the member-States and their administrative authorities but also for the nationals of the member-States. We can deduce this clearly from Articles 187, 189, 191 and 192 of the Treaty.

Nonetheless as far as the broad issues concerning import and export duties were concerned:

The subtle terminology of the Treaty, the material contents and the context surely imply … only an obligation on the member-States.

Further, we find a whole series of provisions which according to their content and context, although drafted in the form of a declaration, clearly envisage only obligations of the member-States and not direct internal legal effects… .

He went on to advise that internal effect was not possible here:

…large parts of the Treaty certainly contain obligations on the member-States only, and do not contain rules with a direct internal effect.

Despite this opinion the Court of Justice found the opposite, declaring a result in favour of van Gend en Loos and against the Dutch government. It expressed its reasons for such a judgment in the following terms:

JUDGMENT

The first question posed by the Tariefcommissie is whether Article 12 of the Treaty has an immediate effect in internal law, in that nationals of the member-States could, on the basis of the Article, enforce rights which the national court should protect.

To know whether the provisions of an international treaty have such an effect it is necessary to look at its spirit, its economic aspect and the terms used.

The purpose of the E.E.C. Treaty—to create a Common Market, the functioning of which directly affects the citizens of the Community—implies that this Treaty is more than an agreement creating only mutual obligations between the contracting parties. This interpretation is confirmed by the preamble to the Treaty which, in addition to mentioning governments, affects individuals. The creation of organs institutionalising

 Decipher
The first two terms are perhaps a little unusual for an English lawyer more familiar with the literal approach.

certain sovereign rights, the exercise of which affects both member-States and citizens is a particular example. In addition, the nationals of the States, united into the Community, are required to collaborate in the functioning of that Community, by means of the European Parliament and the Economic and Social Council. Furthermore, the role of the Court of Justice in the framework of Article 177, the aim of which is to ensure uniformity of interpretation of the Treaty by the national courts, confirms that the States recognised in Community law have an authority capable of being invoked by their nationals before those courts. We must conclude from this that the Community constitutes a new legal order in international law, for whose benefit the States have limited their sovereign rights, albeit within limited fields, and the subjects of which comprise not only the member-States but also their nationals. Community law, therefore, apart from legislation by the member-States, not only imposes obligations on individuals but also confers on them legal rights. The latter arise not only when an explicit grant is made by the Treaty, but also through obligations imposed, in a clearly defined manner, by the Treaty on individuals as well as on member-States and the Community institutions. ...

The text of Article 12 sets out a clear and unconditional prohibition, which is not a duty to act but a duty not to act. This duty is imposed without any power in the States to subordinate its application to a positive act of internal law. The prohibition is perfectly suited by its nature to produce direct effects in the legal relations between the member-States and their citizens.

The carrying out of Article 12 does not require legislative intervention by the States. The fact that the Article designates the member-States as subject to the duty to abstain does not imply that their nationals may not be the beneficiaries of the duty.

The fact that the Treaty, in the aforementioned Articles, allows the Commission and the member-States to bring before the Court a State which has not carried out its obligations, does not imply that individuals may not invoke these obligations, in appropriate cases, before a national court; and likewise, the fact that the Treaty puts at the disposal of the Commission means to ensure respect for the duties imposed on those subject to it does not exclude the possibility of invoking violation of these obligations in litigation between individuals before national courts. To limit the sanctions against violation of Article 12 by member-States merely to the procedures laid down in Articles 169 and 170 would remove all direct judicial protection of the individual rights of their nationals. Reliance on these Articles would risk being ineffective if it had to be exercised after the enforcement of a national decision which misinterpreted the requirements of the Treaty. The vigilance of individuals interested in protecting their rights creates an effective control additional to that entrusted by Articles 169 and 170 to the diligence of the Commission and the member-States.

For these reasons, according to the spirit, the economic aspect and the terms of the Treaty, Article 12 should be interpreted in such a sense as to produce direct effect and to create individual rights which internal courts should protect.

Article 12 of the E.E.C. Treaty has direct application within the territory of a member-State and ensures the benefit of citizens whose individual rights the internal courts should protect. ...

 Alert

 Links
1. Note 'clear and unconditional' legislation is now what is looked for to establish direct effect.
2. By emphasising the negative duty the court created subsequent doubt whether direct effect could apply to a positive duty.

 Decipher
Note the Court of Justice's interchange between direct application and direct effect at this early stage.

Van Gend en Loos is the case that starts the whole direct effect ball rolling. Notice how the Court of Justice does not follow the advice of the Advocate-General, who despite beginning with a recognition that individual rights could exist under the EEC Treaty ultimately pulls back from this conclusion with regard to Article 12 of that Treaty. The Court not only decides that direct effect can apply to the Treaty generally but that it applies to Article 12 in particular.

As seen in this case, a major area of weakness of the EEC Treaty (as originally drafted) was that it failed to provide adequate measures of enforcement against those Member States who infringed Treaty obligations. Article 169 of the Treaty (now Article 258 TFEU), for instance, while allowing the Commission to take an infringing State to the Court of Justice, failed to specify a penalty of value to the individual EU citizen, nor a method by which such an individual could personally seek redress against such a State in their own national courts. *Van Gend en* Loos tackled the issue head on, widening the scope by which the Treaty could be enforced by allowing the individual the right to enforce such obligations. The Court of Justice subsequently held that the direct effect of Articles could be applied to actions between private parties (horizontal direct effect) in *Defrenne v SABENA (No 2)* (Case 43/75) [1976] 2 CMLR 98.

Direct effect was extended in its application from articles to decisions in *Franz Grad v Finanzamt Traunstein* (Case 9/70) [1971] CMLR 1. Part of its reasoning in that case had also declared that regulations could have direct effect. This was confirmed in *Politi a.s.a. v Ministry of Finance of the Italian Republic* (Case 43/71) [1973] CMLR 60. However for a while it had been believed that directives were incapable of receiving direct effect due to their conditional nature (conditional upon implementation by a member state). *Van Duyn* was the case in which the Court of Justice grasped the nettle of unconditionality and decided that a directive could be directly effective.

Van Duyn v Home Office (Case 41/74) [1975] 1 CMLR 1

Panel: Lecourt P, Ó Dálaigh, Lord Mackenzie Stuart, Donner, Monaco, Mertens de Wilmars, Pescatore, Kutscher and Sørensen, JJ, M Henri Mayras, Advocate-General

Legislation: Article 48 EEC (now Article 45 TFEU); Directive 64/221

In the excerpts: Articles 177 and 189 EEC are now Articles 267 and 288 TFEU respectively

Facts: The UK government considered the Church of Scientology of California to be a 'pseudo-philosophical cult' that was socially harmful albeit not unlawful. In an attempt to curb its growth foreign Scientologists were prevented from entering the country to study or work.

Yvonne Van Duyn, a Dutch national, landed at Gatwick airport to take up a secretary's job at the Church's headquarters in East Grinstead, Surrey, only to be sent back to the Netherlands by UK immigration the same day. As a consequence she began a High Court action invoking Article 48 and Directive 64/221 to allege a breach of her right of freedom of movement.

The High Court asked three preliminary questions of the Court of Justice:

1. Was Article 48 EEC (now Article 45 TFEU) directly effective?
2. Was Directive 64/221 directly effective?
3. Could membership of a cult be considered 'personal conduct' entitling the UK to refuse entry for reasons of public policy?

It is question two (could a directive be given direct effect) that is the area of interest here but the examination of question one also served to reinforce the developed principles.

ADVOCATE-GENERAL HENRI MAYRAS

The first question will not delay us.

The criteria which have over several years emerged from your case law to determine whether a provision of Community law, and in particular a rule laid down in the EEC Treaty , is directly applicable in the sense that it confers on individuals rights on which they can rely in proceedings before national courts, are clearly fixed:

—   the provision must impose on the member-States a clear and precise obligation;

—   it must be unconditional, i.e., not accompanied by any reservation; if, however, it is subject to certain exceptions, they must be strictly defined and delimited;

—   finally, the application of the Community rule must not be conditional on any subsequent legislation either of the Community institutions or of those of the member-States, and must not lead to the latter having an effective power of discretionary judgment as to the application of the rule in question.

He goes on to provide justifications for advancing the principle to directives in addition to articles and regulations:

Less obvious is the solution to the second question which concerns, as we have seen, the direct applicability of the Council directive of 25 February 1964.

Article 189 of the Treaty distinguishes between regulations, which are not only binding but also directly applicable in the member-States, and directives, which are also binding, to be sure, for the States but which do not in principle have direct effect in so far as they leave to the States the choice of the methods of bringing them into operation.

But, keeping outside formal legal categories, you have held in *Grad v Finanzamt Traunstein* (9/70), *Transports Lesage et Cie v Hauptzollamt Freiburg* (20/70) and *Haselhorst v Finanzamt Düsseldorf-Altstadt* (23/70) that, apart from regulations, other Community acts mentioned in Article 189 can produce direct effect, particularly in those cases in which the Community authorities have obliged the member-States to adopt a given behaviour; the effective power of such acts, you said, would be weakened if individuals could not, in such circumstances, rely in legal proceedings on the rights which are conferred on them by decisions of such nature, even though they were not enacted in the form of regulations.

Even clearer is the statement in your judgment in *S.A.C.E. v Italian Ministry of Finance* (33/70): a Directive, 'the purpose of which was to impose on a member-State a final date for the performance of a Community obligation, not only affects the relations between the Commission and that State but also entails consequences which may be invoked ... by individuals whenever by its nature the provision establishing this obligation is directly applicable'.

Faced with a directive we must therefore examine in each case whether the wording, the nature and the logic of the provisions in question are capable of producing direct effects between the addressee member-States and their citizens.

The Court of Justice answered the first two questions in the following way:

JUDGMENT

First Question

4.   By the first question, the Court is asked to say whether Article 48 of the E.E.C. Treaty is directly applicable so as to confer on individuals rights enforceable by them in the courts of a member-State.

5.   It is provided, in Article 48 (1) and (2), that freedom of movement for workers shall be secured by the end of the transitional period and that such freedom shall entail 'the abolition of any discrimination based on nationality between workers of member-States as regards employment, remuneration and other conditions of work and employment' .

6.   These provisions impose on member-States a precise obligation which does not require the adoption of any further measure on the part either of the Community institutions or of the member-States and which leaves them, in relation to its implementation, no discretionary power.

7.   Paragraph (3), which defines the rights implied by the principle of freedom of movement for workers, subjects them to limitations justified on grounds of public policy, public security or public health. The application of these limitations is, however, subject to judicial control, so that a member-State's rights to invoke the limitations does not prevent the provisions of Article 48, which enshrine the principle of freedom of movement for workers, from conferring on individuals rights which are enforceable by them and which the national courts must protect.

8.   The reply to the first question must therefore be in the affirmative.

 Decipher
In these paragraphs the Court of Justice confirms that Article 45 satisfies the *van Gend en Loos* criteria.

Second Question

9. The second question asks the Court to say whether Council Directive 64/221 of 25 February 1964 on the co-ordination of special measures concerning the movement and residence of foreign nationals which are justified on grounds of public policy, public security or public health is directly applicable so as to confer on individuals rights enforceable by them in the courts of a member-State.

10. It emerges from the order making the reference that the only provision of the Directive which is relevant is that contained in Article 3 (1) which provides that 'measures taken on grounds of public policy or public security shall be based exclusively on the personal conduct of the individual concerned'.

11. The United Kingdom observes that, since Article 189 of the Treaty distinguishes between the effects ascribed to regulations, directives and decisions, it must therefore be presumed that the Council, in issuing a directive rather than making a regulation, must have intended that the directive should have an effect other than that of a regulation and accordingly that the former should not be directly applicable.

12. If, however, by virtue of the provisions of Article 189 regulations are directly applicable and, consequently, may by their very nature have direct effects, it does not follow from this that other categories of acts mentioned in that Article can never have similar effects. It would be incompatible with the binding effect attributed to a directive by Article 189 to exclude, in principle, the possibility that the obligation which it imposes may be invoked by those concerned. In particular, where the Community authorities have, by directive, imposed on member-States the obligation to pursue a particular course of conduct, the useful effect of such an act would be weakened if individuals were prevented from relying on it before their national courts and if the latter were prevented from taking it into consideration as an element of Community law. Article 177, which empowers national courts to refer to the Court questions concerning the validity and interpretation of all acts of the Community institutions, without distinction, implies furthermore that these acts may be invoked by individuals in the national courts. It is necessary to examine, in every case, whether the nature, general scheme and wording of the provision in question are capable of having direct effects on the relations between member-States and individuals.

13. By providing that measures taken on grounds of public policy shall be based exclusively on the personal conduct of the individual concerned, Article 3 (1) of Directive 64/221 is intended to limit the discretionary power which national laws generally confer on the authorities responsible for the entry and expulsion of foreign nationals. First, the provision lays down an obligation which is not subject to any exception or condition and which, by its very nature, does not require the intervention of any act on the part either of the institutions of the Community or of member-States. Secondly, because member-States are thereby obliged, in implementing a clause which derogates from one of the fundamental principles of the Treaty in favour of individuals, not to take account of factors extraneous to

 Decipher
Here the Court of Justice answers the UK arguments and justifies the extension of direct effect to the directives.

personal conduct, legal certainty for the persons concerned requires that they should be able to rely on this obligation even though it has been laid down in a legislative act which has no automatic direct effect in its entirety.

14. If the meaning and exact scope of the provision raise questions of interpretation, these questions can be resolved by the courts, taking into account also the procedure under Article 177 of the Treaty.

15. Accordingly, in reply to the second question, Article 3 (1) of Council Directive 64/221 of 25 February 1964 confers on individuals rights which are enforceable by them in the courts of a member-State and which the national courts must protect.

With regard to the third question, the Court of Justice went on to find that associations which a person makes were part of 'personal conduct' and as such fell under the discretionary power to refuse entry given to member states under 'public policy'. Van Duyn lost her case.

The Court of Justice's justification for the extension of direct effect to directives in *Van Duyn* has been criticised for being weak. Certain courts in Germany and France initially refused to give direct effect to directives. The Court of Justice subsequently refined its rationale in *Ratti* where it also clarified when a directive will have direct effect.

Pubblico Ministero v Tullio Ratti (Case 148/78) [1980] 1 CMLR 96

Panel: Mertens de Wilmars P, Lord Mackenzie Stuart PPC, Pescatore, Sørensen, O'Keeffe, Bosco and Touffait JJ. Herr Gerhard Reischl, Advocate-General

Legislation: Directives 73/173 and 77/728

Facts: An Italian company Silvam (represented in all that occurred in this case by Mr Ratti) packaged its solvents in containers the labels of which complied with EU Directive 73/173 and its varnishes in containers the labels of which complied with Directive 77/728. Neither Directive had been implemented by the Italian state (although the Government still had time to implement Directive 77/728). Italy still enforced its own more stringent earlier law in this area. Mr Ratti was duly prosecuted for breaching this Italian law. The national court referred a number of issues to the Court of Justice amongst which the following two are of relevance here:

(a) Did Directive 73/173 have direct effect and so confer individual rights which ought to be protected by the Italian court?

(b) Did Directive 77/728 protect a person acting upon a legitimate expectation in complying with the requirements of a directive before the expiry of the period within which the member state must comply with the directive?

JUDGMENT

The answer to question one was self evident as long as the *van Gend en Loos* criteria could be satisfied and the Court duly announced this:

1. As far as solvents are concerned, that legislation ought, at the material time, to have been amended in order to comply with Directive 73/173 of 4 June 1973, the provisions of which member-States were supposed to incorporate into their internal legal orders by 8 December 1974 at the latest, an obligation which the Italian Government has not fulfilled. ...

4. That amendment would have resulted in the repeal of the provision of the Italian Act which the accused is charged with contravening and would consequently have altered the conditions for applying the criminal sanctions contained in the law in question...

21. Particularly in cases in which the Community authorities have, by means of directive, placed member-States under a duty to adopt a certain course of action, the effectiveness of such an act would be weakened if persons were prevented from relying on it in legal proceedings and national courts prevented from taking it into consideration as an element of Community law.

22. Consequently a member-State which has not adopted the implementing measures required by the directive in the prescribed periods may not rely, as against individuals, on its own failure to perform the obligations which the directive entails.

23. It follows that a national court requested by a person who has complied with the provisions of a directive not to apply a national provision incompatible with the directive not incorporated into the internal legal order of a defaulting member-State, must uphold that request if the obligation in question is unconditional and sufficiently precise

24. Therefore the answer to the first question must be that after the expiration of the period fixed for the implementation of a directive a member-State may not apply its internal law — even if it is provided with penal sanctions — which has not yet been adapted in compliance with the directive, to a person who has complied with the requirements of the directive.

Question two, however was not so clear:

5. As regards the packaging and labelling of varnishes, Directive 77/728 of 7 November 1977 had, at the material time, been adopted by the Council, but by virtue of Article 12 thereof member-States have until 9 November 1979 to bring into force the laws, regulations and administrative provisions necessary to comply therewith.

 Decipher
Here the Court of Justice advances a more refined justification for the extension of direct effect to the directives.

As a result could Directive 77/728 be:

39. ...[I]immediately and directly applicable with regard to the obligations imposed on member-States to refrain from action as from the date of notification of that directive in a case where a person, acting upon a legitimate expectation, has complied with the provisions of that directive before the expiry of the period within which the member-State must comply with the said directive.

40. The objective of that directive is analogous to that of Directive 73/173 in that it lays down similar rules for preparations intended to be used as paints, varnishes, printing inks, adhesives and similar products, and containing dangerous substances.

41. Article 12 of that directive provides that member-States must implement it within 24 months of its notification, which took place on 9 November 1977.

42. That period has not yet expired and the States to which the directive was addressed have until 9 November 1979 to incorporate the provisions of Directive 77/728 into their internal legal orders.

43. It follows that, for the reasons expounded in the grounds of the answer to the national court's first question, it is only at the end of the prescribed period and in the event of the member-State's default that the directive — and in particular Article 9 thereof — will be able to have the effects described in the answer to the first question.

44. Until that date is reached the member-States remain free in that field.

45. If one member-State has incorporated the provisions of a directive into its internal legal order before the end of the period prescribed therein, that fact cannot produce any effect with regard to the other member-States.

46. In conclusion, since a directive by its nature imposes obligations only on member-States, it is not possible for an individual to plead the principle of 'legitimate expectation' before the expiry of the period prescribed for its implementation.

47. Therefore the answer to the fifth question must be that Directive 77/728 of the Council of the European Communities of 7 November 1977 ... cannot bring about with respect to any individual who has complied with the provisions of the said directive before the expiration of the adaptation period prescribed for the member-State any effect capable of being taken into consideration by national courts.

 Decipher
It was the fact that Germany had already incorporated the directive and Silvam exported to Germany that had prompted Silvam to the early use of the directive.

Thus, directives will have direct effect when date for implementation has passed and the Member State has not adopted the measures required by the directive.

As noted above, the Court of Justice had held in *Defrenne v SABENA (No 2)* (Case 43/75) [1976] 2 CMLR 98 that a Treaty article could have direct effect against a private party. Further case law was necessary to establish whether a directive can be enforced against a private company or individual.

Marshall v Southampton and South West Hampshire Area Health Authority (Teaching) Case 152/84 [1986] 1 CMLR 688

Panel: Lord Mackenzie Stuart CJ, Everling and Bahlmann PPC, Bosco, Koopmans, Due and O'Higgins JJ, Sir Gordon Slynn, Advocate-General

Legislation: Directive 76/207

In the excerpts: Articles 189 and 191 EEC are now Articles 288 and 297(1) TFEU respectively.

Facts: Miss Marshall had been employed as a Senior Dietician by the Health Authority from 1974 until 1980 when she was dismissed solely because she had reached the Authorities compulsory retirement age (of 60 for women and 65 for men). While she had in fact been allowed to work until she had reached 62 she claimed the differing retirement ages to be contrary to the Sex Discrimination Directive 76/207 as a result of which she had suffered financially and in terms of the satisfaction she obtained from her job. Her case reached the Employment Appeals Tribunal before a number of questions were raised as preliminary references to the Court of Justice. For our purpose the central issue was the contention of both the Authority and the UK government that a directive which has not been implemented cannot be relied on by one private individual against another; and that where the State is acting as an employer, it should be treated in the same way as a private employer.

ADVOCATE-GENERAL SLYNN

I remain, despite the arguments in this case and in the case of Roberts, of the view expressed in my opinion in Becker that a directive not addressed to an individual cannot of itself impose obligations on him. It is, in cases like the present, addressed to member-States and not to the individual. The obligations imposed by such a directive are on the member-States. Such a directive does not have to be notified to the individual and it is only published in the Official Journal by way of information—in my view far too tenuous a link with the individual concerned to create a legal obligation.

Despite the general phrases to which I have referred, I read the Court's judgment as saying implicitly, as I said explicitly, that a directive comes into play only to enable rights to be claimed by individuals against the State in default. The State cannot rely on its own failure to confer those rights. The citizen may assert them against the State either as a sword or as a shield.

To give what is called 'horizontal effect' to directives would totally blur the distinction between regulations and directives which the Treaty establishes in Articles 189 and 191.

This reasoning was to be accepted by the Court of Justice:

JUDGMENT

43.   The respondent and the United Kingdom propose ... that a directive may, in certain specific circumstances, have direct effect as against a member-State in so far as the latter may not rely on its failure to perform its obligations under the directive. However, they maintain that a directive can never impose obligations directly on individuals and that it can only have direct effect against a member-State *qua* public authority and not against a member-State *qua* employer. As an employer a State is no different from a private employer. It would not therefore be proper to put persons employed by the State in a better position than those who are employed by a private employer.

48.   With regard to the argument that a directive may not be relied upon against an individual, it must be emphasised that according to Article 189 of the EEC Treaty the binding nature of a directive, which constitutes the basis for the possibility of relying on the directive before a national court, exists only in relation to 'each member-State to which it is addressed'. It follows that a directive may not of itself impose obligations on an individual and that a provision of a directive may not be relied upon as such against such a person. It must therefore be examined whether, in this case, the respondent must be regarded as having acted as an individual.

Alert

49.   In that respect it must be pointed out that where a person involved in legal proceedings is able to rely on a directive as against the State he may do so regardless of the capacity in which the latter is acting, whether as employer or public authority. In either case it is necessary to prevent the State from taking advantage of its own failure to comply with Community law.

Decipher
A Directive has direct effect against an organ of the State, including a public authority.

50.   It is for the national court to apply those considerations to the circumstances of each case; the Court of Appeal has, however, stated in the order for reference that the respondent, Southampton and South West Hampshire Area Health Authority (Teaching), is a public authority.

51.   The argument submitted by the United Kingdom that the possibility of relying on provisions of the directive against the respondent *qua* organ of the State would give rise to an arbitrary and unfair distinction between the rights of State employees and those of private employees does not justify any other conclusion. Such a distinction may easily be avoided if the member-State concerned has correctly implemented the directive in national law.

In *Marshall* Miss Marshall had been able to bring her action because the Health Authority could be made out to be an organ of the state allowing for vertical direct effect. Given that there was no horizontal direct effect granted to directives the definable parameters of the state were clearly going to be of great importance. Not surprisingly the Court of Justice has taken an expansive definition of the state over the course of a number of cases. *Foster* is the seminal case in establishing the guidelines as to what ought to be seen as state, public body or emanation of the state.

The ground rules for the direct effect of a directive were beginning to slot into place. But the question remained: for the application of direct effect, how far did the concept of the 'State' extend?

Foster and Others v British Gas Plc (Case 188/89) [1990] 2 CMLR 833

Panel: Slynn PC, Kakouris, Schockweiler and Zuleeg PPC, Mancini, Joliet, O'Higgins, Mohitinho de Almeida, Rodriguez Iglesias, Grévisse and Díez de Velasco JJ. Walter Van Gerven, Advocate-General

Legislation: Article 5(1) of Directive 76/207

Facts: Mrs Foster and other appellants were taking a sex discrimination action under Directive 76/207 against their compulsory retirement at 60 instead of the 65 required for male employees of the British Gas Corporation. The House of Lords submitted to the Court of Justice the sole question whether the BGC was a state body against which a directive could be applied.

ADVOCATE-GENERAL VAN GERVAN

'...in *Marshall* the Court stated that persons may only rely on provisions such as Article 5(1) of Directive 76/207 in their relations with 'the State,' in its capacity as 'employer or public authority,' since 'it is necessary to prevent the State from taking advantage of its own failure to comply with Community law.' In paragraph 48, on the other hand, the possibility of relying upon such a provision against an individual is excluded, inasmuch as a directive may not of itself impose obligations on an individual. In academic terminology, that means that where the period for their implementation has expired provisions of directives which from the point of view of their content are unconditional and sufficiently precise have 'vertical direct effect' but no 'horizontal direct effect.'

The reference for a preliminary ruling thus concerns the issue whether at the material time the BGC was 'the State' or 'an individual.'...

He summarised the legal status of BGC in the following terms:

...The BGC was a body with legal personality operating under the supervision of the authorities and having a monopoly on the supply of gas to homes and businesses in Great Britain. The members of the BGC were appointed by the Secretary of State, and he also determined their remuneration. ...The task of the BGC was to develop and maintain an efficient, co-ordinated and economical system of gas supply for Great Britain. ...The Secretary of State was empowered to require the BGC to report on its activities and, after laying that report before both Houses of Parliament, to give the BGC such directions as he considered appropriate on the basis of that report for the most efficient management of the undertaking. ... The Secretary of State could also, after consultation with the BGC, give the BGC general directions for the exercise and performance of its functions...

JUDGMENT

16.   As the Court has consistently held (see Case 8/81, *Becker v Hauptzollamt Münster-Innenstadt*), where the Community authorities have, by means of a

directive, placed member-States under a duty to adopt a certain course of action, the effectiveness of such a measure would be diminished if persons were prevented from relying upon it in proceedings before a court and national courts were prevented from taking it into consideration as an element of Community law. Consequently, a member-State which has not adopted the implementing measures required by the directive within the prescribed period may not plead, as against individuals, its own failure to perform the obligations which the directive entails. Thus, wherever the provisions of a directive appear, as far as their subject-matter is concerned, to be unconditional and sufficiently precise, those provisions may, in the absence of implementing measures adopted within the prescribed period, be relied upon as against any national provision which is incompatible with the directive or in so far as the provisions define rights which individuals are able to assert against the State.

17. The Court further held in *Marshall*, at paragraph 49, that where a person is able to rely on a directive as against the State he may do so regardless of the capacity in which the latter is acting, whether as employer or as public authority. In either case it is necessary to prevent the State from taking advantage of its own failure to comply with Community law.

18. On the basis of those considerations, the Court has held in a series of cases that unconditional and sufficiently precise provisions of a directive could be relied on against organisations or bodies which were subject to the authority or control of the State or had special powers beyond those which result from the normal rules applicable to relations between individuals.

Decipher
The Bipartite Test is specified here.

19. The Court has accordingly held that provisions of a directive could be relied on against tax authorities (Case 8/81, *Becker*, and 22 February 1990 in Case C-221/88, *ECSC v Acciaierie E Ferriere Busseni*), local or regional authorities (Case 103/88, *Fratelli Costanzo v Comune di Milano*), constitutionally independent authorities responsible for the maintenance of public order and safety (Case 222/84, *Johnston v Chief Constable of the Royal Ulster Constabulary*), and public authorities providing public health services (Case 152/84, *Marshall*).

20. It follows from the foregoing that a body, whatever its legal form, which has been made responsible, pursuant to a measure adopted by the State, for providing a public service under the control the State and has for that purpose special powers beyond those which result from the normal rules applicable in relations between individuals is included in any event among the bodies against which the provisions of a directive capable of having direct effect may be relied upon.

Decipher
The Tripartite Test is specified here.

21. With regard to Article 5(1) of Directive 76/207 it should be observed that in Case 152/84, *Marshall*, at paragraph 52, the Court held that that provision was unconditional and sufficiently precise to be relied on by an individual and to be applied by the national courts.

22. The answer to the question referred by the House of Lords must therefore be that Article 5(1) of Council Directive 76/207 of 9 February 1976 may be relied upon in a claim for damages against a body, whatever its legal form, which has been made responsible, pursuant to a measure adopted by the State, for providing a public service under the control of the State and has for that purpose special powers beyond those which result from the normal rules applicable in relations between individuals.

1.2 Indirect Effect

Sabine Von Colson and Elisabeth Kamann v Land Nordrhein-Westfalen (Case 14/83) [1986] 2 CMLR 430

Panel: Martens de Wilmars CJ, Koopmans, Bahlmann and Galmot PPC, Pescatore, Lord Mackenzie Stuart, O'Keeffe, Bosco, Due, Everling and Kakouris JJ. Mme. Simone Rozès, Advocate-General

Legislation: Directive 76/207

In the excerpt: Articles 5 and 189 EEC are now Article 4(3) TEU and Article 288 TFEU respectively.

Facts: Two female plaintiffs applied for work as social workers at Werl prison in Germany. They were not appointed and the posts went to less well qualified male applicants. The German labour court established that this was a result of sex discrimination but that the Directive did not require any particular remedy to be available. In consequence the only penalty provided under German law amounted to damages for actual loss, that is, the reimbursement of transport expenses.

In a number of questions put to the Court of Justice the German court asked in essence for guidance as to what an appropriate sanction was in a case such as this.

As a side point note how the Court of Justice deals with the issue that although it was possible to see the prison service as a state emanation this case would have had difficulty passing the van Gend en Loos criteria in direct effect on the basis of the lack of clarity concerning the appropriate penalty – the very reason this case needed to be brought!

JUDGMENT

21. In its fifth question the Arbeitsgericht essentially asks whether it is possible to infer from the directive any sanction in the event of discrimination other than the right to the conclusion of a contract of employment. Question 6 asks whether the directive, as properly interpreted, may be relied on before national courts by persons who have suffered injury.

Decipher
The Arbeitsgericht was the West German Labour Court.

22. It is impossible to establish real equality of opportunity without an appropriate system of sanctions. That follows not only from the actual purpose of the directive but more specifically from Article 6 thereof which, by granting applicants for a post who have been discriminated against recourse to the courts, acknowledges that those candidates have rights of which they may avail themselves before the courts.

23. Although, as has been stated in the reply to Question 1, full implementation of the directive does not require any specific form of sanction for unlawful discrimination, it does entail that that sanction be such as to guarantee real and effective judicial protection. Moreover it must also have a real deterrent effect on the employer. It follows that where a member-State chooses to penalise the breach of the prohibition of discrimination by the award of compensation, that compensation must in any event be adequate in relation to the damage sustained.

24. In consequence it appears that national provisions limiting the right to compensation of persons who have been discriminated against as regards access to employment to a purely nominal amount, such as, for example, the reimbursement of expenses incurred by them in submitting their application, would not satisfy the requirements of an effective transposition of the directive. ...

Decipher
A national court, as an authority of the Member State. It must comply with the obligation of the Member State to fulfil the purpose of the directive.

26. ... [T]he member-States' obligation arising from a directive to achieve the result envisaged by the directive and their duty under Article 5 of the Treaty to take all appropriate measures, whether general or particular, to ensure the fulfilment of that obligation, is binding on all the authorities of member-States including, for matters within their jurisdiction, the courts. It follows that, in applying the national law and in particular the provisions of a national law specifically introduced in order to implement Directive 76/207, national courts are required to interpret their national law in the light of the wording and the purpose of the directive in order to achieve the result referred to in Article 189(3).

Alert

27. On the other hand, as the above considerations show, the directive does not include any unconditional and sufficiently precise obligation as regards sanctions for discrimination which, in the absence of implementing measures adopted in good time may be relied on by individuals in order to obtain specific compensation under the directive, where that is not provided for or permitted under national law.

28. It should, however, be pointed out to the national court that although Directive 76/207/EEC, for the purpose of imposing a sanction for the breach of the

prohibition of discrimination, leaves the member-States free to choose between the different solutions suitable for achieving its objective, it nevertheless requires that if a member-State chooses to penalise breaches of that prohibition by the award of compensation, then in order to ensure that it is effective and that it has a deterrent effect, that compensation must in any event be adequate in relation to the damage sustained and must therefore amount to more than purely nominal compensation such as, for example, the reimbursement only of the expenses incurred in connection with the application. It is for the national court to interpret and apply the legislation adopted for the implementation of the directive in conformity with the requirements of Community law, in so far as it is given discretion to do so under national law.

 Alert

With regard to the concept of direct effect the Court of Justice seemed to have painted itself into a corner in that while an action based upon a directive could be brought, it could only be brought against a state, public body or emanation of the state. As seen in some earlier cases this left a rankling awareness of injustice among lawyers that employees of private concerns could not rely upon direct effect. This awareness goes some way to explaining the persistence of some Advocates-General who kept unsuccessfully pushing the Court of Justice in the direction of a finding in favour of horizontal direct effect (Lenz in *Faccini Dori v Recreb Srl* (Case C-91/92) [1995] 1 CMLR 665 and Van Gervan in *Marshall v Southampton and South-West Hampshire Area Health Authority (No.2)* (Case C-271/91) [1993] 3 CMLR 293 ('*Marshall II*')). *Von Colson* is the seminal case in establishing a different approach and a line of cases, which have gone some way to resolving the problem created by horizontality in direct effect.

Note however that the very last line of the judgment illuminates the limitation to the *Von Colson* principle. Indirect effect entails only an interpretive obligation. In *Von Colson*, the Court of Justice only obliged the national court to interpret and apply national legislation in conformity with Community law "in so far as it is given discretion to do so under national law". In *Marleasing SA v La Comercial Internacional de Alimentacion SA* (Case C-106/89) [1992] 1 CMLR 305, it simply stated that a national court was required to interpret its national law "as far as possible". Therefore, the Court of Justice in *Wagner Miret v Fondo de Garantía Salarial* (Case C-334/92) [1996] 1 CMLR 889 accepted that, in the light of *Marleasing*, national provisions which expressly excluded higher management staff could not be interpreted in a way that conformed with a directive which applied to all categories of employee.

As a final point it is worth noticing that the Court of Justice removed any potential for vertical and horizontal problems within the context of *Von Colson* in its decision in *Harz v Deutsche Tradax* (Case 79/83) [1986] 2 CMLR 430 where in almost identical circumstances a female employee of a private company was entitled to a similar redress.

1.3 State Liability

Andrea Francovich, Danila Bonifaci and others v Italian Republic (Cases 6/90 & 9/90) [1993] 2 CMLR 66

Panel: Due CJ, Slynn, Joliet, Schockweiler, Grévisse and Kapteyn PPC, Mancini, Moitinho de Almeida, Rodríguez Iglesias, Díez de Velasco and Zuleeg JJ, M Jean Mischo, Advocate-General

Legislation: Directive 80/987

In the excerpts: Articles 169-171 and 189 EEC are now Articles 258-260(1) and 288 TFEU respectively.

Facts: Directive 80/987 sought to ensure that in the event of the bankruptcy of a company its employees would be able to claim their outstanding wages from a guarantee institution established by the Member States. The Italian state had failed to implement the Directive. Andrea Francovich had worked for an Italian company CDN Elletronica SnC which became bankrupt and from which he had been unable to claim his outstanding wages, even after court action. He therefore submitted that he was entitled to obtain from the Italian State the guarantees provided for by Directive 80/987 or, in the alternative, damages. Danila Bonifaci and 33 other employees brought a similar claim against the State for their outstanding wages owed by a separate company. The Italian courts concerned in these claims referred the question of whether a private individual affected by the failure of a member state to implement a directive could require the state to give effect to the directive and/or pay compensation for damage suffered.

ADVOCATE-GENERAL MISCHO

3.   In the event of failure to implement a directive or its incorrect implementation, a member-State deprives Community law of the desired effect. It also commits a breach of Article 5 and Article 189(3) EEC, which affirm the binding nature of the directive and require the member-State to take all the measures necessary for its implementation.

4.   Where the breach of that obligation is confirmed by a judgment of the Court of Justice delivered pursuant to Articles 169 to 171 EEC, the binding authority of a judicial decision and Article 171 EEC requires the member-State, which cannot raise any obstacle whatsoever, to take all appropriate measures to make good its default and give the desired effect to Community law. In so doing it may also be required to pay compensation for the harm which it has caused to individuals as a result of its unlawful conduct.

5.   By virtue of Community law, it must be possible for the member-State to be held liable at least in cases where the conditions are met under which the Community incurs liability as a result of the breach of Community law by one of its institutions. In the case of a directive which should have been implemented by means of a legislative measure, it is therefore sufficient that the relevant

provisions of the directive should have the purpose of protecting the interests of individuals. The condition of a sufficiently serious breach of a superior rule of law must be considered to have been met where the Court has declared the member-State in default in a judgment delivered under Articles 169 to 171.

The Court accepted the Advocate Generals' reasoning but began its judgment by establishing that direct effect was not possible.

JUDGMENT

1. ...[E]ven though the provisions of the directive in question are sufficiently precise and unconditional as regards the determination of the persons entitled to the guarantee and as regards the content of that guarantee, those elements are not sufficient to enable individuals to rely on those provisions before the national courts. Those provisions do not identify the person liable to provide the guarantee, and the State cannot be considered liable on the sole ground that it has failed to take transposition measures within the prescribed period.

It then went on to give its judgment concerning state liability:

31. It must be recalled first of all that the EEC Treaty has created its own legal system which is an integral part of the legal systems of the member-States and which their courts are bound to apply; the subjects of that legal system are not only the member-States but also their nationals. Just as it imposes obligations on individuals, Community law is also intended to create rights which become part of their legal patrimony; those rights arise not only where they are expressly granted by the Treaty but also by virtue of obligations which the Treaty imposes in a clearly defined manner both on individuals and on the member-States and the Community institutions: see Case 26/62, *Van Gend en Loos* and Case 6/64, *Costa v Enel.*

32. Furthermore, it has been consistently held that the national courts whose task it is to apply the provisions of Community law in cases within their jurisdiction must ensure that those rules have full effect and protect the rights which they confer on individuals: see in particular Case 106/77, *Amministrazione delle Finanze dello Stato v Simmenthal,* and Case C-213/89, *Factortame.*

33. It must be held that the full effectiveness of Community rules would be impaired and the protection of the rights which they grant would be weakened if individuals were unable to obtain compensation when their rights are infringed by a breach of Community law for which a member-State can be held responsible.

34. The possibility of compensation by the member-State is particularly indispensable where, as in this case, the full effectiveness of Community rules is subject to prior action on the part of the State and consequently individuals cannot, in the absence of such action, enforce the rights granted to them by Community law before the national courts.

35.   It follows that the principle of State liability for harm caused to individuals by breaches of Community law for which the State can be held responsible is inherent in the system of the Treaty.

36.   Further foundation for the obligation on the part of member-States to pay compensation for such harm is to be found in Article 5 EEC, under which the member-States are required to take all appropriate measures, whether general or particular, to ensure fulfilment of their obligations under Community law. Among these is the obligation to nullify the unlawful consequences of a breach of Community law: see, in relation to the analogous provision of Article 86 ECSC, Case 6/60, *Humblet v Belgium*.

37.   It follows from all the foregoing that it is a principle of Community law that the member-States are obliged to pay compensation for harm caused to individuals by breaches of Community law for which they can be held responsible.

Having established that State liability was now an additional remedy to use against a recalcitrant Member State the Court of Justice stated the conditions under which the remedy would be available:

39.   Where, as in this case, a member-State fails to fulfil its obligations under Article 189(3) EEC to take all the measures necessary to achieve the result prescribed by a directive the full effectiveness of that rule of Community law requires that there should be a right to compensation where three conditions are met.

40.   The first of those conditions is that the result prescribed by the directive should entail the grant of rights to individuals. The second condition is that it should be possible to identify the content of those rights on the basis of the provisions of the directive. Finally, the third condition is the existence of a causal link between the breach of the State's obligation and the harm suffered by the injured parties.

41.   Those conditions are sufficient to give rise to a right on the part of individuals to obtain compensation, a right which is founded directly on Community law.

When a Member State failed to implement an EU measure the Commission, as the watchdog of the Treaty, could ultimately take action in the Court of Justice which could have resulted in a fine upon that State. This normally enforced the Treaty so far as the institutions were concerned but it did not resolve the ongoing problem of what to do when EU citizens suffered damage or loss when a malingering State failed to implement a directive. This provided the spur to the development of direct and indirect effect but what could be done if neither of these two routes failed to provide a solution?

Note that in *Francovich* direct effect was not possible because the Directive lacked clarity about where exactly the money was coming from with which to pay the workers (see below) and indirect effect was not possible because of the absence of any national law capable of interpretation in line with the objectives of the directive. A double whammy prompting Advocate-General Mischo to begin his opinion by pointing out:

'Rarely has the Court been called upon to decide a case in which the adverse consequences for the individuals concerned of failure to implement a directive..[have been]… as shocking as in the case now before us'

The inequality that results when a Member State fails to comply with a directive affects not just the nationals of that state who lose out on their specific Treaty rights, but those other Member States which have complied with the directive often to their cost. Additionally such compliant States may well find their private companies are affected and no longer as competitive.

While *Francovich* established that at least individuals would obtain some redress in such a situation it left open the extent to which such an obligation could be pursued. A key question remained: did this ruling only apply where there was a total failure to implement a directive or did it apply to other EU law and if so, to what extent?

The following case went some way to addressing these questions.

Brasserie du Pecheur SA v Germany; R v Secretary of State for Transport, ex parte Factortame (Factortame III) (Joined Cases 46 & 48/93) [1996] 1 CMLR 889

Panel: Rodríguez Iglesias (Rapporteur) P, Kakouris, Edward and Hirsch, PPC, Mancini, Schockweiler, Moitinho de Almeida, Gulmann and Murray, JJ, Sig Giuseppe Tesauro, Advocate-General

Legislation: Articles 30 and 52 EEC (now Articles 34 and 49 TFEU respectively)

In the excerpts: Articles 5, 189 and 215 EEC are now Articles 4(3) TEU, 288 TFEU and 340 TFEU respectively.

Facts: Brasserie du Pêcheur SA was a French brewery based at Schiltigheim (Alsace), which exported beer to Germany. These exports were stopped by the German government as they failed to comply with the German Reinheitsgebot (purity requirement). It was held that this prohibition was not compatible with Article 30 EEC (now Article 34 TFEU). As a consequence Brasserie brought an action against the German government for compensation for the losses suffered to the amount of 1,800,000 DM.

In *Factortame III*, Spanish fishermen challenged the compatibility of the UK Merchant Shipping Act 1988 with the Treaty. The registration requirement created by the Act imposed conditions concerning nationality, residence and domicile upon the owners of the fishing vessels that were found incompatible with Article 52 EEC (now Article 49 TFEU) in *R v Secretary of State for Transport, ex parte Factortame Ltd* (Case 213/89) [1991] 3 CMLR 589 ('*Factortame II*').

A number of questions were referred to the Court of Justice principally (for present purposes) of whether damages could be claimed where a Member State does not change a statute to comply with Community law (*Brasserie*) and whether damages could be claimed for all or any of the infringements of the Treaty committed against Factortame?

JUDGMENT

18. The German, Irish and Netherlands Governments contend that Member States are required to make good loss or damage caused to individuals only where the provisions breached are not directly effective: in *Francovich and Others* the Court simply sought to fill a lacuna in the system for safeguarding rights of individuals. In so far as national law affords individuals a right of action enabling them to assert their rights under directly effective provisions of Community law, it is unnecessary, where such provisions are breached, also to grant them a right to reparation founded directly on Community law.

19. That argument cannot be accepted.

20. The Court has consistently held that the right of individuals to rely on the directly effective provisions of the Treaty before national courts is only a minimum guarantee and is not sufficient in itself to ensure the full and complete implementation of the Treaty (see, in particular, Case 168/85 *Commission v Italy* [1986] ECR 2945, paragraph 11, Case C-120/88 *Commission v Italy* [1991] ECR I-621, paragraph 10, and C-119/89 *Commission v Spain* [1991] ECR I-641, paragraph 9). The purpose of that right is to ensure that provisions of Community law prevail over national provisions. It cannot, in every case, secure for individuals the benefit of the rights conferred on them by Community law and, in particular, avoid their sustaining damage as a result of a breach of Community law attributable to a Member State. As appears from paragraph [33] of the judgment in *Francovich and Others*, the full effectiveness of Community law would be impaired if individuals were unable to obtain redress when their rights were infringed by a breach of Community law.

21. This will be so where an individual who is a victim of the non-transposition of a directive and is precluded from relying on certain of its provisions directly before the national court because they are insufficiently precise and unconditional, brings an action for damages against the defaulting Member State for breach of the third paragraph of Article 189 of the Treaty. In such circumstances, which obtained in the case of *Francovich* and Others, the purpose of reparation is to redress the injurious consequences of a Member State's failure to transpose a directive as far as beneficiaries of that directive are concerned.

22. It is all the more so in the event of infringement of a right directly conferred by a Community provision upon which individuals are entitled to rely before the national courts. In that event, the right to reparation is the necessary corollary of the direct effect of the Community provision whose breach caused the damage sustained.

23. In this case, it is undisputed that the Community provisions at issue, namely Article 30 of the Treaty in Case C-46/93 and Article 52 in Case C-48/93, have direct effect in the sense that they confer on individuals rights upon which they are entitled to rely directly before the national courts. Breach of such provisions may give rise to reparation...

State liability will be available where the criteria for direct effect fail to be made out. State liability will also be available where direct effect can be made out. In *Brasserie* and *Factortame III* direct effect could be made out on the facts of each case.

37. ...[T]he national courts ask the Court to specify the conditions under which a right to reparation of loss or damage caused to individuals by breaches of Community law attributable to a Member State is, in the particular circumstances, guaranteed by Community law.

38. Although Community law imposes State liability, the conditions under which that liability gives rise to a right to reparation depend on the nature of the breach of Community law giving rise to the loss and damage (*Francovich and Others*).

39. In order to determine those conditions, account should first be taken of the principles inherent in the Community legal order which form the basis for State liability, namely, first, the full effectiveness of Community rules and the effective protection of the rights which they confer and, second, the obligation to co-operate imposed on Member States by Article 5 of the Treaty (*Francovich and Others*).

40. In addition, as the Commission and the several governments which submitted observations have emphasised, it is pertinent to refer to the Court's case law on non-contractual liability on the part of the Community.

41. First, the second paragraph of Article 215 of the Treaty refers, as regards the non-contractual liability of the Community, to the general principles common to the laws of the Member States, from which, in the absence of written rules, the Court also draws inspiration in other areas of Community law.

 Decipher The court includes general principles of EU among these sources.

42. Second, the conditions under which the State may incur liability for damage caused to individuals by a breach of Community law cannot, in the absence of particular justification, differ from those governing the liability of the Community in like circumstances. The protection of the rights which individuals derive from Community law cannot vary depending on whether a national authority or a Community authority is responsible for the damage.

43. The system of rules which the Court has worked out with regard to Article 215 of the Treaty, particularly in relation to liability for legislative measures, takes into account, *inter alia*, the complexity of the situations to be regulated, difficulties in the application or interpretation of the texts and, more particularly, the margin of discretion available to the author of the act in question.

 Decipher Note the argument here is that a EU institution would be liable where it has a wide discretion in how it may act only if it has excessively disregarded the limits of this discretion. This 'manifest and grave' formula will become part of its final decision and applied to Member States also.

44. Thus, in developing its case law on the non-contractual liability of the Community, in particular as regards legislative measures involving choices of economic policy, the Court has had regard to the wide discretion available to the institutions in implementing Community policies.

45. The strict approach taken towards the liability of the Community in the exercise of its legislative activities is due to two considerations. First, even where the legality of measures is subject to judicial review, exercise of the legislative function must

not be hindered by the prospect of actions for damages whenever the general interest of the Community requires legislative measures to be adopted which may adversely affect individual interests. Second, in a legislative context characterised by the exercise of a wide discretion, which is essential for implementing a Community policy, the Community cannot incur liability unless the institution concerned has manifestly and gravely disregarded the limits on the exercise of its powers. ... That said, the national legislature—like the Community institutions—does not systematically have a wide discretion when it acts in a field governed by Community law. Community law may impose upon it obligations to achieve a particular result or obligations to act or refrain from acting which reduce its margin of discretion, sometimes to a considerable degree. This is so, for instance, where, as in the circumstances to which the judgment in *Francovich and Others* relates, Article 189 of the Treaty places the Member State under an obligation to take, within a given period, all the measures needed in order to achieve the result required by a directive. In such a case, the fact that it is for the national legislature to take the necessary measures has no bearing on the Member State's liability for failing to transpose the directive.

47. In contrast, where a Member State acts in a field where it has a wide discretion, comparable to that of the Community institutions in implementing Community policies, the conditions under which it may incur liability must, in principle, be the same as those under which the Community institutions incur liability in a comparable situation.

48. In the case which gave rise to the reference in Case C-46/93, the German legislature had legislated in the field of foodstuffs, specifically beer. In the absence of Community harmonisation, the national legislature had a wide discretion in that sphere in laying down rules on the quality of beer put on the market.

49. As regards the facts of Case C-48/93, the United Kingdom legislature also had a wide discretion. The legislation at issue was concerned, first, with the registration of vessels, a field which, in view of the state of development of Community law, falls within the jurisdiction of the Member States and, secondly, with regulating fishing, a sector in which implementation of the common fisheries policy leaves a margin of discretion to the Member States.

50. Consequently, in each case the German and United Kingdom legislatures were faced with situations involving choices comparable to those made by the Community institutions when they adopt legislative measures pursuant to a Community policy.

51. In such circumstances, Community law confers a right to reparation where three conditions are met: the rule of law infringed must be intended to confer rights on individuals; the breach must be sufficiently serious; and there must be a direct causal link between the breach of the obligation resting on the State and the damage sustained by the injured parties.

 Decipher
Again, a Member State must expect to be liable where an EU institution would be. A wide discretion must be manifestly and gravely exceeded.

 Decipher
In both *Brasserie* and *Factortame III* the States had a wide discretion.

 Alert

52.   First, those conditions satisfy the requirements of the full effectiveness of the rules of Community law and of the effective protection of the rights which those rules confer.

53.   Secondly, those conditions correspond in substance to those defined by the Court in relation to Article 215 in its case law on liability of the Community for damage caused to individuals by unlawful legislative measures adopted by its institutions.

54.   The first condition is manifestly satisfied in the case of Article 30 of the Treaty, the relevant provision in Case C-46/93, and in the case of Article 52, the relevant provision in Case C-48/93. Whilst Article 30 imposes a prohibition on Member States, it nevertheless gives rise to rights for individuals which the national courts must protect. Likewise, the essence of Article 52 is to confer rights on individuals.

55.   As to the second condition, as regards both Community liability under Article 215 and Member State liability for breaches of Community law, the decisive test for finding that a breach of Community law is sufficiently serious is whether the Member State or the Community institution concerned manifestly and gravely disregarded the limits on its discretion.

56.   The factors which the competent court may take into consideration include the clarity and precision of the rule breached, the measure of discretion left by that rule to the national or Community authorities, whether the infringement and the damage caused was intentional or involuntary, whether any error of law was excusable or inexcusable, the fact that the position taken by a Community institution may have contributed towards the omission, and the adoption or retention of national measures or practices contrary to Community law.

 Alert

57.   On any view, a breach of Community law will clearly be sufficiently serious if it has persisted despite a judgment finding the infringement in question to be established, or a preliminary ruling or settled case law of the Court on the matter from which it is clear that the conduct in question constituted an infringement.

An inevitable consequence of any ground breaking legal decision is a degree of opaqueness about how far the newly created obligation extends. Milestone as it was, *Francovich* attracted the same problem. It was a decision about a Member State's total failure to implement a Directive. Did this apply to other EU measures? Did it apply to a partial failure to implement a directive? *Brasserie du Pecheur/Factortame III* addressed these issues by providing a formulaic set of conditions which can be used to deal with a wider range of factors such as partial breaches as opposed to the total breach situation in *Francovich*. The requirement that a breach needs to be sufficiently serious to be actionable is the effective difference between the *Francovich* criteria and those laid out in this case. Subsequent case law has gone on to illustrate and refine State liability further. In this context note *Dillenkofer and Others v Germany* (Joined cases C-178/94, C-179/94, C-188/94, C-189/94 and C-190/94) [1996] 3 CMLR 469.

This involved the non-implementation of a Directive very similar to that in *Francovich*. Here the court did not need to invoke the *Brasserie* conditions, simply deciding that the non-implementation by the German government was sufficiently serious in its own right.

Conclusion

The Treaty allowed the Commission to enforce obligations by fines imposed upon Member States which failed to fulfil their obligations. However, there was nothing in the original Treaty which allowed redress for individuals in their national courts. While the development of the concepts seen in this Chapter have gone a long way to making up for this defect in the Treaty it is true that there are still many gaps through which an individual action may fall. The lack of horizontal direct effect pushes the employees of private companies outside the shelter of *van Gend en Loos*. The lack of national law or the opportunity to provide the correct interpretation of it removes indirect effect. A failure to make out one of the factors in paragraph 56 of *Brasserie* would defeat State liability. In conclusion, despite the cumulative nature of the potential remedies, a private individual could still find no remedy covering their particular situation.

Further Reading

Drake, S: '20 Years After Von Colson: the Impact of 'Indirect Effect' on the Protection of the Individuals Community Rights' (2005) 30 ELR 329

Fairhurst, J: *Law of the European Union*. 9th ed, Longman/Pearson, Chapter 9

Granger, MPF: 'National Application of Francovich and the Construction of a European Administrative Jus Commune' (2007) 32 ELR 157

Horspool, M. and Humphreys, M: *European Union Law*. 7th ed, OUP, Chapter 7

Jacobs, F: 'The Evolution of the European Legal Order' (2004) CMLR 303

Nassimdian, D: 'And We Keep on Meeting: (De)fragmenting State Liability' (2007) 32 ELR 819

Steiner, J. and Woods, L: *EU Law*. 11th ed, OUP, Chapters 5 and 9

2

Free Movement of Goods

Topic List

Introduction

One of the fundamental aims of the EU is to lay the foundation for the free movement of goods between Member States. It is one of the four cornerstone freedoms, the others being the free movement of persons (see Chapter 3), services (see Chapter 4) and capital. These freedoms are necessary to bring about a genuine common market.

Member States can resist this freedom by attempting to protect those producing goods within their territory from goods imported from other Member States. This protectionism can take a number of forms from outright and obvious prohibitions or extra charges on those goods to more subtle forms of restriction. A number of Articles deal with each of these forms of protectionism.

These are Articles 30 and 110 TFEU which concern fiscal barriers and Articles 34 to 36 TFEU which concern non-fiscal barriers.

2.1 Definition of Goods

Commission v Italy (Case 7/68) [1969] CMLR 1 ('*Art Treasures*')

Panel: Lecourt P, A Trabucchi, Mertens de Wilmars, Donner, Strauss, Monaco and Pescatore JJ, M Joseph Gand, Advocate-General

Legislation: Articles 9, 16 and 36 EEC (now Articles 28, 30 and 36 TFEU respectively)

Facts: The Italian government imposed a charge on artistic works and argued that such works do not come within the definition of goods. The Court of Justice reviewed the definition of "goods".

JUDGMENT

Under Article 9 of the Treaty the community is based on a customs union ' which shall cover all trade in goods '. By goods, within the meaning of that provision, there must be understood products which can be valued in money and which are capable, as such, of forming the subject of commercial transactions.

2.2 Fiscal Barriers

2.2.1 Customs Duties and Charges Having Equivalent Effect

From the outset, the EEC Treaty included an obligation on the Member States to abolish customs duties and measures having equivalent effect to customs duties. The result has been that goods should be free to move within the common market without being subject to such duties, even if the purpose of the duty is stated to be something other than protectionism, as in the *Italian Glass* case where the purpose stated was the retention of art. It is the effect which is the important factor.

The more subtle forms of border based levy are "charges having equivalent effect" (CEE). The most comprehensive case which provides a clear idea as to the nature of a CEE is:

Commission v Italy (Case 24/68) [1971] CMLR 611 ('*Statistical Levy*')

Panel: Lecourt P, Trabucchi, Mertens de Wilmars, Donner, Strauss, Monaco and Pescatore JJ, Herr Karl Roemer, Advocate-General

Legislation: Article 16 EEC (replaced by Article 30 TFEU)

In the excerpt: Article 9 EEC is now Article 28 TFEU. Articles 12 and 13 EEC have been replaced by Article 30 TFEU.

Facts: The Italian government imposed a small levy on goods exported to other Member States claiming that the levy was imposed for the purpose of collecting statistical data for use in the analysis of trade patterns.

JUDGMENT

7. It follows from the system as a whole and from the general and absolute nature of the prohibition of any customs duty applicable to goods moving between Member States that customs duties are prohibited independently of any consideration of the purpose for which they were introduced and the destination of the revenue obtained therefrom.

    The justification for this prohibition is based on the fact that any pecuniary charge, however small, imposed on goods by reason of the fact that they cross a frontier constitutes an obstacle to the movement of such goods.

8. The extension of the prohibition of customs duties to charges having equivalent effect is intended to supplement the prohibition against obstacles to trade created by such duties by increasing its efficiency.

    The use of these two complementary concepts thus tends, in trade between Member States, to avoid the imposition of any pecuniary charge on goods circulating within the community by virtue of the fact that they cross a national frontier.

9. Thus, in order to ascribe to a charge an effect equivalent to a customs duty, it is important to consider this effect in the light of the objectives of the Treaty, in the parts, titles and chapters in which Articles 9, 12, 13 and 16 are to be found, particularly in relation to the free movement of goods.

    Consequently, any pecuniary charge, however small and whatever its designation and mode of application, which is imposed unilaterally on domestic or foreign goods by reason of the fact that they cross a frontier, and which is not a customs duty in the strict sense, constitutes a charge having equivalent effect within the meaning of Articles 9, 12, 13 and 16 of the Treaty, even if it is not imposed for the benefit of the state, is not discriminatory or protective in effect and if the product on which the charge is imposed is not in competition with any domestic product.

 Alert

10. It follows from all the provisions referred to and from their relationship with the other provisions of the Treaty that the prohibition of new customs duties or charges having equivalent effect, linked to the principle of the free movement of goods, constitutes a fundamental rule which, without prejudice to the other provisions of the Treaty, does not permit of any exceptions.

2.2.1.1 Charges That Do Not Constitute a Customs Duty or a Charge Having Equivalent Effect

Although there are no defences to Article 30, the Court of Justice has recognised three circumstances where a charge on imports will not constitute a customs duty or a CEE. These were discussed in:

Commission v Germany (Case 18/87) [1990] 1 CMLR 561

Panel: Lord Mackenzie Stuart CJ, Due, Moitinho de Almeida and Rodriguez Iglesias PPC, Koopmans, Everling, Galmot, Kakouris and O'Higgins JJ, Sig Federico Mancini, Advocate-General

Legislation: Articles 9 and 12 EEC (now Articles 28 and 30 TFEU)

In the excerpt: Articles 13 and 16 EEC have been replaced by Article 30 TFEU.

Facts: The German government charged a fee to cover the costs of veterinary inspections on imported live animals. The inspections were required under a Directive regulating the protection of animals during international transport. The Court of Justice discussed whether the inspection fee was a CEE and laid down four requirements for when an inspection fee would not constitute a CEE.

JUDGMENT

5. It should be observed in the first place that, as the Court has held on a number of occasions, the justification for the prohibition of customs duties and any charges having an equivalent effect lies in the fact that any pecuniary charge, however small, imposed on goods by reason of the fact that they cross a frontier, constitutes an obstacle to the movement of goods which is aggravated by the resulting administrative formalities. It follows that any pecuniary charge, whatever its designation and mode of application, which is imposed unilaterally on goods by reason of the fact that they cross a frontier and is not a customs duty in the strict sense constitutes a charge having an equivalent effect to a customs duty within the meaning of Articles 9, 12, 13 and 16 of the Treaty.

6. However, the Court has held that such a charge escapes that classification if it relates to a general system of internal dues applied systematically and in accordance with the same criteria to domestic products and imported products alike (judgment of 31 May 1979 in Case 132/78 *Denkavit v France* [1979] ECR 1923), if it constitutes payment for a service in fact rendered to the economic operator of a sum in proportion to the service (judgment of 9 November 1983 in Case 158/82 *Commission v Denmark* [1983] ECR 3573), or again, subject to certain conditions, if it attaches to inspections carried out to

 Alert

fulfil obligations imposed by Community law (judgment of 25 January 1977 in Case 46/76 *Bauhuis v Netherlands* [1977] ECR 5).

7. The contested fee, which is payable on importation and transit, cannot be regarded as relating to a general system of internal dues. Nor does it constitute payment for a service rendered to the operator, because this condition is satisfied only if the operator in question obtains a definite specific benefit (see judgment of 1 July 1969 in Case 24/68 *Commission v Italy* [1969] ECR 193), which is not the case if the inspection serves to guarantee, in the public interest, the health and life of animals in international transport (see judgment of 20 March 1984 in Case 314/82 *Commission v Belgium* [1984] ECR 1543).

8. Since the contested fee was charged in connection with inspections carried out pursuant to a Community provision, it should be noted that according to the case-law of the Court (judgment of 25 January 1977 in *Bauhuis*, cited above; judgment of 12 July 1977 *Commission v Netherlands* [1977] ECR 1355; judgment of 31 January 1984 in Case 1/83 *IFG v Freistaat Bayern* [1984] ECR 349) such fees may not be classified as charges having an effect equivalent to a customs duty if the following conditions are satisfied :

    (a) they do not exceed the actual costs of the inspections in connection with which they are charged;

    (b) the inspections in question are obligatory and uniform for all the products concerned in the Community;

    (c) they are prescribed by Community law in the general interest of the Community;

    (d) they promote the free movement of goods, in particular by neutralizing obstacles which could arise from unilateral measures of inspection adopted in accordance with Article 36 of the Treaty.

9. In this instance these conditions are satisfied by the contested fee.

 Alert

2.2.2 Discriminatory Internal Taxation: Article 110(1)

Article 110 TFEU prohibits forms of internal taxation which discriminate against imported goods or have the effect of protecting domestically produced goods against competition from imported goods. It is well established that this Article cannot be applied at the same time as Article 30 TFEU:

Alfons Lütticke GmbH v Hauptzollamt Sarrelouis (Case 57/65) [1971] CMLR 674

Panel: Hammes CJ; L. Delvaux, W Strauss, A M Donner, A Trabucchi, R Lecourt and R Monaco JJ.

Legislation: Article 12 and 13 EEC (since replaced by Article 30 TFEU) and Article 95 EEC (now Article 110 TFEU)

JUDGMENT

10.   ... It should however be stated that Article 12 and 13 on the one hand and Article 95 on the other could not be applied jointly to one and the same case. Taxes with effect equivalent to customs duties on the one hand and internal taxes on the other are subject to different systems. In that respect it should be mentioned that a tax aimed at compensating the effect of an internal tax thereby takes on the internal character of the tax the effect of which it is intended to compensate.

It is not always entirely straightforward to determine whether a charge or levy is a CEE or an internal tax. This was considered by the Court of Justice in the following case in which a definition of internal taxation was also provided:

Commission v France (Case 90/79) [1981] 3 CMLR 1 ('*Reprographic Machinery*')

Panel: Mertens de Wilmars CJ; Pescatore, Lord Mackenzie Stuart and Koopmans PPC; O'Keeffe, Touffait and Due JJ, Mr Jean-Pierre Warner, Advocate-General

Legislation: Article 9 EEC (now Article 28 TFEU), Articles 12 and 13 EEC (now replaced by Article 30 TFEU) and Article 95 EEC (now Article 110 TFEU)

Facts: France had introduced a levy on the use of certain types of reprographic machinery, such as photocopiers and microfiche scanners. This was charged at the rate of 3% on sales, otherwise than for export, by undertakings which had manufactured them and on imports of such machines. The money was to be used to subsidize the publication of quality works, the purchase of both French and foreign books by libraries and the translation of foreign works into French. The production of reprographic machinery was extremely small in French compared to the import of such machines. The Commission maintained that this was a CEE. The French Government argued that it was an internal tax which did not breach Article 95 EEC (now Article 110 TFEU).

The same law had also introduced a levy on the publication of books which was charged at a rate of 0.2% and was payable by publishers on their sales, other than export sales, of any kind of works published by them.

JUDGMENT

12.   Well-established case-law of the court is to the effect that the prohibition laid down by Articles 9, 12 and 13 of the Treaty in regard to charges having equivalent effect covers any charge exacted at the time of or on account of importation which, being borne specifically by an imported product to the exclusion of the similar domestic product, has the result of altering the cost price of the imported product thereby producing the same restrictive effect on the free movement of goods as a customs duty.

13.   The essential feature of a charge having an effect equivalent to a customs duty which distinguishes it from an internal tax therefore resides in the fact that the

former is borne solely by an imported product as such whilst the latter is borne both by imported and domestic products.

14. The court has however recognized that even a charge which is borne by a product imported from another member state, when there is no identical or similar domestic product, does not constitute a charge having equivalent effect but internal taxation within the meaning of Article 95 of the Treaty if it relates to a general system of internal dues applied systematically to categories of products in accordance with objective criteria irrespective of the origin of the products.

 Alert

15. Those considerations demonstrate that even if it were necessary in some cases, for the purpose of classifying a charge borne by imported products, to equate extremely low domestic production with its non-existence, that would not mean that the levy in question would necessarily have to be regarded as a charge having an effect equivalent to a customs duty. In particular, that will not be so if the levy is part of a general system on internal dues applying systematically to categories of products according to the criteria indicated above.

16. The court is of the opinion that the particular features of the levy in issue lead to its being accepted as forming part of such a general system of internal dues. That follows first from its inclusion in taxation arrangements which have their origin in the breach made in legal systems for the protection of copyright by the increase in the use of reprography and which are designed to subject, if only indirectly, the users of those processes to a charge which compensates for that which they would normally have to bear.

17. That conclusion follows in the second place from the fact that the levy in issue forms a single entity with the levy imposed on book publishers by the same internal legislation and from the fact, too, that it is borne by a range of very different machines which are moreover classified under various customs headings but which have in common the fact that they are all intended to be used for reprographic purposes in addition to more specific uses.

18. It follows from those considerations that the alleged failure to fulfil obligations has not been proved and that the action should be dismissed.

2.2.2.1 Similar Goods

When investigating whether there has been discrimination against particular imported goods under Article 110, the courts will first determine whether the relevant goods produced within the Member State are genuinely similar to the imported goods.

Commission v Denmark (Case 106/84) [1987] 2 CMLR 278

Panel: Koopmans PC; Everling, Bahlmann and Joliet PPC; Bosco, Due, Galmot, Kakouris and Schockweiler JJ.

Legislation: Article 95 (now Article 110 TFEU)

Facts: Denmark imposed a duty of 10.72 Dkr per litre on table wine made from grapes whilst imposing a duty of 6.92 Dkr per litre for table wine made from other fruit where the alcoholic strength did not exceed 14% by volume. It also imposed a duty of 19.93 Dkr on wine liqueur made from grapes where the alcoholic strength did not exceed 23% by volume whilst imposing a duty of 11.02 Dkr on liqueur made from other fruit where the strength did not exceed 20% by volume.

JUDGMENT

9. Since the Commission has based its action primarily on the first paragraph of Article 95, it is necessary to consider in the first place whether the conditions for the application of that provision are fulfilled.

10. As the Court recalled in Cases 168/78 (*E.C. Commission v France*), 169/78 (*E.C. Commission v Italy*) and 171/78 (*E.C. Commission v Denmark*), the aim of Article 95 as a whole is to ensure free movement of goods between the member-States in normal conditions of competition by the elimination of all forms of protection which result from the application of internal taxation which discriminates against products from other member-States and to guarantee the complete neutrality of internal taxation as regards competition between domestic products and imported products. With regard to the concept of similar products, the first paragraph of Article 95 prohibits more specifically any tax provision whose effect is to impose, by whatever mechanism, higher taxation on imported goods than on domestic products.

11. It is clear from the documents before the Court that wine made from grapes and consumed in Denmark is exclusively an imported product. With regard to fruit wine, wine of the liqueur type is almost entirely a domestically produced product and wine of the table-wine type, whilst approximately one third of the volume thereof is imported from other member-States, is a typical domestically-produced alcoholic beverage which has traditionally represented an essential outlet for Danish fruit growers.

12. In order to determine whether products are similar within the terms of the prohibition laid down in Article 95(1) it is necessary to consider, as the Court stated in Case 45/75 (*Rewe v Hauptzollamt Landau*), whether they have similar characteristics and meet the same needs from the point of view of consumers. The Court endorsed a broad interpretation of the concept of similarity in its judgments in Case 168/78 (*E.C. Commission v France*) and Case 216/81 (*Cogis v Amministrazione Delle Finanze Dello Stato*) and assessed the similarity of the products not according to whether they were strictly identical, but according to whether their use was similar and comparable. Consequently, in order to determine whether products are similar it is necessary first to consider certain objective characteristics of both categories of beverages, such as their origin, the method of manufacture and their organoleptic properties, in particular taste and alcohol content, and secondly to consider whether or not both categories of beverages are capable of meeting the same need from the point of view of consumers.

 Alert

13. In order to make that assessment, it is necessary to consider separately the two types of beverage to which the Danish tax legislation on wine applies, namely table wine and liqueur wine.

14. With regard to wine of the table-wine type, it should be noted in the first place that wines made from grapes and wines made from other fruit are manufactured from the same kind of basic product, namely agricultural produce, and by the same process, namely natural fermentation. Their organoleptic properties, in particular their taste and their alcohol content, are similar. The fact that the final alcohol content in fruit wine is achieved by the addition of ethyl alcohol must be regarded as irrelevant, since the alcohol content of wine made from grapes may also be increased, particularly in order to improve wine with a low natural alcohol content.

15. Moreover, in view of their similar characteristics the two categories of beverages can meet the same needs from the point of view of consumers inasmuch as they can be consumed in the same way, namely to quench thirst, as refreshments and at meal times. The fact that the two categories of beverage meet the same needs cannot be called in question by the fact that fruit wine has always been less popular with consumers than wine made from grapes. The question whether they meet the same needs must be assessed on the basis not of existing consumer habits but of the prospective development of those habits and, essentially, on the basis of objective characteristics which ensure that a product is capable of meeting the same needs as another product from the point of view of certain categories of consumers.

16. With regard to wine of the liqueur type, the methods of manufacturing wine from grapes and from other fruit may be regarded as identical, since the end product is invariably obtained by the addition of ethyl alcohol following initial fermentation for some length of time and, in some cases, by the addition of other substances, such as juice or honey. Accordingly, in view of their comparable characteristics and similar properties, the two categories of products meet the same needs from the point of view of consumers, since they are consumed as apéritifs by some and as dessert wine by others. Fruit wine of the liqueur-wine type and grape wine of the liqueur-wine type must consequently be regarded as similar products for the purposes of the first paragraph of Article 95 EEC.

17. The similarity between the two types of wine concerned cannot be denied, as the Danish Government maintains, on the ground that wine made from grapes and wine made from other fruit are classified under different tariff headings. As the Court held in Case 169/78, *Re Italian Taxation Of Spirits*, the customs classification of alcoholic beverages, which was designed to meet the requirements of external trade, cannot provide conclusive evidence with regard to the appraisal of the criterion of similarity laid down in the first paragraph of Article 95 EEC.

18. Similarly, the fact that wine made from grapes is not covered by a common organisation of the market cannot be considered relevant to the question whether products are similar, since the absence of such an organisation cannot justify discriminatory taxation which favours the use, for the manufacture of products which are in other respects similar, of certain categories of agricultural produce to the detriment of other categories of produce originating largely in other member-States.

This can be contrasted with another case from Denmark which was decided on the same day:

John Walker & Sons Limited v Ministeriet for Skatter og Afgifter (Ministry for Fiscal Affairs) (Case 234/84) [1987] 2 CMLR 278

Panel: Koopmans PC; Everling, Bahlmann and Joliet PPC; Bosco, Due, Galmot, Kakouris and Schockweiler JJ.

Legislation: Article 95 EEC (now Article 110 TFEU); Directive 75/439/EEC

Facts: In Denmark, spirits, fruit liqueur wine of exceeding 20% alcohol by volume and grape liqueur wine exceeding 23% by volume taxed on the basis of a specific duty imposed per litre of pure ethyl alcohol and a duty proportionate to the highest selling price charged by wholesalers. Fruit liqueur wine not exceeding 20% alcohol by volume were only subject to a specific duty calculated per litre of the product.

In determining whether spirits and fruit wine liqueur were similar products, the Court of Justice set out an identical paragraph to that in paragraph 12 of *Commission v Denmark* (Case 106/84) [1987] 2 CMLR 278 above and then continued:

JUDGMENT

12. It should be noted that the two categories of beverages exhibit manifestly different characteristics. Fruit wine of the liqueur type is a fruit-based product obtained by natural fermentation, whereas Scotch whisky is a cereal-based product obtained by distillation. The organoleptic properties of the two products are also different. As the Court held in *Rewe*, the fact that the same raw material, for example alcohol, is to be found in the two products is not sufficient reason to apply the prohibition contained in Article 95(1). For the products to be regarded as similar that raw material must also be present in more or less equal proportions in both products. In that regard, it must be pointed out that the alcoholic strength of Scotch whisky is 40 per cent. by volume, whereas the alcoholic strength of fruit wine of the liqueur type, to which the Danish tax legislation applies, does not exceed 20 per cent. by volume.

13. The contention that Scotch whisky may be consumed in the same way as fruit wine of the liqueur type, as an apéritif diluted with water or with fruit juice, even if it were established, would not be sufficient to render Scotch whisky similar to fruit wine of the liqueur type, whose intrinsic characteristics are fundamentally different.

14. The answer to the first question must therefore be that the first paragraph of Article 95 of the EEC Treaty must be interpreted as meaning that products such as Scotch whisky and fruit wine of the liqueur type may not be regarded as similar products.

2.2.2.2 Direct and Indirect Forms of Discrimination

Where the goods imported from another Member State are similar to the domestically produced goods, the Member State will be prohibited by the first paragraph of Article 110 TFEU from imposing, directly or indirectly, a higher tax burden on the imported goods than that it imposes on its domestic goods. This has been interpreted widely by the Court of Justice to require not only that imported goods are subject to the same rates of taxation as domestically produced goods but also that they are treated equally with domestic goods in respect of all taxation procedures including the modes of assessment and other detailed rules of application (*Commission v Italy* (Case 169/78) [1980] ECR 385).

The prohibition in the first paragraph of Article 110 encompasses both direct and indirect forms of discrimination. Direct discrimination is easily identifiable. It arises where the tax system openly treats imported goods less favourably than similar domestic goods on the basis of their origin. Indirect discrimination is harder to identify. It covers more covert forms of discrimination where tax measures do not appear on their face to be discriminatory but have the practical effect of placing a greater burden on imported goods than on domestic goods.

The Court of Justice has consistently refused to accept that instances of direct discrimination can be justified. For example:

Commission v Italy (Case 21/79) [1980] 2 CMLR 613 ('*Regenerated Oil*')

Panel: Kutscher CJ; O'Keefe and Touffait PPC; Mertens de Wilmers, Pescatore, Lord Mackenzie Stuart, Bosco, Koopmans and Due, JJ.

Legislation: Article 95 EEC (now Article 110 TFEU)

Facts: Italy imposed an internal production tax on oil and processed products derived from it. Oil which had been regenerated from used oil was taxed at only 25% of this rate. A similar tax was charged on imported oil and processed products but no reduction was provided for imported regenerated oil.

JUDGMENT

19. It is an established fact, which the Italian Republic does not dispute, that imported and home-produced regenerated oils are not only like products but are even identical so that the relationship between them is undeniably covered by the first paragraph of Article 95 of the Treaty.

20. The Government of the Italian Republic, in order to justify the retention of the rules disqualifying imported regenerated oils from the benefit of the lower rates of tax allowed on home-product regenerated oils, relies in substance on the following three arguments: (1) it is impossible to distinguish, by means of the experimental testing methods, regenerated oils from oils of primary distillation, and this would be likely to lead to tax evasion when the products in question are imported; (2) the tax exemption is justified by the very high production cost of regenerated oils with the result that without the tax reduction at issue these oils could not compete with oils of primary distillation; (3) the aims of the exemption correspond to the aims of Council Directive 75/439/EEC and the exemption is in actual fact the indemnity which Articles 13 and 14 of the directive authorise the member-States to grant.

21. The first argument cannot be accepted as justification of the alleged differential treatment. It is for the importers of mineral oils from the other member-States who wish to qualify for the reduced rate to produce evidence that the oils imported by them into Italy are regenerated oils and the Italian administration, without being able nonetheless to set a higher standard of proof than is necessary, is entitled to require in particular that the evidence be adduced in a form that removes the risk of tax evasion, for example by producing certificates from the authorities or other appropriate bodies of the exporting member-State permitting the regenerated oil to be identified as from the premises where it was regenerated. The practice in the Community, especially in relation to the discontinuance of public health inspections at the frontiers between member-States, offers numerous examples of such forms of permissible inspection.

In contrast, taxation measures which appear to discriminate indirectly against imported goods will be examined to determine whether they can be legitimately justified on an objective non-discriminatory basis:

Chemial Farmaceutici SpA v DAF SpA (Case 140/79) [1981] 3 CMLR 350

Panel: Mertens de Wilmars CJ; Pescatore and Koopmans PPC; Lord Mackenzie Stuart, O'Keeffe, Bosco and Touffait JJ.

Legislation: Article 95 EEC (now Article 110 TFEU)

Facts: Synthetic alcohol and alcohol produced by fermentation can be used interchangeably. Italy imposed a tax of 6,000 lire per hectolitre on synthetic alcohol but only 1,000 lire per hectolitre on alcohol produced by fermentation. No synthetic alcohol was produced in Italy which meant that, in practice, only imports were subject to the higher tax. Chemial Farmaceutici SpA placed an order with DAF SpA for denatured synthetic alcohol at 30,000 lire per hectolitre. The agreement stated that this price included the tax at 6,000 lire per hectolitre. A month later, the tax on synthetic alcohol was increased to 12,000 lire per hectolitre. DAF requested that Chemial either pay the increase in tax or consider the contract null and void. Chemial insisted upon performance of the contract and argued that the tax was contrary to EEC law.

JUDGMENT

 Alert

14. As the Court has stated on many occasions, particularly in the judgments cited by the Italian government, in its present stage of development Community law does not restrict the freedom of each member state to lay down tax arrangements which differentiate between certain products on the basis of objective criteria, such as the nature of the raw materials used or the production processes employed. Such differentiation is compatible with Community law if it pursues economic policy objectives which are themselves compatible with the requirements of the Treaty and its secondary law and if the detailed rules are such as to avoid any form of discrimination, direct or indirect, in regard to imports from other member states or any form of protection of competing domestic products.

15. Differential taxation such as that which exists in Italy for denatured synthetic alcohol on the one hand and denatured alcohol obtained by fermentation on the other satisfies these requirements. It appears in fact that that system of taxation pursues an objective of legitimate industrial policy in that it is such as to promote the distillation of agricultural products as against the manufacture of alcohol from petroleum derivatives. That choice does not conflict with the rules of Community law or the requirements of a policy decided within the framework of the Community.

16. The detailed provisions of the legislation at issue before the national Court cannot be considered as discriminatory since, on the one hand, it is not disputed that imports from other member states of alcohol obtained by fermentation qualify for the same tax treatment as Italian alcohol produced by fermentation and, on the other hand, although the rate of tax prescribed for synthetic alcohol results in restraining the importation of synthetic alcohol originating in other member states, it has an equivalent economic effect in the national territory in that it also hampers the establishment of profitable production of the same product by Italian industry.

17. The reply to the questions submitted by the national Court should therefore be that tax arrangements which impose heavier charges on denatured synthetic alcohol than on denatured alcohol obtained by fermentation on the basis of the raw materials and the manufacturing processes employed for the two products are not at variance with the first paragraph of Article 95 of the EEC Treaty if they are applied identically to the two categories of alcohol originating in other member states.

18. Where, by reason of the taxation of synthetic alcohol, it has been impossible to develop profitable production of that type of alcohol on national territory, the application of such tax arrangements cannot be considered as constituting indirect protection of national production of alcohol obtained by fermentation within the meaning of the second paragraph of Article 95 on the sole ground that their consequence is that the product subject to the heavier taxation is in fact a product which is exclusively imported from other member states of the Community.

Whereas the Court of Justice referred to economic policy objectives in *Chemial Farmaceutici*, it should be noted that other policy objectives, such as those concerning social policy, may also be capable of justifying taxation measures (as, for example, the Court of Justice indicated in *Commission v Greece* (Case 132/88) [1991] 3 CMLR 1 below).

Chemial Farmaceutici is an example of a case in which the two taxes were imposed at a flat rate. The situation in which the rate of taxation increases progressively across a range of goods of a particular kind was addressed in:

Humblot v Directeur des Services Fiscaux (Case 112/84) [1986] 2 CMLR 338

Panel: Bosco PC, Pescatore, Koopmans, Everling, Bahlmann, Galmot and Joliet JJ, Mr Pieter Verloren Van Themaat Advocate-General

Legislation: Article 95 EEC (now Article 110 TFEU)

Facts: Humblot had acquired a car with an engine power rating of 36CV. The French law imposed a two-tier system of annual taxation on cars. The first tier applied to all cars with engine power ratings of up to 16 CV. This consisted of a differential tax, the rate of which increased progressively and uniformly on the basis of the power of the car engines up to a maximum tax rate of 1,100 frs. The second tier applied to cars with an engine power rating over 16CV. They were subject to a special tax at a flat rate of 5,000 frs. France did not produce any cars with an engine size over 16CV.

ADVOCATE GENERAL VERLOREN VAN THEMAAT

4.3. ... In so far as a Member State, according to previous decisions of the Court, may tax certain products more heavily on account of their being luxury goods, the differentiation criterion employed must — the Commission argues — be consistent with the specified objective and there must be no direct or indirect discrimination. In this case there is no such consistency between the taxation criterion and the luxury character of the products. Many cars rated at less than 16 CV are also manifestly luxury goods irrespective of whether the price in particular or other details demonstrating luxury characteristics are taken into consideration. In addition, as far as petrol consumption is concerned (in so far as energy conservation is one of the objectives of the special tax), the Commission considers that it is clear from actual figures that no such connection exists between the criterion applied for differentiation and any objective of that kind as to make that criterion consistent with the aim of energy conservation. Finally, the Commission considers that, even if it is regarded as a luxury tax, the special tax does not in any case fulfil the requirement laid down by the Court in its previous decisions, namely that it may not result in any direct or indirect discrimination in regard to imports from other Member States. A progressive rate of taxation may only lead to higher taxation on imported goods in so far as the progression of the tax rates is commensurate with the aims pursued by the tax. In no case would a leap in the rate as in this case fulfil the objectives assumed for purposes of argument (luxury tax, energy conservation).

4.4. I concur with the view taken by the Commission, which, as regards its chief aspects, is also supported by the plaintiff in the main proceedings. In that regard no significantly new aspects were adduced at the hearing. Nevertheless, I consider it desirable to go into greater detail than the Commission's proposed answers in two respects. First, I consider it desirable to be more explicit about the applicability of the first paragraph of Article 95 to cases of this kind. Secondly, I consider it desirable to make it clear that although a leap in the rate of tax of the kind involved in this case is at variance with the first paragraph of Article 95 a gradual progression in the rate of tax is not at variance therewith, provided that the gradual increase is commensurate with the non-fiscal aims pursued by the progressive tax rate. Finally, I would point out that it follows from the nature of a special excise tax that the rate of taxation may be adjusted more precisely to suit the products concerned than may general turnover tax.

JUDGMENT

10. The Commission considers that the special tax is contrary to the first paragraph of Article 95 of the Treaty. It argues that all cars, irrespective of their power rating for tax purposes, are similar within the meaning of the case-law of the court. That being so, it is no longer possible for a Member State to create discrimination between imported and domestically-produced vehicles. The only exception is where a Member State taxes products differently - even identical products - on the basis of neutral criteria consistent with objectives of economic policy which are compatible with the Treaty, whilst avoiding discrimination between domestic and imported products. The Commission contends, however, that the criterion adopted by France in this instance, namely power rating for tax purposes, is not geared to an economic policy objective, such as heavier taxation of luxury products or vehicles with high fuel consumption. Accordingly, the Commission considers that the special tax, which is almost five times the highest rate of differential tax, affects imported vehicles only and does not pursue an economic policy objective compatible with the Treaty, is contrary to the first paragraph of Article 95 of the Treaty.

11. The United Kingdom government considers that vehicles of more than 16 CV are in a competitive relationship with some cars with a lower power rating for tax purposes, from which it follows that the special tax is contrary to the second paragraph of Article 95 of the Treaty since it diverts consumers from imported cars to French prestige models.

12. It is appropriate in the first place to stress that as community law stands at present the Member States are at liberty to subject products such as cars to a system of road tax which increases progressively in amount depending on an objective criterion, such as the power rating for tax purposes, which may be determined in various ways.

13. Such a system of domestic taxation is, however, compatible with Article 95 only in so far as it is free from any discriminatory or protective effect.

14. That is not true of a system like the one at issue in the main proceedings. Under that system there are two distinct taxes: a differential tax which increases progressively and is charged on cars not exceeding a given power rating for tax purposes and a fixed tax on cars exceeding that rating which is almost five times as high as the highest rate of the differential tax. Although the system embodies no formal distinction based on the origin of products it manifestly exhibits discriminatory or protective features contrary to Article 95, since the power rating determining liability to the special tax has been fixed at a level such that only imported cars, in particular from other Member States, are subject to the special tax whereas all cars of domestic manufacture are liable to the distinctly more advantageous differential tax.

Alert

15. In the absence of considerations relating to the amount of the special tax, consumers seeking comparable cars as regards such matters as size, comfort, actual power, maintenance costs, durability, fuel consumption and price would naturally choose from among cars above and below the critical power rating laid down by French law. However, liability to the special tax entails a much larger increase in taxation than passing from one category of car to another in a system of progressive taxation embodying balanced differentials like the system on which the differential tax is based. The resultant additional taxation is liable to cancel out the advantages which certain cars imported from other Member States might have in consumers' eyes over comparable cars of domestic manufacture, particularly since the special tax continues to be payable for several years. In that respect the special tax reduces the amount of competition to which cars of domestic manufacture are subject and hence is contrary to the principle of neutrality with which domestic taxation must comply.

16. In the light of the foregoing considerations the question raised by the national court for a preliminary ruling should be answered as follows: Article 95 of the EEC treaty prohibits the charging on cars exceeding a given power rating for tax purposes of a special fixed tax the amount of which is several times the highest amount of the progressive tax payable on cars of less than the said power rating for tax purposes, where the only cars subject to the special tax are imported, in particular from other Member States.

It is worth noting that the Court of Justice drew no distinction here between the first and second paragraphs of Article 95 EEC (now Article 110 TFEU). Its conclusion concerned both.

The outcome on the facts in *Humblot* can be contrasted with that in the following case:

Commission v Greece (Case 132/88) [1991] 3 CMLR 1

Panel: Due CJ, Kakouris and Zuleeg PPC, Joliet, Moitinho de Almeida, Rodríguez Iglesias and Grévisse JJ, M Jean Mischo, Advocate-General

Legislation: Article 95 EEC (now Article 110 TFEU)

Facts: Greek law imposed a special consumption tax on the purchase and importation of cars and a single supplementary special tax on the first registration of cars. These both increased progressively with the cylinder capacity of the car. Each involved a more pronounced increase at 1,200cc and another sharp rise at 1,800cc. In the case of the single supplementary special tax, the increase at 1,800cc was by more than 50%. All of the cars produced in Greece had a cylinder capacity of less than 1,600cc.

JUDGMENT

5. By letter of 16 September 1986, the Commission informed the Hellenic Republic that it considered that the system of taxation of private cars, in the form of the two taxes described above, infringed Article 95 of the Treaty.

6. In the first place, it pointed out that the only cars produced in Greece were of a cylinder capacity of less than 1 600 cc. In the judgment of 9 May 1985 in Case 112/84 *Humblot v Directeur des Services Fiscaux* (1985) ECR 1367, the Court had stated that, in order to be free of any discriminatory or protective effect, a progressive system of taxation of cars had to be based on objective criteria and embody balanced differentials. The Commission maintained that neither the special consumption tax nor the single supplementary special tax satisfied those requirements. No objective criterion justified the excessive tax charged on cars of a cylinder capacity over 1 800 cc, since all cars were similar products, regardless of their cylinder capacity.

    ...

9. On 15 December 1986, the Hellenic Republic replied that it contested the complaints made by the Commission. It contended that both the special consumption tax and the single supplementary special tax affected domestically produced cars and those manufactured abroad without distinction, on the basis of an objective criterion, that of cylinder capacity. It stated that in Greece cars of a cylinder capacity over 1800 cc were regarded as luxury products, exclusively for people with extremely high incomes, and that it was therefore legitimate to subject them to particularly heavy taxation. Moreover, in view of the poor infrastructure of the road network and the problems of pollution prevailing in Greece, tax legislation discouraging the purchase of large-engined cars was justified. The Hellenic Republic also pointed out the increase in taxes became steeper not only above 1 800 cc but also above 1 200 cc. Since most of the cars produced in Greece had a cylinder capacity of 1 300 cc, it was apparent that the taxes in question were not designed to protect domestic production.

    ...

Alert

16. With regard to that complaint, the Hellenic Republic contended in the course of the written procedure that the differential thresholds adopted for the two taxes in question, namely 1200 cc and 1800 cc, were objectively justified because they reflected the social circumstances prevailing in Greece and, to some extent, in Europe as a whole: cars of less than 1200 cc are for people with modest incomes; those with a cylinder capacity of between 1201 and 1800 cc are bought by people whose income is in the middle range; and those of above 1800 cc are, above all in Greece, only for people with very substantial incomes.

17. It must be emphasized in this regard that Article 95 of the Treaty does not provide a basis for censuring the excessiveness of the level of taxation which the Member States might adopt for particular products in the light of considerations of social policy. As the Court held in particular in Humblot, cited above, paragraphs 12 and 13, and in the judgment of 16 December 1986 in Case 200/85 Commission v Italy [1986] ECR 3953, paragraphs 8 and 10, as Community law stands at present, the Member States are at liberty to subject products such as cars to a system of tax which increases progressively in amount according to an objective criterion, such as cylinder capacity, provided that the system of taxation is free from any discriminatory or protective effect.

18. It must be made clear that a system of taxation cannot be regarded as discriminatory solely because only imported products, in particular those from other Member States, come within the most heavily taxed category (see judgment of 14 January 1981 in Case 140/79 Chemial Farmaceutici v DAF [1981] ECR 1, paragraph 18).

19. In order to determine whether the special consumption tax and the single supplementary special tax have a discriminatory or protective effect, it is necessary to consider whether they are capable of discouraging consumers from purchasing cars of a cylinder capacity in excess of 1800 cc, which are all manufactured abroad, in such a way as to benefit domestically produced cars.

20. If it is assumed that the particular features of the system of taxation at issue actually discourage certain consumers from purchasing cars of a cylinder capacity greater than 1800 cc, those consumers will choose either a model in the range of cars having cylinder capacities between 1600 and 1800 cc or a model in the range of cars having cylinder capacities below 1600 cc. All the models in the first-mentioned range are of foreign manufacture. The second range includes cars of both foreign and Greek manufacture. Consequently, the Commission has not shown how the system of taxation at issue might have the effect of favouring the sale of cars of Greek manufacture.

2.2.3 Non-Similar Products: Article 110(2)

If the goods are non-similar, the Court will carry out an analysis to determine whether the products fall within the second paragraph of Article 110. The function of this paragraph was outline by the Court of Justice in:

Commission v France (Case 168/78) [1981] 2 CMLR 631 ('Spirits')

Panel: Kutscher C.J.; O'Keeffe and Touffait PP.C.; Mertens de Wilmars, Pescatore, Lord Mackenzie Stuart, Bosco, Koopmans and Due JJ.

Legislation: Article 95 EEC (now Article 110 TFEU)

JUDGMENT

6. The function of the second paragraph of Article 95 is to cover, in addition, all forms of indirect tax protection in the case of products which, without being similar within the meaning of the first paragraph, are nevertheless in competition, even partial, indirect or potential, with certain products of the importing country.

If an importer is able to point to goods produced within a Member State which are non-similar, but compete with the goods of the importer and which enjoy some form of beneficial treatment as a result of the internal tax regime within that Member State, the importer may have a valid case against that Member State.

The following case provides a useful demonstration of the approach taken when reviewing non-similar products.

Commission v United Kingdom (Case 170/78) [1980] 1 CMLR 716 ('Wine and Beer')

Panel: Kutscher CJ; O'Keeffe and Touffait PPC; Mertens de Wilmars, Pescatore, Lord Mackenzie Stuart, Bosco, Koopmans and Due JJ.

Legislation: Article 95(2) EEC (now Article 110(2) TFEU)

Facts: The Commission accused the United Kingdom of imposing 50% higher tax burden on wine than on beer and thereby affording indirect protection to its national beer production. The British Government denied this.

JUDGMENT

6. In order to determine the existence of a competitive relationship under the second paragraph of Article 95, it is necessary to consider not only the present state of the market but also the possibilities for development within the context of free movement of goods at the Community level and the further potential for the substitution of products for one another which may be revealed by intensification of trade, so as fully to develop the complementary features of the economies of the member-States in accordance with the objectives laid down by Article 2 of the Treaty.

7. Where there is a competitive relationship between an imported product and national production characterised as stated above, the second paragraph of Article 95 prohibits tax practices 'of such a nature as to afford indirect protection' to the production of the importing member-State.

8. It follows from the arguments put before the Court that the parties are not fully in agreement as to the conditions for the application of that provision to this case.

The Commission has above all been concerned to show the difference between the tax burden imposed on the products in question. For its part, the Government of the United Kingdom points out that in the case of the second paragraph of Article 95 it is insufficient to establish that there is a difference in taxation; the Treaty requires that the protective effect of the tax system in question must be shown actually to exist. It considers however that this has not been shown.

9. It is true that the first and second paragraphs of Article 95 lay down different conditions as regards the characteristics of the tax practices prohibited by that Article. Under the first paragraph of that Article, which relates to products which are similar and therefore hypothetically broadly comparable, the prohibition applies where a tax mechanism is of such a nature as to impose higher taxation on imported products than on domestic products. On the other hand, the second paragraph of Article 95, precisely in view of the difficulty of making a sufficiently precise comparison between the products in question, employs a more general criterion, in other words the indirect protection afforded by a domestic tax system.

10. It is however appropriate to emphasise that the above-mentioned provision is linked to the 'nature' of the tax system in question so that it is impossible to require in each case that the protective effect should be shown statistically. It is sufficient for the purposes of the application of the second paragraph of Article 95 for it to be shown that a given tax mechanism is likely, in view of its inherent characteristics, to bring about the protective effect referred to by the Treaty. Without, therefore, disregarding the importance of the criteria which may be deduced from statistics from which the effects of a given tax system may be measured, it is impossible to require the Commission to supply statistical data on the actual foundation of the protective effect of the tax system complained of.

11. It is appropriate to appraise the facts of the case and the arguments put forward by the parties in the light of this interpretation of Article 95.

The question of competition between wine and beer

12. According to the Commission, there is a competitive relationship between wine and beer; in the case of certain consumers they may therefore actually be substituted for one another and in the case of others they may, at least potentially, be so substituted. The two beverages in fact belong to the same category of alcoholic beverages which are the product of natural fermentation; both may be used for the same purposes, as thirst-quenching drinks or to accompany meals.

13. The Government of the United Kingdom contests this attitude. Without denying the common characteristics of the two beverages, it emphasises that they are both the products of entirely different manufacturing processes. The alcoholic content of wine is three times (11% to 12%) that of beer (3% on average). The price structure of the two products is entirely different, since wine is appreciably more expensive than beer. As regards consumer habits, the Government of the United Kingdom states that, in accordance with long established tradition in the United

Kingdom, beer is a popular drink consumed preferably in public-houses or in connection with work; domestic consumption and consumption with meals is negligible. In contrast, the consumption of wine is more unusual and special from the point of view of social custom.

14. The Court considers that the Commission's argument is well-founded in that it is impossible to deny that to a certain extent the two beverages in question are capable of meeting identical needs, so that it must be acknowledged that there is a certain degree of substitution for one another. For the purpose of measuring the possible degree of substitution, it is impossible to restrict oneself to consumer habits in a member-State or in a given region. In fact, those habits, which are essentially variable in time and space, cannot be considered to be a fixed rule; the tax policy of a member-State must not therefore crystallise given consumer habits so as to consolidate an advantage acquired by national industries concerned to comply with them.

 Alert

15. At the same time it is however necessary to recognise, together with the Government of the United Kingdom, the great differences between wine and beer from the point of view of the manufacturing processes and the natural properties of those beverages. Wine is an agricultural product which is the outcome of intensive farming methods and is closely linked to the properties of the soil and climatic factors; for that reason its characteristics are extremely variable, whereas beer, which is produced from raw materials less susceptible to risks of that nature, is at the same time better suited to methods of industrial manufacture. The difference between the conditions of production leads, in the case of both products, to price structures which are so extremely different that in spite of the competitive relationship between the finished products it seems particularly difficult to make comparisons from the tax point of view.

The Court of Justice moved on to consider arguments about the methods for comparing the tax burden on the two products and the protective nature of the tax system before drawing the following conclusion:

24. The Court considers that a comparison of the development of the two tax systems in question shows a protective trend as regards imports of wine in the United Kingdom. However, in view of the uncertainties remaining both as to the characteristics of the competitive relationship between wine and beer and as to the question of the appropriate tax ratio between the two products from the point of view of the whole of the Community, the Court considers that it is unable to give a ruling at this stage on the failure to fulfil its obligations under the Treaty for which the United Kingdom is criticised. It therefore requests the Commission and the United Kingdom to resume examination of the question at issue in the light of the foregoing considerations and to report to the Court within a prescribed period either on any solution of the dispute which they have reached or on their respective viewpoints, taking into consideration the legal factors arising from this judgment. The intervener will be able to present its observations to the Court at the appropriate time.

Having considered further argument, Court delivered a final judgment in:

Commission v United Kingdom (Case 170/78) [1983] 3 CMLR 512 ('Wine and Beer')

Panel: Mertens de Wilmars CJ; Pescatore, O'Keeffe and Everling PPC; Lord Mackenzie Stuart, Bosco, Koopmans, Due, Bahlmann, Galmot and Kakouris JJ.

Legislation and facts: As above.

The Court of Justice began by providing a summary of its observations on the question of competitive relation between wine and beer in its earlier judgement and then continued:

JUDGMENT

10.   The Government of the United Kingdom did not give any opinion on that question in its subsequent statements. The Commission expressed the view that the difference in the conditions of production, to which the Court had attached some importance, was not significant from the point of view of the price structures of the two products, particularly in relation to the competitive relationship between beer and wines of popular quality.

11.   The Italian Government contended in that connection that it was inappropriate to compare beer with wines of average alcoholic strength or, a fortiori, with wines of greater alcoholic strength. In its opinion, it was the lightest wines with an alcoholic strength in the region of 9 per cent., that is to say the most popular and cheapest wines, which were genuinely in competition with beer. It therefore took the view that those wines should be chosen for purposes of comparison where it was a question of measuring the incidence of taxation on the basis of either alcoholic strength or the price of the products.

12.   The Court considers that observation by the Italian Government to be pertinent. In view of the substantial differences in the quality and, therefore, in the price of wines, the decisive competitive relationship between beer, a popular and widely consumed beverage, and wine must be established by reference to those wines which are the most accessible to the public at large, that is to say, generally speaking, the lightest and cheapest varieties. Accordingly, that is the appropriate basis for making fiscal comparisons by reference to the alcoholic strength or to the price of the two beverages in question.

 Alert

The Court of Justice then moved on to consider how to determine the tax ratio between the products:

25.   The Commission's calculations, which relate to the United Kingdom market in its present state and the relevance of which is not challenged by the United Kingdom Government, show that wine is subject to an additional tax burden of around 58 and 77 per cent., whereas the Italian Government's calculations relating to the cheapest wine show that wine is subject to an additional tax burden of up to 286 per cent. Those findings are indirectly confirmed by the United Kingdom

Government's analysis of the selling prices of the two German wines. Indeed, one of those two wines represents almost exactly the point of parity between beer and wine, from the point of view of the incidence of taxation on the price. That example shows that all cheaper wines marketed in the United Kingdom are taxed, by reference to price, more heavily in relative terms than beer. It appears from the price lists provided by the Commission that on the United Kingdom market there are an appreciable number of wines falling within that definition, and among them practically all the Italian wines, which are therefore subject to an additional tax burden which increases in inverse proportion to their price.

26. After considering the information provided by the parties, the court has come to the conclusion that, if a comparison is made on the basis of those wines which are cheaper than the types of wine selected by the United Kingdom and of which several varieties are sold in significant quantities on the United Kingdom market, it becomes apparent that precisely those wines which, in view of their price, are most directly in competition with domestic beer production are subject to a considerably higher tax burden.

 Alert

27. It is clear, therefore, following the detailed inquiry conducted by the court — whatever criterion for comparison is used, there being no need to express a preference for one or the other — that the United Kingdom's tax system has the effect of subjecting wine imported from other Member States to an additional tax burden so as to afford protection to domestic beer production, inasmuch as beer production constitutes the most relevant reference criterion from the point of view of competition. Since such protection is most marked in the case of the most popular wines, the effect of the United Kingdom tax system is to stamp wine with the hallmarks of a luxury product which, in view of the tax burden which it bears, can scarcely constitute in the eyes of the consumer a genuine alternative to the typical domestically produced beverage.

28. It follows from the foregoing considerations that, by levying excise duty on still light wines made from fresh grapes at a higher rate, in relative terms, than on beer, the United Kingdom has failed to fulfil its obligations under the second paragraph of Article 95 of the EEC Treaty

The outcome of this case can be contrasted with the following case which also involved the taxation of wine and beer:

Commission v Belgium (Case 356/85) [1988] 3 CMLR 277

Panel: Lord Mackenzie Stuart CJ; O'Higgins and Schockweiler PPC.; Bosco, Due, Everling, Bahlmann, Joliet and Moitinho de Almeida JJ.

Legislation: Article 95 EEC (now Article 110 TFEU)

Facts: Belgium imposed VAT on wine at a rate of 25% and on beer at a rate of 19%. It did not produce any wine but it did produce a substantial amount of beer.

JUDGMENT

12. With regard to the question whether or not the tax system at issue is protective in nature, the Commission and the French Government take the view that once a competitive relationship is established between two products any difference in the rates of tax applied to the same basis of assessment, in this case the value, is contrary to the second paragraph of Article 95 of the Treaty, and it is not necessary also to take into account the impact of that difference of rates on the retail price and hence on consumer preference.

13. According to the Belgian Government, on the other hand, if the second paragraph of Article 95 is to apply it is also necessary, by contrast with the position under the first paragraph, for a further condition to be satisfied, namely that the discrepancy in the tax burden must be liable to have a protective effect favouring domestic products. It is therefore necessary to consider the possible economic effects of the tax in question.

14. In its judgment in Case 168/78, *E.C. Commission v France*, the Court held that whilst the criterion indicated in the first paragraph of Article 95 consists in the comparison of tax burdens whether in terms of the rate, the mode of assessment or other detailed rules for their application, in view of the difficulty of making sufficiently precise comparisons between the products in question the second paragraph of that Article is based upon a more general criterion, namely the protective nature of the system of internal taxation.

15. It follows that any assessment of the compatibility of a given tax with the second paragraph of Article 95 must take account of the impact of that tax on the competitive relationship between the products concerned. The essential question is therefore whether or not the tax is of such a kind as to have the effect, on the market in question, of reducing potential consumption of imported products to the advantage of competing domestic products.

 Alert

16. Consequently, in considering to what extent a protective effect actually exists, the difference between the respective selling prices of beer and wine competing with beer cannot be disregarded. The Belgian Government has stated that the price of a litre of beer, including tax, is on average 29.75 Bfr, whereas the corresponding price of a litre of ordinary wine is around 125 Bfr, four times the price of beer, giving a difference in price per litre of 95.25 Bfr. In the Belgian Government's view it follows that even if a single rate were applied to both products, the price difference between the two would continue to be substantial; the reduction in that difference would be so insignificant that it would not influence consumer preference.

17. In response to that argument the Commission drew attention to the fact that in two Belgian establishments named by it the wine most commonly consumed is sold at 61 Bfr per litre, including tax. The Belgian Government did not challenge that figure but stated that, according to the information given to it by one of those establishments, the sales of wines priced at less than 80 Bfr, which include wines

sold in five-litre plastic containers and cooking wines, account for only about 15.6 per cent. of total wine sales. According to the Belgian Government, it is more appropriate to compare such wines with table beer which is sold for as little as 17 Bfr per litre.

18. In view of those observations, it must be concluded that the Commission has not shown that the difference between the respective prices for comparable qualities of beer and wine is so small that the difference of 6 per cent. between the VAT rates applied to the two products is capable of influencing consumer behaviour. The Commission has thus not shown that that difference gives rise to any protective effect favouring beer intended for domestic consumption.

19. Nor do the statistics produced by the Commission comparing trends in beer and wine consumption indicate the existence of any protective effect. The Commission stated that beer consumption in Belgium reached a peak in 1973 and has been on the decline since then. By contrast, wine consumption has tripled during the last 20 years; however, from 1980 onwards, the grown in wine consumption slowed down and it levelled off in 1982 and 1983.

20. Whilst those figures show the general trends in the consumption of the products in question, they do not show with any certainty that there is any causal connection between the patterns of consumption described and the introduction in 1977 of a higher rate of VAT for wine. Consequently, the Commission cannot successfully rely upon them to support its view that the progressive increase in wine consumption was slowed down and finally brought to a halt precisely because of the introduction of a higher rate of VAT for wine. Moreover, that view does not appear to be borne out by the fact, pointed out by the Belgian Government and not contested by the Commission, that between 1978 and 1983 the rate of VAT applicable to beer was increased on three occasions without there being in the medium term any restrictive effect on the consumption of beer to the advantage of wine.

21. It follows that the Commission has not established that the tax system in question actually has a protective effect. Accordingly, the application must be dismissed.

2.3 Non-Fiscal Barriers

Whereas Articles 30 and 110 TFEU deal with fiscal measures which affect trade between Member States, Articles 34 to 36 TFEU deal with non-fiscal measures, ie measures other than customs duties, CEE's and internal taxation. Such measures can take a wide range of forms. In addition, by their nature customs duties, CEE's and internal taxation can only be put in place by a government. In contrast, non-fiscal measures can also be put in place by non-governmental organisations. For instance a pressure group could implement a road blockade to further its cause. In such cases the member state Government can be liable for failing to take appropriate action against the relevant parties within their territory.

2.3.1 Article 34 TFEU: Restrictions on Imports

Article 34 prohibits quantitative restrictions and all measures having equivalent effect between Member States.

2.3.1.1 Quantitative Restrictions

Quantitative restrictions are simply overt restrictions on quantity. They were defined by the Court of Justice in:

Geddo v Ente Nazionale Risi **(Case 2/73) [1974] 1 CMLR 13**

Legislation: Articles 20 (2) and 23 of Regulation 359/67 which prohibited quantitative restrictions on rice and measures having equivalent effect

JUDGMENT:

7. The ban on any quantitative restriction or measure having equivalent effect in Article 20 (2) of the said regulation [i.e. Regulation 359/67] has among its objects to prevent Member States from taking unilateral measures to limit exports to third countries unless otherwise permitted by the regulations.

    The prohibition of such a measure as between members of the community in Article 23 is intended to ensure the free movement of goods within the community.

    The prohibition on quantitative restrictions covers measures which amount to a total or partial restraint of, according to the circumstances, imports, exports or goods in transit.

 Alert

Such measures usually take the form of bans or quotas on imports. Such behaviour may be justified under Article 36 TFEU which is discussed further below at 3.3.1. Otherwise it will constitute a breach of Article 34 TFEU.

2.3.1.2 Measures Having Equivalent Effect ('MEQRs')

Whereas quotas and bans are clear forms of restriction on the quantity of imports, there can be other more subtle forms of non-fiscal measure which have an equivalent effect to such restrictions by acting as barriers to trade. They often take the form of requirements that a product must comply with before it can be marketed within a member state. Such measures having equivalent effect ('MEQRs') are also prohibited by Article 34 TFEU. The jurisprudence in this area can be fairly complex. That is because there are a large number of ways in which a Member State can impose MEQR's and by definition they are not necessarily obvious on the face of the provision. In addition, this area more than any other within free movement of goods, steps on the toes of the traditions and customs of the various Member States.

Before considering the case law in this area students should be familiar with the content of Directive 70/50. This was a transitional measure which only applied to measures that were operative when the EEC Treaty initially came into force. It is now redundant but it undoubtedly influenced the Court of Justice in its assessment of MEQR's.

Commission Directive 70/50

Article 1

The purpose of this Directive is to abolish the measures referred to in Articles 2 and 3, which were operative at the date of entry into force of the EEC Treaty.

Article 2

1. This Directive covers measures, other than those applicable equally to domestic or imported products, which hinder imports which could otherwise take place, including measures which makes importation more difficult or costly than the disposal of domestic production.

...

Article 3.

The Directive also covers measures governing the marketing of products which deal, in particular, with shape, size, weight, composition, presentation, identification or putting up and which are equally applicable to domestic and imported products, where the restrictive effect of such measures on the free movement of goods exceeds effects intrinsic to trade rules.

This is the case, in particular, where:

— the restrictive effects on the free movement of goods are out of proportion to their purpose;

— the same objective cam be attained by other methods which are less of a hindrance to trade.

Measures which do not apply equally to domestic and imported goods are now known as distinctly applicable measures. Those which do apply equally to domestic and imported good are now known as indistinctly applicable measures.

The most important early decision in relation to MEQR's followed only a few years after the Directive was adopted. This was the decision of the Court of Justice in *Procureur du Roi v Benoit and Gustave Dassonville* (Case 8/74) [1974] ECR 83 in which the concept of an MEQR was defined. The Directive was considered by Advocate General Trabucchi in his opinion in that case but it was not mentioned at all by the Court in its decision.

Procureur du Roi v Benoit and Gustave Dassonville (Case 8/74) [1974] ECR 837

Legislation: Article 30 EEC (now Article 34 TFEU)

In the excerpt: Article 36 EEC is now Article 36 TFEU

Facts: The Belgium law imposed a rule preventing the sale of certain products, such as Scotch whisky, without a certificate of authenticity. A trader in whisky purchased his whisky in France and made his own certificate of authenticity. The trader was accused of forging the certificate. The trader argued that the requirement for a certificate amounted to a measure having equivalent effect to a quantitative restriction on trade.

JUDGMENT:

5. All trading rules enacted by Member States which are capable of hindering, directly or indirectly, actually or potentially, intra-community trade are to be considered as measures having an effect equivalent to quantitative restrictions.

 Alert

6. In the absence of a community system guaranteeing for consumers the authenticity of a product's designation of origin, if a Member State takes measures to prevent unfair practices in this connexion, it is however subject to the condition that these measures should be reasonable and that the means of proof required should not act as a hindrance to trade between Member States and should, in consequence, be accessible to all community nationals.

7. Even without having to examine whether or not such measures are covered by Article 36, they must not, in any case, by virtue of the principle expressed in the second sentence of that Article, constitute a means of arbitrary discrimination or a disguised restriction on trade between Member States.

8. That may be the case with formalities, required by a Member State for the purpose of proving the origin of a product, which only direct importers are really in a position to satisfy without facing serious difficulties.

9. Consequently, the requirement by a Member State of a certificate of authenticity which is less easily obtainable by importers of an authentic product which has been put into free circulation in a regular manner in another Member State than by importers of the same product coming directly from the country of origin constitutes a measure having an effect equivalent to a quantitative restriction as prohibited by the Treaty.

The definition in paragraph 5 is now known as the *Dassonville* formula. It was strikingly wide, extending even to indirect and potential hindrances to intra-Community trade. It was also framed in terms that were wide enough not only to cover distinctly applicable measures but also to be capable of covering indistinctly applicable measures.

Distinctly Applicable MEQR's

A determination of whether or not a distinctly applicable measure is an MEQR requires a careful assessment in order to determine whether it is capable of hindering intra-Community trade. For example, a requirement that imported goods should be inspected will be an MEQR as it can add costs to the product because of the delay and extra transport requirements. As this illustrates, there are evident parallels between such a measure and CEE's which are prohibited under Article 30 TFEU.

Firma Denkavit Futtermittel GmbH v Minister für Ernährung (Case 251/78) [1979] ECR 3369

Legislation: Articles 30 and 36 EEC (now Articles 34 and 36 TFEU respectively)

Facts: An importer of animal foodstuffs from the Netherlands into North Rhine-Westphalia in Germany was required by a law of that German region:

i) to produce a certificate from the competent authorities in the exporting State confirming that the consignment of goods had undergone a heating process to destroy any salmonellae present in them; and

ii) to undergo inspection of samples from that consignment before being permitted to import the it.

However, an exemption could be granted by the responsible Minister, under certain conditions, where there was no reason to fear that the importation and transit of the feeding-stuffs in question were a source of introduction or propagation of epizootic disease germs.

JUDGMENT

10. As the national court has rightly pointed out the court in its decided cases continues to interpret the concept of measures having an effect equivalent to quantitative restrictions in Article 30 of the Treaty as applying to systematic veterinary and public health inspections carried out at the intra-community frontiers. The same interpretation applies, as the court has acknowledged in its judgment of 24 January 1978 in Case 82/77 *Openbaar Ministerie of the Kingdom of the Netherlands v Jacobus Philippus van Tiggele* [1978] ECR 25, to a system under which a trader finds that he has to apply to be exempted or to derogate from a domestic measure which is itself a quantitative restriction or a measure having equivalent effect .

11. The concept of a measure having an effect equivalent to a quantitative restriction also applies to the obligation to produce a certificate to the effect that the imported feeding-stuffs have undergone specified treatment in the exporting country. The fact that there are often provisions in Community directives which are designed to harmonize and bring to an end as far as possible national veterinary and public health inspections at the frontier does not result in the requirement under national law in the importing Member State to produce a certificate from the authorities of the exporting state no longer being treated as a measure having equivalent effect. As far as their restrictive effect on intra-Community trade is concerned it is in fact impossible to compare a legal requirement laid down unilaterally by a Member State to produce a certificate, to the production of which it attaches such legal effects as it deems advisable , with the obligation imposed by a directive on all the member states to issue , in order to facilitate intra-Community trade , a standard veterinary and public health certificate in a system the aim of which is to transfer supervision to the exporting member state and to replace in this way the systematic protective measures at the frontier with a uniform system so as to make multiple frontier inspections unnecessary and at the same time to give the Member State of destination the opportunity of ensuring that the guarantees provided by the system of inspection thus standardized are in fact given.

12.   It follows from the foregoing considerations that the concept of a measure having an effect equivalent to quantitative restrictions covers national measures such as those provided for by Articles 1, 2 and 9 of the Viehseuchenverordnung [the North Rhine-Westphalian Regulation on Infectious Diseases of Animals] 1957 and that such measures fall within the prohibition in Article 30 of the Treaty unless they fall within the exception provided for in Article 36.

Note that it is possible for a Member State to breach both Article 30 TFEU and Article 34 TFEU by not only imposing an inspection in breach of Article 34 but also by charging for that inspection in breach of Article 30. Indeed, this happened in *Denkavit* itself.

Furthermore, it is also important to note that the *Dassonville* formula does not require the Commission or courts to show that any particular MEQR actually hindered trade. It is enough that the measure could hinder trade, even if it does not involve any binding legislative measures:

Commission v Ireland (Case 249/81) [1982] ECR 4005 ('*Buy Irish*')

Legislation: Article 30 EEC (now Article 34 TFEU)

Facts: The Irish Government sought to promote the sale of Irish goods by encouraging the use of a "Buy Irish" symbol on Irish made goods and by the organisation of a publicity campaign.

JUDGMENT

21.   The Irish Government maintains that the prohibition against measures having an effect equivalent to quantitative restrictions in Article 30 is concerned only with "measures", that is to say, binding provisions emanating from a public authority. However, no such provision has been adopted by the Irish government, which has confined itself to giving moral support and financial aid to the activities pursued by the Irish industries.

22.   The Irish Government goes on to emphasize that the campaign has had no restrictive effect on imports since the proportion of Irish goods to all goods sold on the Irish market fell from 49.2% in 1977 to 43.4% in 1980.

23.   The first observation to be made is that the campaign cannot be likened to advertising by private or public undertakings, or by a group of undertakings, to encourage people to buy goods produced by those undertakings. Regardless of the means used to implement it, the campaign is a reflection of the Irish Government's considered intention to substitute domestic products for imported products on the Irish market and thereby to check the flow of imports from other Member States.

24.   It must be remembered here that a representative of the Irish Government stated when the campaign was launched that it was a carefully thought-out set of initiatives constituting an integrated programme for promoting domestic products; that the Irish goods council was set up at the initiative of the Irish Government a

few months later; and that the task of implementing the integrated programme as it was envisaged by the Government was entrusted, or left, to that council.

25. Whilst it may be true that the two elements of the programme which have continued in effect, namely the advertising campaign and the use of the "guaranteed Irish" symbol, have not had any significant success in winning over the Irish market to domestic products, it is not possible to overlook the fact that, regardless of their efficacy, those two activities form part of a Government programme which is designed to achieve the substitution of domestic products for imported products and is liable to affect the volume of trade between Member States.

26. The advertising campaign to encourage the sale and purchase of Irish products cannot be divorced from its origin as part of the Government programme, or from its connection with the introduction of the "Guaranteed Irish" symbol and with the organization of a special system for investigating complaints about products bearing that symbol. The establishment of the system for investigating complaints about Irish products provides adequate confirmation of the degree of organization surrounding the "Buy Irish" 'campaign and of the discriminatory nature of the campaign.

 Alert

27. In the circumstances the two activities in question amount to the establishment of a national practice, introduced by the Irish Government and prosecuted with its assistance, the potential effect of which on imports from other Member States is comparable to that resulting from Government measures of a binding nature.

28. Such a practice cannot escape the prohibition laid down by Article 30 of the Treaty solely because it is not based on decisions which are binding upon undertakings. Even measures adopted by the Government of a member state which do not have binding effect may be capable of influencing the conduct of traders and consumers in that state and thus of frustrating the aims of the community as set out in Article 2 and enlarged upon in Article 3 of the Treaty.

29. That is the case where, as in this instance, such a restrictive practice represents the implementation of a programme defined by the Government which affects the national economy as a whole and which is intended to check the flow of trade between Member States by encouraging the purchase of domestic products, by means of an advertising campaign on a national scale and the organization of special procedures applicable solely to domestic products, and where those activities are attributable as a whole to the Government and are pursued in an organized fashion throughout the national territory.

30. Ireland has therefore failed to fulfil its obligations under the Treaty by organizing a campaign to promote the sale and purchase of Irish goods within its territory.

Indistinctly Applicable MEQR's

Indistinctly applicable measures are the most subtle form of provision prohibited under Article 34 TFEU. Many of the cases involve packaging and presentation rules. Some rules and requirements pre-dated the entry of the relevant member state into the union and sometimes reflected particular traditions of that member state. However, an important component of the enforcement of Article 34 TFEU was the removal of these rules where they could not be justified.

The *Dassonville* formula defined MEQRs in terms that were wide enough to include indistinctly applicable measures. The Court of Justice confirmed that such rules are capable of infringing Article 34 in its seminal decision in:

Rewe-Zentrale AG v Bundesmonopolverwaltung für Branntwein (Case 120/78) [1979] ECR 649 ('Cassis de Dijon')

Legislation: Articles 30 and 37 EEC (now Articles 34 and 37 TFEU respectively)

Facts: An importer wanted to import the liqueur 'Cassis de Dijon' from Germany into France. German law specified that such liqueurs had to have an alcohol content of 25 per cent. Cassis de Dijon had an alcohol content of between 15 and 20 per cent and therefore it importation into Germany was not permitted.

JUDGMENT

6. The national court is thereby asking for assistance in the matter of interpretation in order to enable it to assess whether the requirement of a minimum alcohol content may be covered either by the prohibition on all measures having an effect equivalent to quantitative restrictions in trade between Member States contained in Article 30 of the Treaty or by the prohibition on all discrimination regarding the conditions under which goods are procured and marketed between nationals of Member States within the meaning of Article 37.

The Court of Justice first concluded that Article 37 EEC (now Article 37 TFEU), which concerns State monopolies of a commercial character, was irrelevant. It then turned to consider Article 30 EEC (now Article 34 TFEU).

8. In the absence of common rules relating to the production and marketing of alcohol — a proposal for a regulation submitted to the council by the Commission on 7 December 1976 (Official Journal C309, P.2) not yet having received the council's approval — it is for the Member States to regulate all matters relating to the production and marketing of alcohol and alcoholic beverages on their own territory.

Obstacles to movement within the community resulting from disparities between the national laws relating to the marketing of the products in question must be accepted in so far as those provisions may be recognized as being necessary in order to satisfy mandatory requirements relating in particular to the effectiveness of fiscal supervision, the protection of public health, the fairness of commercial transactions and the defence of the consumer.

The Court of Justice then discussed whether or not the measure could be justified on the basis of the protection of public health or the defence of the consumer. This part of the judgement, which established the mandatory requirements (rule of reason) defence, is extracted and discussed further below at 3.3.2. The Court of Justice concluded that the restriction could not be justified and continued with the following:

14. ... In practice, the principle effect of requirements of this nature is to promote alcoholic beverages having a high alcohol content by excluding from the national market products of other Member States which do not answer that description.

It therefore appears that the unilateral requirement imposed by the rules of a member state of minimum alcohol content for the purposes of the sale of alcoholic beverages constitutes an obstacle to trade which is incompatible with the provisions of Article 30 of the Treaty.

There is therefore no valid reason why, provided that they have been lawfully produced and marketed in one of the Member States, alcoholic beverages should not be introduced into any other member state; the sale of such products may not be subject to a legal prohibition on the marketing of beverages with an alcohol content lower than the limit set by the national rules.

 Alert

15. Consequently, the first question should be answered to the effect that the concept of "measures having an effect equivalent to quantitative restrictions on imports" contained in Article 30 of the Treaty is to be understood to mean that the fixing of a minimum alcohol content for alcoholic beverages intended for human consumption by the legislation of a Member State also falls within the prohibition laid down in that provision where the importation of alcoholic beverages lawfully produced and marketed in another member state is concerned.

This gave rise to the presumption of mutual recognition which presumes that there will be no valid reason why goods which have been lawfully produced and marketed in one member state cannot be introduced and marketed in another member state. In effect, each Member State must recognise and accept the legal requirements governing the production and marketing of products in the other member states and so must refrain from imposing additional requirements.

An example of the application of Article 34 in relation to a form of packaging that had become "traditional" in a particular Member State can be found in *Walter Rau Lebensmittelwerke v Smedt PvbA* (Case 261/81) [1982] ECR 3961 which is discussed in 3.3.2 below. Another example of the Court of Justice identifying an indistinctly applicable MEQR can be found in:

Commission v Ireland (Case 45/87) [1988] ECR 4929 ('Dundalk Water Supply')

Facts: Contractors tendering for the contract to supply water to Dundalk, whether from Ireland or elsewhere, were required by Dundalk Urban District Council to supply pipes which complied with 'Irish Standard Mark 188'. An Irish undertaking had made the lowest bid to supply pipes but its bid had been refused because the pipes, which had been manufactured in Spain, had not been certified as complying with the Irish Standard Mark, even though they met an equivalent international standard. The Irish undertaking and the Spanish manufacturer of the pipes complained to the Commission which brought infringement proceedings against Ireland in the Court of Justice.

JUDGMENT

12. It must be observed at the outset that the Commission maintains that Dundalk Urban District Council is a public body for whose acts the Irish Government is responsible. Moreover, before accepting a tender, Dundalk Council has to obtain the authorization of the Irish Department of the Environment. Those facts have not been challenged by the Irish Government.

13. It must also be noted that according to the Irish Government the requirement of compliance with Irish standards is the usual practice followed in relation to public works contracts in Ireland.

14. The Irish Government points out that the contract at issue relates not to the sale of goods but to the performance of work, and the clauses relating to the materials to be used are completely subsidiary. Contracts concerned with the performance of work fall under the Treaty provisions relating to the free supply of services, without prejudice to any harmonization measures which might be taken under Article 100. Consequently, Article 30 cannot apply to a contract for works.

15. In that connection, the Irish Government cites the case-law of the Court and, in particular, the judgment of 22 March 1977 in Case 74/76 *Iannelli & Volpi v Meroni* [1977] ECR 557, according to which the field of application of Article 30 does not include obstacles to trade covered by other specific provisions of the Treaty.

16. That argument cannot be accepted. Article 30 envisages the elimination of all measures of the Member States which impede imports in intra-Community trade, whether the measures bear directly on the movement of imported goods or have the effect of indirectly impeding the marketing of goods from other Member States. The fact that some of those barriers must be considered in the light of specific provisions of the Treaty, such as the provisions of Article 95 relating to fiscal discrimination, in no way detracts from the general character of the prohibitions laid down by Article 30.

17. The provisions on the freedom to supply services invoked by the Irish Government, on the other hand, are not concerned with the movement of goods but the freedom to perform activities and have them carried out; they do not lay down any specific rule relating to particular barriers to the free movement of goods. Consequently, the fact that a public works contract relates to the provision of services cannot remove a clause in an invitation to tender restricting the materials that may be used from the scope of the prohibitions set out in Article 30.

18. Consequently, it must be considered whether the inclusion of Clause 4.29 in the invitation to tender and in the tender specifications was liable to impede imports of pipes into Ireland.

19. In that connection, it must first be pointed out that the inclusion of such a clause in an invitation to tender may cause economic operators who produce or utilize pipes equivalent to pipes certified as complying with Irish standards to refrain from tendering.

20. It further appears from the documents in the case that only one undertaking has been certified by the IIRS to IS 188:1975 to apply the Irish Standard Mark to pipes of the type required for the purposes of the public works contract at issue. That undertaking is located in Ireland. Consequently, the inclusion of Clause 4.29 had the effect of restricting the supply of the pipes needed for the Dundalk scheme to Irish manufacturers alone.

2.3.2 Defences

Article 36 sets out the defences available to Member States in respect of a potential breach of Article 34. The defences are available in respect of both QR's and MEQR's. Additional defences are available in respect of indistinctly applicable MEQR's under the 'rule of reason' as described further below.

2.3.2.1 Article 36 Derogations

Article 36 sets out 6 derogations: public morality; public policy; public security; the protection of health and life of humans, animals or plants; the protection of national treasures possessing artistic, historic or archaeological value and finally the protection of industrial and commercial property. Set out below are cases two of the most used derogations: public morality and the protection of health and life of humans, animals or plants.

Public Morality

Conegate Ltd v Commissioners of Customs and Excise (Case 121/85) [1986] ECR 1007

Note: Article 177 is now Article 267

Facts: The UK sought to prevent the import of life-size inflatable 'love-love' dolls from Germany. The production of such dolls was legal within the UK.

JUDGMENT

15. However, although community law leaves the Member States free to make their own assessments of the indecent or obscene character of certain articles, it must be pointed out that the fact that goods cause offence cannot be regarded as sufficiently serious to justify restrictions on the free movement of goods where the member state concerned does not adopt, with respect to the same goods manufactured or marketed within its territory, penal measures or other serious and effective measures intended to prevent the distribution of such goods in its territory.

 Alert

16. It follows that a Member State may not rely on grounds of public morality in order to prohibit the importation of goods from other Member States when its

legislation contains no prohibition on the manufacture or marketing of the same goods on its territory.

17. It is not for the court, within the framework of the powers conferred upon it by Article 177 of the EEC Treaty, to consider whether, and to what extent, the United Kingdom legislation contains such a prohibition. However, the question whether or not such a prohibition exists in a state comprised of different constituent parts which have their own internal legislation, can be resolved only by taking into consideration all the relevant legislation. Although it is not necessary, for the purposes of the application of the above-mentioned rule, that the manufacture and marketing of the products whose importation has been prohibited should be prohibited in the territory of all the constituent parts, it must at least be possible to conclude from the applicable rules, taken as a whole, that their purpose is, in substance, to prohibit the manufacture and marketing of those products.

18. In this instance, in the actual wording of its first question the high court took care to define the substance of the national legislation the compatibility of which with community law is a question which it proposes to determine. Thus it refers to rules in the importing Member State under which the goods in question may be manufactured freely and marketed subject only to certain restrictions, which it sets out explicitly, namely an absolute prohibition on the transmission of such goods by post, a restriction on their public display and, in certain areas of the Member State concerned, a system of licensing of premises for the sale of those goods to customers aged 18 years and over. Such restrictions cannot however be regarded as equivalent in substance to a prohibition on manufacture and marketing.

The protection of health and life of humans, animals or plants

Officer van Justice v Santoz BV (Case 174/82) [1983] ECR 2445

Facts: The Dutch authorities refused to allow the sale of muesli bars containing added vitamins on the grounds that excessive consumption of vitamins could be harmful to human health. Scientific data did not provide a clear answer as to the point at which vitamins did become harmful to health.

JUDGMENT

16. As the court found in its judgment of 17 December 1981 in Case 272/80 (*Frans-nederlandse Maatschappij Voor Biologische Producten* (1981) ECR 3277), in so far as there are uncertainties at the present state of scientific research it is for the Member States, in the absence of harmonization, to decide what degree of protection of the health and life of humans they intend to assure, having regard however for the requirements of the free movement of goods within the community.

17. Those principles also apply to substances such as vitamins which are not as a general rule harmful in themselves but may have special harmful effects solely if taken to excess as part of the general nutrition, the composition of which is unforeseeable and cannot be monitored. In view of the uncertainties inherent in the scientific assessment, national rules prohibiting, without prior authorization, the marketing of foodstuffs to which vitamins have been added are justified on principle within the meaning of Article 36 of the Treaty on grounds of the protection of human health.

 Alert

18. Nevertheless the principle of proportionality which underlies the last sentence of Article 36 of the Treaty requires that the power of the Member States to prohibit imports of the products in question from other Member States should be restricted to what is necessary to attain the legitimate aim of protecting health. Accordingly, national rules providing for such a prohibition are justified only if authorizations to market are granted when they are compatible with the need to protect health.

19. Such an assessment is, however, difficult to make in relation to additives such as vitamins the abovementioned characteristics of which exclude the possibility of foreseeing or monitoring the quantities consumed as part of the general nutrition and the degree of harmfulness of which cannot be determined with sufficient certainty. Nevertheless, although in view of the present stage of harmonization of national laws at the community level a wide discretion must be left to the Member States, they must, in order to observe the principle of proportionality, authorize marketing when the addition of vitamins to foodstuffs meets a real need, especially a technical or nutritional one.

20. The first question must therefore be answered to the effect that community law permits national rules prohibiting without prior authorization the marketing of foodstuffs lawfully marketed in another Member State to which vitamins have been added, provided that the marketing is authorized when the addition of vitamins meets a real need, especially a technical or nutritional one.

Second question

21. In the second question the national court asks in essence whether community law precludes national rules such as those referred to by the national court where the authorization to market is subject to proof by the importer that the product in question is not harmful to health.

22. In as much as the question arises as to where the onus of proof lies when there is a request for authorization, in view of the answer to the first question, it must be remembered that Article 36 of the Treaty creates an exception, which must be strictly interpreted, to the rule of free movement of goods within the community which is one of the fundamental principles of the common market. It is therefore for the national authorities who rely on that provision in order to adopt a measure restricting intra-community trade to check in each instance that the measure contemplated satisfies the criteria of that provision.

23. Accordingly, although the national authorities may, in so far as they do not have it themselves, ask the importer to produce the information in his possession relating to the composition of the product and the technical or nutritional reasons for adding vitamins, they must themselves assess, in the light of all the relevant information, whether authorization must be granted pursuant to community law.

24. The second question must therefore be answered to the effect that community law does not permit national rules which subject authorization to market to proof by the importer that the product in question is not harmful to health, without prejudice to the right of the national authorities to ask the importer to submit all the information in his possession needed to assess the facts

2.3.2.2 Mandatory Requirements (the 'Rule of Reason')

The Court of Justice had suggested in *Dassonville* that a Member State may be able to justify indistinctly applicable MEQRs on grounds which do not fall within Article 36:

Procureur du Roi v Benoit and Gustave Dassonville (Case 8/74) [1974] ECR 837

Facts: See 3.1.2 above.

JUDGMENT:

6. In the absence of a community system guaranteeing for consumers the authenticity of a product's designation of origin, if a Member State takes measures to prevent unfair practices in this connexion, it is however subject to the condition that these measures should be reasonable and that the means of proof required should not act as a hindrance to trade between Member States and should, in consequence, be accessible to all community nationals.

This was confirmed and developed by the Court of Justice in its seminal judgement in *Cassis de Dijon*. The Court of Justice established that indistinctly applicable MEQRs could be justified by mandatory requirements which serve purposes in the general interest. These mandatory requirements are effectively additional grounds of defence, beyond those in Article 36, which are recognised by the Court of Justice. They serve to rebut the presumption of mutual recognition.

Rewe-Zentrale AG v Bundesmonopolverwaltung für Branntwein (Case 120/78) [1979] ECR 649 ('*Cassis de Dijon*')

Facts: see 3.1.2 above

JUDGMENT

8. ... Obstacles to movement within the community resulting from disparities between the national laws relating to the marketing of the products in question must be accepted in so far as those provisions may be recognized as being necessary in order to satisfy mandatory requirements relating in particular to the effectiveness of fiscal supervision, the protection of public health, the fairness of commercial transactions and the defence of the consumer.

9. The Government of the Federal Republic of Germany, intervening in the proceedings, put forward various arguments which, in its view, justify the application of provisions relating to the minimum alcohol content of alcoholic beverages, adducing considerations relating on the one hand to the protection of public health and on the other to the protection of the consumer against unfair commercial practices.

10. As regards the protection of public health the German Government states that the purpose of the fixing of minimum alcohol contents by national legislation is to avoid the proliferation of alcoholic beverages on the national market, in particular alcoholic beverages with a low alcohol content, since, in its view, such products may more easily induce a tolerance towards alcohol than more highly alcoholic beverages.

11. Such considerations are not decisive since the consumer can obtain on the market an extremely wide range of weakly or moderately alcoholic products and furthermore a large proportion of alcoholic beverages with a high alcohol content freely sold on the German market is generally consumed in a diluted form.

12. The German Government also claims that the fixing of a lower limit for the alcohol content of certain liqueurs is designed to protect the consumer against unfair practices on the part of producers and distributors of alcoholic beverages.

This argument is based on the consideration that the lowering of the alcohol content secures a competitive advantage in relation to beverages with a higher alcohol content, since alcohol constitutes by far the most expensive constituent of beverages by reason of the high rate of tax to which it is subject.

Furthermore, according to the German government, to allow alcoholic products into free circulation wherever, as regards their alcohol content, they comply with the rules laid down in the country of production would have the effect of imposing as a common standard within the community the lowest alcohol content permitted in any of the Member States, and even of rendering any requirements in this field inoperative since a lower limit of this nature is foreign to the rules of several Member States.

13. As the Commission rightly observed, the fixing of limits in relation to the alcohol content of beverages may lead to the standardization of products placed on the market and of their designations, in the interests of a greater transparency of commercial transactions and offers for sale to the public.

However, this line of argument cannot be taken so far as to regard the mandatory fixing of minimum alcohol contents as being an essential guarantee of the fairness of commercial transactions, since it is a simple matter to ensure that suitable information is conveyed to the purchaser by requiring the display of an indication of origin and of the alcohol content on the packaging of products.

14. It is clear from the foregoing that the requirements relating to the minimum alcohol content of alcoholic beverages do not serve a purpose which is in the general interest and such as to take precedence over the requirements of the free movement of goods, which constitutes one of the fundamental rules of the community.

...

An indistinctly applicable MEQR will only be justified by a mandatory requirement if it is proportionate to the public interest objective embodied in the mandatory requirement. This was made clear by the Court of Justice in:

Walter Rau Lebensmittelwerke v Smedt PvbA (Case 261/81) [1982] ECR 3961

Facts: Belgian statute required all margarine in Belgium to be sold in cubic packages. The Belgian Government argued that this applied to all sellers of margarine and the measure was in place to avoid customer confusion. One of the questions the Court of Justice considered is whether customers could be informed in other ways rather than just by standard packaging.

JUDGMENT

10. The question submitted by the Landgericht seeks to ascertain whether the application in one member state to margarine imported from another member state of legislation which does not allow that product to be retailed unless packaged in a particular form, in this case in cube-shaped blocks or packs, constitutes a measure having an effect equivalent to a quantitative restriction within the meaning of Article 30.

11. The defendant in the main action and the Belgian government maintain that the Belgian royal decree may not be classified as a measure equivalent to a quantitative restriction. The previous judgments of the court concerned only a prohibition against the importation and marketing of products arising from national legislation on product quality, which was not the case in this instance because it was sufficient to adapt the presentation of the product in order to market it. Furthermore the form of packaging does not constitute a real obstacle to trade. In any case, even if sale by retail were prohibited, there are alternative possibilities such as the wholesale trade.

12. In this regard it must be recalled, as the court has repeatedly held since its judgment of 20 February 1979 in Case 120/78 *Rewe* [1979] ECR 649, that in the absence of common rules relating to the marketing of the products concerned, obstacles to free movement within the community resulting from disparities between the national laws must be accepted in so far as such rules, applicable to domestic and to imported products without distinction, may be recognized as being necessary in order to satisfy mandatory requirements relating inter alia to consumer protection. It is also necessary for such rules to be proportionate to the aim in view. If a member state has a choice between various measures to attain

 Alert

the same objective it should choose the means which least restricts the free movement of goods.

13. Although the requirement that a particular form of packaging must also be used for imported products is not an absolute barrier to the importation into the member state concerned of products originating in other member states , nevertheless it is of such a nature as to render the marketing of those products more difficult or more expensive either by barring them from certain channels of distribution or owing to the additional costs brought about by the necessity to package the products in question in special packs which comply with the requirements in force on the market of their destination.

14. In this case the protective effect of the Belgian rules is moreover demonstrated by the fact, affirmed by the Commission and not disputed by the Belgian government, that despite prices appreciably higher than those in some other member states there is practically no margarine of foreign origin to be found on the Belgian market.

15. Therefore it may not be claimed that the requirement of special packaging for the product is not an obstacle to marketing.

16. Furthermore, the Belgian government contends that the requirement of the cubic form is necessary for the protection of the consumer in order to prevent confusion between butter and margarine. It states that the cubic form used for the sale of margarine is "rooted" in the habits of Belgian consumers and is therefore an effective safeguard in that respect.

17. It cannot be reasonably denied that in principle legislation designed to prevent butter and margarine from being confused in the mind of the consumer is justified. However, the application by one member state to margarine lawfully manufactured and marketed in another member state of legislation which prescribes for that product a specific kind of packaging such as the cubic form to the exclusion of any other form of packaging considerably exceeds the requirements of the object in view. Consumers may in fact be protected just as effectively by other measures, for example by rules on labelling, which hinder the free movement of goods less.

A proportionality test is essentially a test of the suitability and necessity of the measure for achieving the objective. For example:

Commission v Ireland (Case 45/87) [1988] ECR 4929 (*'Dundalk Water Supply'*)

Facts: See above

JUDGMENT

21. The Irish Government maintains that it is necessary to specify the standards to which materials must be manufactured, particularly in a case such as this where the pipes utilized must suit the existing network. Compliance with another

standard, even an international standard such as ISO 160:1980, would not suffice to eliminate certain technical difficulties.

22. That technical argument cannot be accepted. The Commission' s complaint does not relate to compliance with technical requirements but to the refusal of the Irish authorities to verify whether those requirements are satisfied where the manufacturer of the materials has not been certified by the IIRS to IS 188. By incorporating in the notice in question the words "or equivalent" after the reference to the Irish standard, as provided for by Directive 71/305 where it is applicable, the Irish authorities could have verified compliance with the technical conditions without from the outset restricting the contract only to tenderers proposing to utilize Irish materials.

Some question the need for additional defences beyond those set out in Article 36 TFEU. Subsequent case law made it clear that the principle of mutual recognition would often provide a useful weapon for the importer. However, the court has not treated the list of mandatory requirements set out in *Cassis de Dijon* as an exhaustive list. Therefore, additional requirements have been permitted, such as the protection of the environment in *Commission v Denmark* (Case 302/86) [1988] ECR 460.

2.3.3 Selling Arrangements

The judgment in *Cassis de Dijon* is not without controversy. Critics became concerned that the principle of mutual recognition had become too strong a weapon for importers and that, in some cases, the principle was being applied incorrectly. This criticism was particularly directed at cases concerning indistinctly applicable measures which restricted the promotion and sale of products without placing any additional requirements on the products themselves. In *Cinéthèque SA and others v Fédération Nationale des Cinémas Français* (Joined cases 60 and 61/84) [1985] ECR 2605, the Court of Justice held that an indistinctly applicable prohibition on the commercial 'exploitation' (which, in that case, involved distribution) of videos of any film that were intended for sale or hire within one year of that film being authorised to be shown in cinemas constituted an MEQR because it hindered the importation of videos from other member states, even though, as the Advocate General noted, the importation of videos was not itself prohibited. An indistinctly applicable prohibition on Sunday trading was also held to be an MEQR on the strength of *Cinéthèque* in *Torfaen Borough Council v B&Q plc* (Case C-145/88) [1989] ECR 3851, a conclusion that was reaffirmed in *Stoke-on-Trent and Norwich City Councils v B&Q plc* (Case 169/91) [1992] ECR I-6635. The decisions in these cases were open to the criticism that, in contrast to *Cassis de Dijon*, the importers did not suffer a dual burden. Indeed, the measures imposed a burden on importers which was equal to that suffered by domestic producers. The concerns expressed by critics were not abated by the fact that the restrictions in these cases were held either to be justified on the basis of a mandatory requirement (*Stoke-on-Trent*) or at least to be capable of being so justified (*Cinéthèque* and *Torfean*).

The Court of Justice subsequently sought to deal with this concern by designating such restrictions as selling arrangements and distinguishing them from MEQRs:

Criminal Proceedings against Keck and Mithouard (Cases C-267 & C-268/91) [1993] ECR I-6097

Note: Article 30 EEC (now Article 34 TFEU)

Facts: Keck and Mithouard sold goods at a loss in contravention of French law. They argued that the law deprived them of a method of promoting goods imported by them into France.

JUDGMENT

12. National legislation imposing a general prohibition on resale at a loss is not designed to regulate trade in goods between Member States.

13. Such legislation may, admittedly, restrict the volume of sales, and hence the volume of sales of products from other Member States, in so far as it deprives traders of a method of sales promotion. But the question remains whether such a possibility is sufficient to characterize the legislation in question as a measure having equivalent effect to a quantitative restriction on imports.

14. In view of the increasing tendency of traders to invoke Article 30 of the Treaty as a means of challenging any rules whose effect is to limit their commercial freedom even where such rules are not aimed at products from other Member States, the Court considers it necessary to re-examine and clarify its case-law on this matter.

 Alert

15. It is established by the case-law beginning with "Cassis de Dijon" (Case 120/78 *Rewe-Zentral v Bundesmonopolverwaltung für Branntwein* [1979] ECR 649) that, in the absence of harmonization of legislation, obstacles to free movement of goods which are the consequence of applying, to goods coming from other Member States where they are lawfully manufactured and marketed, rules that lay down requirements to be met by such goods (such as those relating to designation, form, size, weight, composition, presentation, labelling, packaging) constitute measures of equivalent effect prohibited by Article 30. This is so even if those rules apply without distinction to all products unless their application can be justified by a public-interest objective taking precedence over the free movement of goods.

16. By contrast, contrary to what has previously been decided, the application to products from other Member States of national provisions restricting or prohibiting certain selling arrangements is not such as to hinder directly or indirectly, actually or potentially, trade between Member States within the meaning of the *Dassonville* judgment (Case 8/74 [1974] ECR 837), so long as those provisions apply to all relevant traders operating within the national territory and so long as they affect in the same manner, in law and in fact, the marketing of domestic products and of those from other Member States.

17. Provided that those conditions are fulfilled, the application of such rules to the sale of products from another Member State meeting the requirements laid down by that State is not by nature such as to prevent their access to the market or to

impede access any more than it impedes the access of domestic products. Such rules therefore fall outside the scope of Article 30 of the Treaty.

18.   Accordingly, the reply to be given to the national court is that Article 30 of the EEC Treaty is to be interpreted as not applying to legislation of a Member State imposing a general prohibition on resale at a loss.

This clarification proved useful in defeating claims from importers such as claims that Sunday trading laws could be an indistinctly applicable MEQR (see *Punto Casa SpA v Sindaco del Comune di Capena et Comune di Capena* (Joined cases C-69/93 and C-258/93) [1994] ECR I-2355)

Further Reading

Barents, R: 'Charges of Equivalent Effect to Customs Duties' (1978) 15 CMLRev 415

Chalmers, D: 'Repackaging the Internal Market – The Ramifications of the Keck Judgment' (1994) 19 ELR 385

Easson, A: 'The Spirits, Wine and Beer Judgements: A Legal Mickey Finn?' (1980) 5 ELR 318

Shuibhne, N: 'The Free Movement of Goods and Article 28: An Evolving Framework' (2002) 27 ELR 408

3

Free Movement of Persons

Topic List

Introduction

This chapter deals with the free movement of workers and other persons which is one of the central elements of the new legal order created by the Treaties and secondary legislation. It is regularly in the news headlines and is of huge significance, providing EU citizens with a range of important rights and privileges. The European Union has successfully created the largest (in terms of numbers of states) area without borders in the world today and probably in all human history.

3.1 Defining a 'Worker'

3.1.1 An Employment Relationship

Deborah Lawrie-Blum v Land Baden-Württemberg (Case 66/85) [1987] 3 CMLR 389

Panel: Lord Mackenzie Stuart CJ, Koopmans, Everling and Bahlmann PPC, Bosco, Due and Schockweiler JJ, Herr Carl Otto Lenz, Advocate-General

Legislation: Article 48 EEC (now Article 45 TFEU)

Facts: The applicant was a British national who attended the University of Freiburg to train to be a teacher. The German authorities claimed she was not a worker because, although paid for a few hours teaching each week, she was in reality training. This raised the question of how much work an individual had to undertake to qualify as a worker, particularly in a context in which they were clearly carrying out some other activity within the host state.

JUDGMENT

On the meaning of 'worker' in Article 48(1)

12. Mrs. Lawrie-Blum considers that any paid activity must be regarded as an economic activity and that the sphere in which it is exercised must necessarily be of an economic nature. A restrictive interpretation of Article 48(1) would reduce freedom of movement to a mere instrument of economic integration, would be contrary to its broader objective of creating an area in which Community citizens enjoy freedom of movement and would deprive the exception in Article 48(4) of any meaning of its own. The term 'worker' covers any person performing for remuneration work the nature of which is not determined by himself for and under the control of another, regardless of the legal nature of the employment relationship.

13. The Land Baden-Württemberg espouses the considerations put forward by the Bundesverwaltungsgericht in its order for reference to the effect that, since a trainee teacher's activity falls under education policy, it is not an economic activity within the meaning of Article 2 of the Treaty. The term 'worker' within the meaning of Article 48 of the Treaty and Regulation 1612/68 covers only persons whose relationship to their employer is governed by a contract subject to private

law and not persons whose employment relationship is subject to public law. The period of preparatory service should be regarded as the last stage of the professional training of future teachers.

14. The United Kingdom considers that a distinction between students and workers must be made on the basis of objective criteria and that the term 'worker' in Article 48 must be given a Community definition. Objectively defined, a 'worker' is a person who is obliged to provide services to another in return for monetary reward and who is subject to the direction or control of the other person as regards the way in which the work is done. In the present case, account must be taken of the fact that a trainee teacher is required, at least towards the end of the period of preparatory service, to conduct lessons and therefore provides an economically valuable service for which he receives remuneration which is based on the starting salary of a duly appointed teacher.

15. The Commission takes the view that the criterion for the application of Article 48 is the existence of an employment relationship, regardless of the legal nature of that relationship and its purpose. The fact that the period of preparatory service is a compulsory stage in the preparation for the practice of a profession and that it is spent in the public service is irrelevant if the objective criteria for defining the term 'worker', namely the existence of a relationship of subordination vis-à-vis the employer, irrespective of the nature of that relationship, the actual provision of services and the payment of remuneration, are satisfied.

16. Since freedom of movement for workers constitutes one of the fundamental principles of the Community, the term 'worker' in Article 48 may not be interpreted differently according to the law of each member-State but has a Community meaning. Since it defines the scope of that fundamental freedom, the Community concept of a 'worker' must be interpreted broadly Case 53/81 *Levin v Staatssecretaris Van Justitie*.

17. That concept must be defined in accordance with objective criteria which distinguish the employment relationship by reference to the rights and duties of the persons concerned. The essential feature of an employment relationship, however, is that for a certain period of time a person performs services for and under the direction of another person in return for which he receives remuneration.

 Alert

18. In the present case, it is clear that during the entire period of preparatory service the trainee teacher is under the direction and supervision of the school to which he is assigned. It is the school that determines the services to be performed by him and his working hours and it is the school's instructions that he must carry out and its rules that he must observe. During a substantial part of the preparatory service he is required to give lessons to the school's pupils and thus provides a service of some economic value to the school. The amounts which he receives may be regarded as remuneration for the services provided and for the duties involved in completing the period of preparatory service. Consequently, the three criteria for the existence of an employment relationship are fulfilled in this case.

19. The fact that teachers' preparatory service, like apprenticeships in other occupations, may be regarded as practical preparation directly related to the actual pursuit of the occupation in point is not a bar to the application of Article 48(1) if the service is performed under the conditions of an activity as an employed person.

20. Nor may it be objected that services performed in education do not fall within the scope of the EEC Treaty because they are not of an economic nature. All that is required for the application of Article 48 is that the activity should be in the nature of work performed for remuneration, irrespective of the sphere in which it is carried out (Case 36/74 *Walrave v Union Cycliste Internationale*). Nor may the economic nature of those activities be denied on the ground that they are performed by persons whose status is governed by public law since, as the Court pointed out in its judgment in Case 152/73 *(Sotgiu v Deutsche Bundespost)*, the nature of the legal relationship between employee and employer, whether involving public law status or a private law contract, is immaterial as regards the application of Article 48 .

21. The fact that trainee teachers give lessons for only a few hours a week and are paid remuneration below the starting salary of a qualified teacher does not prevent them from being regarded as workers. In its judgment in *Levin*, cited above, the Court held that the expressions 'worker' and 'activity as an employed person' must be understood as including persons who, because they are not employed full time, receive pay lower than that for full-time employment, provided that the activities performed are effective and genuine. The latter requirement is not called into question in this case.

 Alert

22. Consequently, the reply to the first part of the question must be that a trainee teacher who, under the direction and supervision of the school authorities, is undergoing a period of service in preparation for the teaching profession during which he provides services by giving lessons and receives remuneration must be regarded as a worker within the meaning of Article 48(1) EEC, irrespective of the legal nature of the employment relationship. ...

3.1.2 An 'Effective and Genuine Activity'

A worker for the purposes of Article 45 is defined as a person who is pursuing an 'effective and genuine activity'. This seeks to exclude people who are only carrying out marginal activity (i.e. of very little genuine economic significance). It should be noted that the ECJ has been reluctant to categorise activity in this way.

Levin v Staatssecretaris van Justitie (Case 53/81) [1982] 2 CMLR 454

Panel: Mertens de Wilmars CJ, Bosco, Touffait and Due PPC, Pescatore, Lord Mackenzie Stuart, O'Keeffe, Koopmans, Everling, Chloros and Grévisse JJ, Sir Gordon Slynn, Advocate-General

Legislation: Regulation 1612/68 (now Regulation 492/2011)

In the excerpt: Directive 68/360 has now been replaced by Directive 2004/38; Articles 2 and 3 EEC have been replaced by Article 3 TEU and Articles 2 to 6 TFEU.

Facts: the applicant was a British national who had been refused a residence permit in the Netherlands on the basis that she was not working at the time of application. She argued that she had in fact begun part-time employment and, in any event, she and her husband (who was not an EU national) had sufficient resources to maintain themselves even without working. The applicant could thus be distinguished from other cases in that they were only a part time worker. The question for the ECJ was what level of activity was sufficient for an individual to be classified as a worker.

JUDGMENT

10. The Dutch and Danish Governments have each argued that only persons whose wages are at least equal to the subsistence level regarded as necessary by the laws of the member-State where they work, or who work at least as many hours as is considered normal for full-time work in the sector concerned, can rely upon Article 48 of the EEC Treaty. Since Community legislation contains no provisions on the matter, recourse must be had, they say, to national criteria in order to determine both the minimum wage and the minimum number of hours.

11. This argument cannot, however, be accepted. As the Court has already declared in its judgment of 19 March 1964, the terms 'worker' and 'work in paid employment' cannot be determined by reference to the legislation of the member-States, but have a meaning in Community law. Otherwise, the Community rules relating to the free movement of workers would be deprived of their effect, because the meaning of these terms could be fixed and varied unilaterally, outside the control of the Community institutions, by the national legislators, who could thus at will exclude particular categories of person from the application of the Treaty.

12. This would particularly be the case if enjoyment of the rights accorded on the basis of the free movement of workers could be made dependent on a wage which the law of the host State regards as the minimum; because of this, the personal area of application of the Community rules on this subject could vary from member-State to member-State. The meaning and scope of the terms 'worker' and 'work in paid employment' must therefore be clarified in the light of the principles of the Community legal order.

13. It must be emphasised in this connection that these terms determine the area of application of one of the fundamental freedoms guaranteed by the Treaty and must on this basis not be interpreted restrictively.

14. In accordance with this view, the recitals to Regulation 1612/68 confirm in general terms the right of all workers of the member-States to do the work of their choice within the Community, regardless of whether they are permanent workers, seasonal workers or frontier workers, or workers who are employed in the framework of a supply of services. Moreover, while, by its Article 4, Directive 68/360 grants workers—on production of the document on which they have

entered the territory, and of a confirmation of engagement or employment made by the employer—the right of residence, it does not make this right dependent on any condition as to the sort of work or the income earned thereby.

15. An interpretation which accords to these terms their full scope is equally in keeping with the objectives of the Treaty, which, under Articles 2 and 3, includes the removal between the member-States of obstacles to the free movement of persons, *inter alia,* in order to promote the harmonious development of economic activity within the whole Community and to improve the standard of living. Since part-time work, although possibly producing less income than that which is regarded as the minimum for subsistence, is for many an effective means of improving their living conditions, the beneficial effect of Community law would be undermined and the achievement of the objectives of the Treaty jeopardised if enjoyment of the rights accorded on the basis of the free movement of workers were reserved to persons who earn by full-time work wages which are at least equal to the minimum wage guaranteed in the sector concerned.

16. Consequently, the terms 'worker' and 'work in paid employment' must be understood as meaning that the provisions relating to the free movement of workers also relate to persons who only perform or wish to perform part-time work in paid employment and who only receive or would only receive therefore a wage which is lower than the minimum wage guaranteed in the sector concerned. No distinction must be made here between those who are prepared to make do with their income from such work and those who supplement this income with other income, either from private resources or from the earnings of an accompanying member of their family.

 Alert

17. It must, however, be observed that, although part-time work does not fall outside the area of application of the provisions relating to the free movement of workers, these provisions only apply to the performance of real and actual work, to the exclusion of work of such small degree that it appears merely minimal and subsidiary. From the formulation of the principle of the free movement of persons and from the place occupied by the provisions relating to this matter in the overall system of the Treaty, it is clear that these provisions only guarantee free movement to persons who perform or wish to perform an activity of an economic nature.

18. It must therefore be said in answer to the first and second questions that the provisions of Community law relating to the free movement of workers also apply to a citizen of a member-State who, on the territory of another member-State, works in paid employment which produces less income than is regarded in the latter member-State as the minimum for subsistence, regardless of whether the person concerned augments his income from such work in paid employment up to that minimum with other income or makes do with means of subsistence below the minimum, so long as he performs real and actual work in paid employment.

The third question

19. The third question seeks in essence to know whether the right of entry to and residence in the territory of a member-State can be denied to a worker who, by his entry or residence, is pursuing principally other aims than the work in paid employment, as defined in the answer to the first and second questions.

20. According to the wording of Article 48(3) of the EEC Treaty, workers have the right to move freely within the territory of the member-States 'for the purpose' of accepting an offer of employment actually made. Under the same provision, they are entitled to remain in one of the member-States 'for the purpose' of carrying out an employed activity there. Moreover, the recitals to Regulation 1612/68 specify that free movement means the right for workers to move freely within the Community 'in order' to work there in paid employment, while, under Article 2 of Directive 68/360, the member-States are obliged to allow workers to leave their territory 'in order' to accept or to perform work in paid employment on the territory of another member-State.

21. From these formulations, however, there emerges only the requirement, inherent in the very principle of the free movement of workers, that the advantages accorded by Community law on the basis of this freedom can only be invoked by persons who are actually working in paid employment or who seriously wish to do so. These formulations, however, do not imply that enjoyment of this freedom can be made dependent on the motives of a citizen of a member-State in applying for entry to or residence on the territory of a member-State, so long as he performs or wishes to perform work which satisfies the above-mentioned criteria, that is to say, real and actual work in paid employment.

22. Once this condition is satisfied, the worker's intentions in seeking work in the member-State concerned are irrelevant and must not be taken into account.

23. It must therefore be said in answer to the third question posed by the Raad van State that any motives with which a worker from a member-State seeks work in another member-State are irrelevant to his right of entry to and residence on the territory of the latter State, so long as he performs or wishes to perform real and actual work in paid employment there. ...

 Alert

3.2 Discrimination

Anita Groener v Minister for Education and City of Dublin Vocational Education Committee (Case 379/87) [1990] 1 CMLR 401

Panel: Due CJ, Slynn, Kakouris, Schockweiler and Zuleeg PPC, Koopmans, Mancini, Joliet, O'Higgins, Moitinho de Almeida and Grevisse JJ, M Marco Darmon, Advocate-General

Legislation: Article 3(1) of Regulation 1612/68 (now Article 3(1) of Regulation 492/2011)

Facts: Groener was a Dutch art teacher who was refused an appointment as a lecturer in an Irish vocational school because she did not speak Irish (Gaeilge). This was not strictly a requirement of the job since the teaching of art in those schools was conducted in English. It was instead intended to assist in promoting the language as an aspect of government cultural policy. The ECJ held that the requirement did indirectly discriminate (not many non-Irish workers spoke Irish), but that the language requirement was not disproportionate to the policy objective and, therefore, was compatible with Article 3 of Regulation 1612/68.

JUDGMENT

14. Since the second indent of Article 3(1) is not applicable where linguistic requirements are justified by the nature of the post, it is appropriate to consider first the second question submitted by the national court, which is essentially whether the nature of a permanent full-time post of lecturer in art in public vocational education institutions is such as to justify the requirement of a knowledge of the Irish language.

15. According to the documents before the Court, the teaching of art, like that of most other subjects taught in public vocational education schools, is conducted essentially or indeed exclusively in the English language. It follows that, as indicated by the terms of the second question submitted, knowledge of the Irish language is not required for the performance of the duties which teaching of the kind at issue specifically entails.

16. However, that finding is not in itself sufficient to enable the national court to decide whether the linguistic requirement in question is justified 'by reason of the nature of the post to be filled' , within the

    414 meaning of the last subparagraph of Article 3(1) of Regulation 1612/68.

17. To apprehend the full scope of the second question, regard must be had to the special linguistic situation in Ireland, as it appears from the documents before the Court. By virtue of Article 8 of the Bunreacht na hEireann (Irish Constitution)

    1. The Irish language as the national language is the first official language.

    2. The English language is recognised as a second official language.

    3. Provision may, however, be made by law for the exclusive use of either of the said languages for any one or more official purposes, either throughout the State or in any part thereof.

18. As is apparent from the documents before the Court, although Irish is not spoken by the whole Irish population, the policy followed by Irish Governments for many years has been designed not only to maintain but also to promote the use of Irish as a means of expressing national identity and culture. It is for that reason that Irish courses are compulsory for children receiving primary education and optional for those receiving secondary education. The obligation imposed on lecturers in public vocational education schools to have a certain knowledge of

the Irish language is one of the measures adopted by the Irish Government in furtherance of that policy.

19. The EEC Treaty does not prohibit the adoption of a policy for the protection and promotion of a language of a member-State which is both the national language and the first official language. However, the implementation of such a policy must not encroach upon a fundamental freedom such as that of the free movement of workers. Therefore, the requirements deriving from measures intended to implement such a policy must not in any circumstances be disproportionate in relation to the aim pursued and the manner in which they are applied must not bring about discrimination against nationals of other member-States.

20. The importance of education for the implementation of such a policy must be recognised. Teachers have an essential role to play, not only through the teaching which they provide but also by their participation in the daily life of the school and the privileged relationship which they have with their pupils. In those circumstances, it is not unreasonable to require them to have some knowledge of the first national language.

21. It follows that the requirement imposed on teachers to have an adequate knowledge of such a language must, provided that the level of knowledge required is not disproportionate in relation to the objective pursued, be regarded as a condition corresponding to the knowledge required by reason of the nature of the post to be filled within the meaning of the last subparagraph of Article 3(1) of Regulation 1612/68.

 Alert

22. It must also be pointed out that where the national provisions provide for the possibility of exemption from that linguistic requirement where no other fully qualified candidate has applied for the post to be filled, Community law requires that power to grant exemptions to be exercised by the Minister in a non-discriminatory manner.

23. Moreover, the principle of non-discrimination precludes the imposition of any requirement that the linguistic knowledge in question must have been acquired within the national territory. It also implies that the nationals of other member-States should have an opportunity to re-take the oral examination, in the event of their having previously failed it, when they again apply for a post of assistant lecturer of lecturer.

24. Accordingly, the reply to the second question must be that a permanent full-time post of lecturer in public vocational education institutions is a post of such a nature as to justify the requirement of linguistic knowledge, within the meaning of the last subparagraph of Article 3(1) of Council Regulation 1612/68, provided that the linguistic requirement in question is imposed as part of a policy for the promotion of the national language which is, at the same time, the first official language and provided that that requirement is applied in a proportionate and non-discriminatory manner. ...

Further Reading

Golynker, O: 'Jobseekers' rights in the European Union: challenges of changing the paradigm of social solidarity' [2005] ELRev 111

4

Establishment and Services

Topic List

4.1 The Concepts of Establishment and Services

Reinhard Gebhard v Consiglio Dell'Ordine degli Avvocati E Procuratori di Milano (Case 55/94) [1996] 1 CMLR 603

Panel: Rodríguez Iglesias P, Kakouris, Edward (Rapporteur), and Hirsch PPC, Mancini, Schockweiler, Moitinho de Almeida, Kapteyn, Gulmann, Murray, Jann, Ragnemalm and Sevon JJ. M. Philippe Léger, Advocate-General

Legislation: Articles 52 EC (now Article 49 TFEU)

In the excerpt: Article 60 EC is now Article 57 TFEU.

Facts: Reinhard Gebhard was a German national and law graduate of the University of Tubingen. In 1977 he was authorised to practise as a member of the Stuttgart Bar in Germany. He married an Italian national and settled in Italy with three children in 1978 where he worked as an associate member of a lawyers chambers in Milan before going on to practise as an Avvocato (lawyer) in his own chambers. His work was non contentious with 65% of his turnover derived from assisting and representing German speakers, 35% from assisting Italians in Germany and Austria and 5% from assisting Italian lawyers dealing with problems of German law. His work was essentially advisory about non-Italian law and when it came to the application of Italian law or court work in Italy he had recourse to Italian practitioners.

In 1992 the Milan Bar denied him the right to use the title of Avvocato from a permanent basis of chambers in Italy in contravention of Italian law and suspended him from acting as a lawyer for six months.

He appealed these findings and preliminary references were made to the Court of Justice concerning how compliant Italian law was with the Treaty and what criteria could be used to distinguish a provider of services from a lawyer established in a Member State.

ADVOCATE-GENERAL M. PHILLIPPE LEGER

18. The right of establishment and the provision of services constitute two separate branches of Community law, which are dealt with in two separate chapters of the EC Treaty and do not overlap.

19. The principle of freedom of establishment aims to foster the free movement of self-employed persons by enabling a self-employed person from one Member State to establish himself in another Member State on the same terms as a national of the latter State. In other words, "…establishment means integration into a national economy".

20. The principle of freedom to provide services merely enables a self-employed person established in a Member State in which he is integrated to exercise his activity in another Member State.

21. Establishment and the provision of services are mutually *exclusive*: it emerges clearly from Article 60 EC that the provisions on freedom to provide services are applicable only on condition that those on freedom of establishment are not applicable.

22. The rules governing those two major freedoms are very different. Thus, the activity of lawyers as providers of services is the subject of harmonising Directive 77/249, which enables services to be freely provided under the original professional qualification, whereas conditions for the establishment of lawyers have not—yet—been the subject of an actual harmonising directive. The establishment of lawyers is governed by Articles 52 et seq. of the Treaty...

 Note:
Now governed by the Lawyers Establishment Directive 98/5

He went on to spell out the problem and ways of resolving it:

86... [T]he distinction between the provision of services and establishment is not based on a single criterion ...

87. Consequently, there is a range of *indicia* which enables the provision of services to be distinguished from establishment.

88. The location of the lawyer's main centre of activity, the place where he has his principal residence, the size of his turnover in the various Member States in which he carries out his activity, the amount of time spent in each of those States and the place at which he is entered on the Bar rolls will each afford evidence for the purpose of determining the nature of his activity in each of the Member States considered.

JUDGMENT

[25] The concept of establishment within the meaning of the Treaty is ... a very broad one, allowing a Community national to participate, on a stable and continuous basis, in the economic life of a Member State other than his State of origin and to profit therefrom, so contributing to economic and social interpenetration within the Community in the sphere of activities as self-employed persons (see, to this effect, Case 2/74, *Reyners v. Belgium*).

Alert

[26] In contrast, where the provider of services moves to another Member State, the provisions of the chapter on services, in particular the third paragraph of Article 60, envisage that he is to pursue his activity there on a temporary basis.

[27] As the Advocate General has pointed out, the temporary nature of the activities in question has to be determined in the light, not only of the duration of the provision of the service, but also of its regularity, periodicity or continuity. The fact that the provision of services is temporary does not mean that the provider of services within the meaning of the Treaty may not equip himself with some form of infrastructure in the host Member State (including an office, chambers or consulting rooms) in so far as such infrastructure is necessary for the purposes of performing the services in question.

[28] However, that situation is to be distinguished from that of Mr Gebhard who, as a national of a Member State, pursues a professional activity on a stable and continuous basis in another Member State where he holds himself out from an established professional base to, amongst others, nationals of that State. Such a national comes

> under the provisions of the chapter relating to the right of establishment and not those of the chapter relating to service.

While this case established the criteria to differentiate between the Establishment and Services, the distinction between these is still a fine one. While the decision in *Gebhard* and similar cases such as *R v Secretary of State for Transport, ex parte Factortame Ltd* (Case 213/89) [1991] 3 CMLR 589 ('*Factortame II*') help to clarify such distinctions, cases brought before the Court of Justice will still often make reference to both of these freedoms, leaving any final decision to be made by the national court.

4.2 Freedom of Establishment

Freedom of Establishment, enshrined in Article 49 TFEU, is one of the fundamental freedoms crucial to the development of the internal market. While the Free Movement of Persons largely covers the employee, Establishment covers the self-employed professional or trade person as well as legal persons such as companies and firms.

A unifying feature across most areas of EU law is the basic goal of achieving a level playing field.

However, there are distinguishing features unique to Establishment and Services. The most obvious of these is existence of the raft of legislation, which is indicative of the importance attached by the Treaty to both professional qualifications and the need for professional expertise to be widely available across the EU.

So we shall see that while case law began the process of 'levelling the field', it was overtaken by measures such as Directive 2005/36. As a result, nearly all professions are now covered by legislation and it is this which lays down the path to be followed by Member States concerned about professional qualification. Nonetheless, the case law is of seminal importance here as the legislation is based upon the case law principles. Wherever there is a gap in the legislation, the case law fills it (the unregulated professions being an obvious example). Even where there is not a gap the case law, Article 49 TFEU can still be relied upon to ensure acquisition of skills is fully taken into account.

4.2.1 *Reyners* and *Thieffry*

Jean Reyners v The Belgian State (Case 2/74) [1974] 2 CMLR 305

Panel: Lecourt P, Donner, Sørensen, Monaco, Mertens de Wilmars, Pescatore, Kutscher, Ó Dálaigh and Lord Mackenzie Stuart JJ. M. Henri Mayras, Advocate-General

Legislation: Articles 52 and 55 EEC (now Articles 49 and 51 TFEU respectively)

In the excerpt: Article 8(7) EEC has now been repealed; Articles 13 and 16 EEC have now been replaced by Article 30 TFEU; Articles 7, 54, 57 and 95 EEC are now Articles 18, 50, 53 and110 TFEU respectively (although references to the transitional period have been removed).

Facts: Jean Reyners was born in Brussels and spent his life in Belgium even though he was born of Dutch parents and retained Dutch nationality. In Belgium he pursued legal studies culminating in his award of Doctor of Belgian Law. Despite this he was not allowed to practise as an avocat in Belgium because he was not of Belgian nationality. This requirement could have been removed by Royal dispensation but this required the home states of such foreign nationals to display reciprocity towards Belgian nationals in similar situations in their states. Holland required Dutch nationality for its legal practitioners. Reyners applied a number of times for the Royal dispensation arguing the Belgian requirement was contrary to the Treaty of Rome.

The Belgian Conseil d'Etat sent a preliminary reference to the Court of Justice, asking two questions:

i) Whether the profession of avocat was exempt from the Treaty on the basis of Article 55 EEC (now Article 51 TFEU) which allowed 'activities which in that State are connected, even occasionally, with the exercise of official authority' to be excluded from the provisions of the Treaty. Particularly did this refer only to those aspects of an avocat's role which required them to exercise official authority or was it referring to the role of avocat per se?

ii) Whether, following the end of the transitional period, Article 52 EEC (now Article 49 TFEU) had direct effect. The problem here was that Article 54 EEC (now Article 50 TFEU) required the Council and Commission to establish a programme for the abolition of restrictions to the freedom of establishment. The completion of this programme thereby seemed a necessary prerequisite to achieving the objectives of Article 52 EEC (now Article 49 TFEU). This meant that Article 52 EEC (now Article 49 TFEU) was conditional upon the achievement of Article 54 EEC (now Article 50 TFEU) and so it appeared to be incapable under the *Van Gend en Loos* criteria of having direct effect until the programme under Article 54 EEC (now Article 50 TFEU) had been completed. Given the difficulty in getting Member State agreement to the harmonisation measures under Article 54 EEC (now Article 50 TFEU), the possibility of Article 52 EEC (now Article 49 TFEU) having direct effect seemed a long way off and, indeed, no Directive had been adopted to provide for the freedom of establishment of lawyers.

ADVOCATE-GENERAL M HENRY MAYRAS.

The Advocate General began by explaining the purpose behind Article 52 EEC (now Article 49 TFEU):

The economic integration which is the basic aim of the Rome Treaty implies the development of trade in a single market as well as the free circulation of goods and men. It opens up to undertakings and to workers a field of action widened to the whole of the Community, multiplies business relations and thus contributes to breaking down the national framework which has become too narrow.

Consequently, it requires also not only that all restrictions should be abolished on the free supply of services within that Community, but also that the nationals of each member country should be recognised as having the right to establish themselves in another member-State and there to carry out their occupations, whether they be industrial, commercial, agricultural or professional, on the same conditions as the nationals of the latter State.

He argued that similar Treaty requirements for transitional periods for the attainment of some of the other Freedoms had not stopped the court establishing direct effect:

The Treaty offers many examples of provisions using the same techniques, whether for the abolition of customs duties on imports (Article 13) or on exports (Article 16) between the member-States, or the prohibition on member-States subjecting the goods of other member-States, either directly or indirectly, to internal taxes of any nature higher than those to which similar national products are subject. In these various cases the obligations imposed on the States were to be gradually complied with: 'during the transitional period' as Article 13 says ...

You have not hesitated to decide that on expiry of the term fixed in [this] case the rules laid down by [this] provision [was] to become directly applicable.

You held so regarding Article 95 in *Alfons Lütticke GmbH v. Hauptzollamt Sarrelouis* (57/65).

While with regard to Article 55 EEC (now Article 51 TFEU) the role of avocat could not be precluded *per se* simply because of a potential exercise of official authority. An avocat is not necessarily in a position to exercise such power. Article 55 EEC was only designed to cover those situations where an avocat was in such a position. Such situations were likely to be limited:

Official authority is that which derives from the sovereignty, the imperium of the state; it implies, for the one exercising it, the power to enjoy prerogatives which fall outside the ordinary law (*exorbittantes du droit commun*), privileges of public power, powers of coercion over the citizens.

The Court was broadly to fall in line with his approach. First, it held that Article 52 EEC (now Article 49 TFEU) did have direct effect from the end of the transitional period:

JUDGMENT

[15] Article 7 of the Treaty, which forms part of the 'principles' of the Community, provides that within the scope of application of the Treaty and without prejudice to any special provisions contained therein, 'any discrimination on grounds of nationality shall be prohibited'.

[16] Article 52 provides for the implementation of this general provision in the special sphere of the right of establishment.

[17] The words 'within the framework of the provision set out below' refer to the Chapter relating to the right of establishment taken as a whole and require, in consequence, to be interpreted in this general context.

[18] After having stated that 'restrictions on the freedom of establishment of nationals of a member-State in the territory of another member-State shall be abolished by

progressive stages in the course of the transitional period', Article 52 expresses the guiding principle in the matter by providing that freedom of establishment shall include the right to take up and pursue activities as self employed persons 'under the conditions laid down for its own nationals by the law of the country where such establishment is effected'.

[19] For the purpose of achieving this objective by progressive stages during the transitional period Article 54 provides for the drawing up by the Council of a 'general programme' and, for the implementation of this programme, directives intended to attain freedom of establishment in respect of the various activities in question.

[20] Besides these liberalising measures, Article 57 provides for directives intended to ensure mutual recognition of diplomas, certificates and other evidence of formal qualifications and in a general way for the co-ordination of laws with regard to establishment and the pursuit of activities as self-employed persons.

[21] It appears from the above that, within the system of the chapter on the right of establishment, the 'general programme' and the directives provided for by the Treaty are intended to perform two functions, the first being to eliminate during the transitional period the obstacles which hinder the attainment of freedom of establishment, the second consisting in introducing into the laws of the member-States a body of provisions aimed at facilitating the effective exercise of such freedom, with a view to favouring economic and social interpenetration within the Community in the field of self-employed activities.

[22] This second objective is the one referred to, first, by certain provisions of Article 54 (3), relating in particular to co-operation between the competent authorities in the member-States and adjustment of administrative procedures and practices, and, secondly, by the set of provisions in Article 57.

[23] The effect of the provisions of Article 52 must be decided within the framework of this system.

[24] The rule on equal treatment with nationals is one of the fundamental legal provisions of the Community.

[25] As a reference to a set of legislative provisions effectively applied by the country of establishment to its own nationals, this rule is, by its essence, capable of being directly invoked by nationals of all the other member-States.

[26] In laying down that freedom of establishment shall be attained at the end of the transitional period, Article 52 thus imposes an obligation to attain a precise result, the fulfilment of which had to be made easier by, but not made dependent on, the implementation of a programme of progressive measures.

[27] The fact that this progression has not been adhered to leaves the obligation itself intact beyond the end of the period provided for its fulfilment

[28] This interpretation is in accordance with Article 8(7) of the Treaty, according to which the expiry of the transitional period shall constitute the latest date by which all the

rules laid down must enter into force and all the measures required for establishing the Common Market must be implemented.

[29] It is not possible to invoke against such an effect the fact that the Council has failed to issue the directives provided for by Articles 54 and 57 or the fact that certain of the directives actually issued have not fully attained the objective of non-discrimination required by Article 52.

[30] After the expiry of the transitional period the directives provided for by the Chapter on the right of establishment have become superfluous with regard to implementing the rule on nationality, since this is henceforth sanctioned by the Treaty itself with direct effect.

[32] It is right therefore to reply to the question raised that, since the end of the transitional period, Article 52 of the Treaty is a directly applicable provision despite the absence in a particular sphere, of the directives prescribed by Articles 54(2) and 57(1) of the Treaty.

With regard to the other question concerning the extent of Article 55 EEC (now Article 51 TFEU):

[34]…[T]he question is whether, within a profession such as that of *avocat*, only those activities inherent in this profession which are connected with the exercise of official authority are excepted from the application of the Chapter on the right of establishment, or whether the whole of this profession is excepted by reason of the fact that it comprises activities connected with the exercise of this authority

…

[38] The plaintiff in the main action, for his part, contends that at most only certain activities of the profession of *avocat* are connected with the exercise of official authority and that they alone therefore come within the exception created by Article 55 to the principle of free establishment.

The court followed the applicant's line of reasoning:

[46] An extension of the exception allowed by Article 55 to a whole profession would be possible only in cases where such activities were linked with that profession in such a way that freedom of establishment would result in imposing on the member-State concerned the obligation to allow the exercise, even occasionally, by non-nationals of functions appertaining to official authority.

[47] This extension is on the other hand not possible when, within the framework of an independent profession, the activities connected with the exercise of official authority are separable from the professional activity in question taken as a whole.

…

[51] Professional activities involving contacts, even regular and organic, with the courts, including even compulsory co-operation in their functioning, do not constitute, as such, connection with the exercise of official authority.

[52] The most typical activities of the profession of *avocat*, in particular, such as consultation and legal assistance and also representation and the defence of parties in court, even when the intervention or assistance of the *avocat* is compulsory or is a legal monopoly, cannot be considered as connected with the exercise of official authority.

[53] The exercise of these activities leaves the discretion of judicial authority and the free exercise of judicial power intact.

[54] It is therefore right to reply to the question raised that the exception to freedom of establishment provided for by the first paragraph of Article 55 must be restricted to those of the activities referred to in Article 52 which in themselves involve a direct and specific connection with the exercise of official authority...

This was a case of direct discrimination in which the refusal had been overtly based on the nationality of the applicant. Subsequent cases have extended the reach of Article 49 TFEU (as it is now) beyond direct discrimination to restrictions which are not based on the nationality of the applicant.

Thieffry v Conseil de l'Ordre des Avocats à la Cour de Paris (Paris Bar Council) (Case 71/76) [1977] 2 CMLR 373

Panel: Kutscher CJ, Donner and Pescatore PPC, Mertens de Wilmars, Sørensen, Lord Mackenzie Stuart, O'Keeffe, Bosco and Touffait JJ. M. Henri Mayras, Advocate-General

Legislation: Articles 52 and 57 EEC (now Articles 49 and 53 TFEU)

In the excerpt: Articles 3 and 53 EEC have since been repealed. Article 5 EEC is now the second and third sentences of Article 4(3) TEU.

Facts: Jean Thieffry was of Belgian nationality and possessed a Doctor of Laws from the University of Louvain (Belgium). He subsequently practised as an advocate at the Brussels Bar for more than 10 years. He then assisted a London barrister for a number of years before finally settling in Paris, where for some years he assisted in the chambers of an advocate of the Paris bar as well as teaching law. He had been effectively practising the profession of advocate for about 20 years and had been offered a partnership by a Parisian advocate, subject to his becoming a member of the Paris Bar. With the aim of being admitted to that Bar, in 1974 Thieffry obtained recognition of equivalence from the University of Paris that his Belgian qualification was equivalent to the French licentiate's degree in law. The power for universities to recognise foreign qualifications as being the equivalent to the French licentiate's degree in various fields had been provided by a French decree dating back to 1921. Thieffry then sat and passed the qualifying certificate for the profession of advocate in 1975. The Paris Bar rejected his application by a decision of 9 March 1976. While the Bar accepted the direct effect of Article 52 EEC (now Article 49 TFEU), it took the view that, as there was no directive relating to the mutual recognition of legal diplomas, it remained bound by the requirement under French law that an advocate had to hold a French licentiate's degree in law. Thieffry did not have this qualification and so his application had to be rejected.

ADVOCATE-GENERAL M. HENRI MAYRAS

In my opinion, it is clear in the light of these provisions that the requirement of the national diploma of a licentiate's degree in law, imposed by Section 11(2) of the Act of 31 December 1971 on the reform of the legal professions, in fact constitutes an indirect and disguised but quite definite restriction with regard to nationals of other member-States desirous of entering the profession of advocate in France. In fact it is a question here of the *nationality of the diploma*, no longer that of the person, constituting an obstacle to the effective exercise of the right of establishment.

According to the current case law of this Court, freedom of establishment is a fundamental right, enforceable by all the nationals of the member-States; any limitation upon the effective exercise of that right can only be interpreted strictly; the attainment of freedom of establishment is in no way subject to the adoption of the directives provided for in Article 57, particularly in Article 57(1), which refers to the mutual recognition of diplomas. The role of those directives is merely secondary and subsidiary; they are intended only, as the Court has held, to facilitate the effective exercise of the right of establishment, and failure or delay on the part of the Council in adopting them cannot paralyse the implementation of Article 52.

JUDGMENT

[7] Under Article 3 of the Treaty, the activities of the Community include, *inter alia*, the abolition of obstacles to freedom of movement for persons and services.

[8] With a view to attaining this objective, the first paragraph of Article 52 provides that restrictions on the freedom of establishment of nationals of a member-State in the territory of another member-State shall be abolished by progressive stages in the course of the transitional period.

[9] Under the second paragraph of the same Article, freedom of establishment includes the right to take up activities as self-employed persons, under the conditions laid down for its own nationals by the law of the country where such establishment is effected.

[10] Article 53 emphasises the irreversible nature of the liberalisation achieved in this regard at any given time, by providing that member-States shall not introduce any new restrictions on the right of establishment in their territories of nationals of other member-States.

[11] With a view to making it easier for persons to take up and pursue activities as self-employed persons, Article 57 assigns to the Council the duty of issuing directives concerning, first, the mutual recognition of diplomas, and secondly, the coordination of the provisions laid down by law or administrative action in member-States concerning the taking up and pursuit of activities as self-employed persons.

[12] That Article is therefore directed towards reconciling freedom of establishment with the application of national professional rules justified by the general good, in particular rules relating to organisation, qualifications, professional ethics, supervision and liability, provided that such application is effected without discrimination.

[13] In the General Programme for the abolition of restrictions on freedom of establishment, adopted on 18 December 1961 pursuant to Article 54 of the Treaty, the Council proposed to eliminate not only overt discrimination, but also any form of disguised discrimination, by designating in Title III (B) as restrictions which are to be eliminated, 'Any requirements imposed, pursuant to any provision laid down by law, regulation or administrative action or in consequence of any administrative practice, in respect of the taking up or pursuit of an activity as a self-employed person where, although applicable irrespective of nationality, their effect is exclusively or principally to hinder the taking up or pursuit of such activity by foreign nationals.'

[14] In the context of the abolition of restrictions on freedom of establishment, that programme provides useful guidance for the implementation of the relevant provisions of the Treaty.

[15] It follows from the provisions cited taken as a whole that freedom of establishment, subject to observance of professional rules justified by the general good, is one of the objectives of the Treaty.

[16] In so far as Community law makes no special provision, these objectives may be attained by measures enacted by the member-States, which under Article 5 of the Treaty are bound to take 'all appropriate measures, whether general or particular, to ensure fulfilment of the obligations arising out of this Treaty or resulting from action taken by the institutions of the Community', and to abstain 'from any measure which could jeopardise the attainment of the objectives of this Treaty' .

[17] Consequently, if the freedom of establishment provided for by Article 52 can be ensured in a member-State either under the provisions of the laws and regulations in force, or by virtue of the practices of the public service or of professional bodies, a person subject to Community law cannot be denied the practical benefit of that freedom solely by virtue of the fact that, for a particular profession, the directives provided for by Article 57 of the Treaty have not yet been adopted.

[18] Since the practical enjoyment of freedom of establishment can thus in certain circumstances depend upon national practice or legislation, it is incumbent upon the competent public authorities—including legally recognised professional bodies—to ensure that such practice or legislation is applied in accordance with the objective defined by the provisions of the Treaty relating to freedom of establishment.

[19] In particular, there is an unjustified restriction on that freedom where, in a member-State, admission to a particular profession is refused to a person covered by the Treaty who holds a diploma which has been recognised as an equivalent qualification by the competent authority of the country of establishment and who furthermore has fulfilled the specific conditions regarding professional training in force in that country, solely by reason of the fact that the person concerned does not possess the national diploma corresponding to the diploma which he holds and which has been recognised as an equivalent qualification.

 Alert

This left one further issue for the Court to address. The French Government had argued that a distinction should be drawn between those decisions of university authorities which have only civil effects and those which have academic effects. Decisions with civil effects confer rights upon their recipients which can be enforced even outside the university. Decisions with academic effects confer rights upon their recipients only in respect of the university institution itself. The French Government argued that the recognition of the qualifications in question only had academic effects as it merely gave the right to follow studies from one university to another. It did not involve any civil effect, in particular the right to practise a profession. This latter aspect ought to remain in the hands of the state. The Court of Justice responded to that argument in the following way:

[20] The national court specifically referred to the effect of a recognition of equivalence 'by the university authority of the country of establishment' , and in the course of the proceedings the question has been raised whether a distinction should be drawn, as regards the equivalence of diplomas, between university recognition, granted with a view to permitting the pursuit of certain studies, and a recognition having 'civil effect', granted with a view to permitting the pursuit of a professional activity.

[21] It emerges from the information supplied in this connection by the Commission and the governments which took part in the proceedings that the distinction between the academic effect and the civil effect of the recognition of foreign diplomas is acknowledged, in various forms, in the legislation and practice of several member-States.

[22] Since this distinction falls within the ambit of the national law of the different States, it is for the national authorities to assess the consequences thereof, taking account, however, of the objectives of Community law.

[23] In this connection it is important that, in each member-State, the recognition of evidence of a professional qualification for the purposes of establishment may be accepted to the full extent compatible with the observance of the professional requirements mentioned above.

[24] Consequently, it is for the national authorities to judge whether a recognition granted by a university authority can, in addition to its academic effect, constitute valid evidence of a professional qualification.

Consequently, the Court of Justice broadly accepted the argument of the French Government on this point. While a university may establish the equivalence of qualifications, it is the competent national authorities which must determine whether such university recognition also constitutes valid evidence of professional qualification. This determination was a question of fact. However, the Court then went on to qualify this:

[25] The fact that a national legislation provides for recognition of equivalence only for university purposes does not of itself justify the refusal to recognise such equivalence as evidence of a professional qualification.

[26] This is particularly so when a diploma recognised for university purposes is supplemented by a professional qualifying certificate obtained according to the legislation of the country of establishment.

[27] In these circumstances, the answer to the question referred to the Court should be that when a national of one member-State desirous of exercising a professional activity such as the profession of advocate in another member-State has obtained a diploma in his country of origin which has been recognised as an equivalent qualification by the competent authority under the legislation of the country of establishment and which has thus enabled him to sit and pass the special qualifying examination for the profession in question, the act of demanding the national diploma prescribed by the legislation of the country of establishment constitutes, even in the absence of the directives provided for in Article 57, a restriction incompatible with the freedom of establishment guaranteed by Article 52 of the Treaty.

 Alert

4.2.2 From Discrimination to Indistinctly Applicable Restrictions

The judgment of the Court of Justice in *Thieffry* was significant for two reasons. The first reason concerned the reach of Article 52 EEC (now Article 49 TFEU). The Paris Bar had not refused Thieffry's application on the basis of his nationality. It had refused the application solely on the basis that he did not hold the French licentiate's degree in law as required by French law. The Court of Justice's decision that such a restriction was capable of being incompatible with Article 52 EEC (now Article 49 TFEU) and its reference in the course of its judgment to the particular proposals in the Council of Minister's General Programme indicated that the prohibition on restrictions to the freedom of establishment in Article 52 EEC (now Article 49 TFEU) extended beyond direct discrimination to include indirect forms of discrimination and potentially even to other indistinctly applicable restrictions which hindered the freedom of establishment. But this was conditioned by the Court's observation that the freedom of establishment had to be reconciled with the need for national professional rules justified by the general good.

This approach was developed over subsequent cases. For example:

Ordre des Avocats Au Barreau de Paris (Paris Bar Council) v Rechtsanwalt Onno Klopp (Case 107/83) [1985] 1 CMLR 99

Panel: Lord Mackenzie Stuart C.J.; Koopmans, Bahlmann, Galmot PP.C.; Pescatore, O'Keeffe, Bosco, Dueand Everling JJ.

Legislation: Article 52 EEC (now Article 49 TFEU)

Facts: Klopp was a German national and an advocate at the Dusseldorf bar in Germany. He had applied to be registered at the Paris Bar in France whilst continuing to maintain an office in Dusseldorf. His application as refused on the sole ground that advocates at the Paris Bar were permitted to maintain chambers solely in the territorial jurisdiction of the Tribunal de Grande Instance with which they are registered. Klopp argued that a Member State cannot prohibit an advocate who is a national of another member-State from maintaining chambers there. The Paris Bar Council and the French Government both argued that the rule did not violate Article 52 EEC (now Article 49 TFEU) as it did not draw any distinction between nationals and non-nationals and it was justified by the need for the advocate to practise within the jurisdiction of a certain court so that both the court and his clients can have ready access to him. This, it was contended, was both objectively necessary and in accordance with the public interest.

JUDGMENT

[17] It should be emphasised that, pursuant to Article 52(2) the freedom of establishment includes the right to take up and pursue activities as self-employed persons 'under the conditions laid down for its own nationals by the law of the country where such establishment is effected.' It follows from this provision and its context that, in the absence of specific Community rules on the subject, each member-State is free to regulate the practice of the profession of advocate in its territory.

[18] However, this rule does not imply that the legislation of a member-State may require an advocate to have no more than one establishment in the whole of Community territory. Such a restrictive interpretation would in practice have the consequence that an advocate, once established in a particular member-State, could no longer invoke the benefit of the freedoms given by the Treaty in order to establish himself in another member-State except at the price of giving up his existing establishment.

[19] The view that the freedom of establishment is not confined to the right to open a single establishment within the Community is confirmed by the very terms of Article 52 of the Treaty, which provide that the gradual abolition of restrictions on the freedom of establishment also applies to restrictions on the setting up of agencies, branches or subsidiaries by nationals of any member-State established in the territory of another member-State. This rule must be regarded as a specific expression of a general principle applying equally to the liberal professions, whereby the right of establishment includes the right to set up and maintain, in compliance with professional rules, more than one centre of activity in Community territory.

[20] However, bearing in mind the particular features of the profession of advocate, it must be accepted that the host State has the right, in the interest of the proper administration of justice, to require advocates who are members of a Bar in its territory to conduct their practice in such a way as to maintain sufficient contact with their clients and the judicial authorities and to comply with professional codes of behaviour. Nevertheless, such requirements should not have the effect of preventing nationals of other member-States from actually exercising the right of establishment guaranteed by the Treaty.

[21] In this connection it should be observed that modern means of transport and telecommunications make it possible to maintain the appropriate contact with the judicial authorities and clients. Likewise, the existence of a second set of chambers in another member-State does not preclude the application of professional codes of behaviour in the host State.

[22] The answer to the question submitted to the Court should therefore be that, even in the absence of a directive on the co-ordination of national provisions governing access to the profession of advocate and the practice of that profession, Articles 52 *et seq.* of the Treaty prevent the competent authorities of any member-State from refusing, in accordance with their national legislation and the professional codes of behaviour ruling there, a national of another member-State the right to join and to practise the profession of advocate merely because he at the same time maintains chambers in another member-State.

The case law eventually reached the point in which the Court of Justice held that Article 49 TFEU (as it is now) prohibited not only discriminatory restrictions but also any indistinctly applicable restriction which hindered the freedom of establishment or made it less attractive, unless that restriction could be justified by imperative requirements in the public interest:

Reinhard Gebhard v Consiglio Dell'Ordine degli Avvocati E Procuratori di Milano (Case 55/94) [1996] 1 CMLR 603

Legislation: Articles 52 EC (now Article 49 TFEU)

Facts: See above in part 1 of this chapter.

JUDGMENT

[35] However, the taking-up and pursuit of certain self-employed activities may be conditional on complying with certain provisions laid down by law, regulation or administrative action justified by the general good, such as rules relating to organisation, qualifications, professional ethics, supervision and liability (see Case C-71/76, *Thieffry v Conseil de l'Ordre des Avocats À la Cour de Paris*). Such provisions may stipulate in particular that pursuit of a particular activity is restricted to holders of a diploma, certificate or other evidence of formal qualifications, to persons belonging to a professional body or to persons subject to particular rules or supervision, as the case may be. They may also lay down the conditions for the use of professional titles, such as *avvocato*.

[37] It follows, however, from the Court's case law that national measures liable to hinder or make less attractive the exercise of fundamental freedoms guaranteed by the Treaty must fulfil four conditions: they must be applied in a non-discriminatory manner; they must be justified by imperative requirements in the general interest; they must be suitable for securing the attainment of the objective which they pursue; and they must not go beyond what is necessary in order to attain it (see Case C-19/92, *Kraus v Land Badenwürttemberg*).

[38] Likewise, in applying their national provisions, Member States may not ignore the knowledge and qualifications already acquired by the person concerned in another Member State (Case C-340/89, *Vlassopoulou v Ministerium für Justiz, Bundesund Europaangelegenheiten Baden-Württemberg*. Consequently, they must take account of the equivalence of diplomas (see the judgment in *Thieffry* and, if necessary, proceed to

 Decipher

Note the four conditions are relevant to all of the fundamental freedoms rendering a common approach to the removal of obstacles across them all.

a comparison of the knowledge and qualifications required by their national rules and those of the person concerned (see the judgment in *Vlassopoulou*).

This is a broadly the same approach as the Court has taken to indistinctly applicable restrictions for the other fundamental freedoms such as the free movement of goods (see *Rewe-Zentrale AG v Bundesmonopolverwaltung für Branntwein* (Case 120/78) [1979] ECR 649 ('Cassis de Dijon') discussed in Chapter 2 above).

4.2.3 The Recognition of Qualifications and the Principle of Equivalence

A second important development in *Thieffry* lay in the approach of the Court of Justice to the recognition of qualifications. Article 57 EEC had provided for the mutual recognition of diplomas, certificates and other evidence of formal qualifications by means of the Council of Ministers issuing directives for this purpose. The Court of Justice in *Thieffry* held that this did not prevent the recognition of qualifications being subject to the obligations in Article 52 EEC (now Article 49 TFEU) relating to the freedom of establishment even where no directive had been adopted to provide for the mutual recognition of qualifications in the particular professional field. Furthermore, it also made it clear that, where national law provided for the recognition of equivalent foreign qualifications by a competent national authority, a person could not be denied admission to a profession solely on the ground that he or she did hold the relevant national qualification once the competent national authority had recognised that his or her qualification was the equivalent to the national qualification and that person had fulfilled the other requirements of professional training. This was the first step in establishing the principle of equivalence. The principle was developed further in *Union Nationale des Entraineurs et Cadres Techniques Professionnels du Football (UNECTEF) v Heylens* (Case 222/86) [1989] 1 CMLR 901. This concerned the recognition of qualifications to be a football trainer, albeit in the context of the free movement of workers. The Court of Justice held that, when determining whether a foreign qualification is the equivalent to that required under national law, national authorities had to make the determination on an objective basis exclusively in the light of the level of knowledge and qualifications which the holder of the foreign qualification can be assumed to possess in the light of the diploma, having regard to the nature and duration of the studies and practical training which the diploma certifies that he has carried out. Reasons also had to be provided for a decision that the qualification was not equivalent.

Heylens, like *Theiffry*, was a case in which national law had provided for the recognition of equivalent foreign qualifications by a competent national authority. The following case saw the Court of Justice extend its approach even further to situations in which no such provision of national law exists:

Irene Vlassopoulou v Ministerium für Justiz, Bundes- und Europaangelegenheiten Baden-Württemberg (Ministry of Justice, Federal and European Affairs of the Province of Baden-Württemberg) (Case 340/89) [1993] 2 CMLR 221

Panel: Due CJ, Rodríguez Iglesias and Díez de Velasco PPC, Slynn , Kakouris, Joliet, Grévisse, Zuleeg and Kapteyn JJ. Mr. Walter Van Gerven, Advocate-General

Legislation: Article 52 EEC (now Article 49 TFEU)

Facts: In 1982 Mrs Irene Vlassopoulou, a Greek national, was both admitted to the Athens Bar and also submitted her doctoral thesis to the University of Tübingen (Germany). In July 1983 she began working in a firm of German lawyers in Mannheim and although practising in Greece, her main practice was in Mannheim dealing with Greek and EU law. As far was German law was concerned, Mrs Vlassopoulou practised under the responsibility of one of her German colleagues in the firm.

In 1988 her application to be admitted as a German lawyer was refused on the grounds that she did not possess the German professional education and training. Her appeal against this led to the Bundesgerichtshof (German appeal body) referring the following question to the Court of Justice for a preliminary ruling:

Is freedom of establishment within the meaning of Article 52 of the EEC Treaty infringed if a Community national who is already admitted and practising as a lawyer in her country of origin and for five years has been admitted in the host country as a legal adviser (Rechtsbeistand) and also practises in a law firm established there can be admitted as a lawyer in the host country only in accordance with the statutory rules of that country?

At an early part of its judgment the Court of Justice pointed out that where there has been no progress made by the Commission in the harmonising of professional qualifications then the Member States have the need to ensure the maintenance of professional standards.

JUDGMENT

[9] In this regard, it must be stated first of all that in the absence of harmonisation of the conditions of access to a particular occupation the member-States are entitled to lay down the knowledge and qualifications needed in order to pursue it and to require the production of a diploma certifying that the holder has the relevant knowledge and qualifications: see Case 222/86, *Union Nationale des Entraineurs et Cadres Techniques Professionnels du Football (UNECTEF) v Heylens*.

[14] Moreover, it is also clear from Case 71/76, *Thieffry v Conseil de l'Ordre des Avocats À la Cour de Paris* that, in so far as Community law makes no special provision, the objectives of the Treaty, and in particular freedom of establishment, may be achieved by measures enacted by the member-States, which, under Article 5 EEC, must take 'all appropriate measures, whether general or particular, to ensure fulfilment of the obligations arising out of this Treaty or resulting from action taken by the institutions of the Community' and abstain from 'any measure which could jeopardise the attainment of the objectives of this Treaty.'

[15] It must be stated in this regard that, even if applied without any discrimination on the basis of nationality, national requirements concerning qualifications may have the effect of hindering nationals of the other member-States in the exercise of their right of

establishment guaranteed to them by Article 52 of the EEC Treaty. That could be the case if the national rules in question took no account of the knowledge and qualifications already acquired by the person concerned in another member-State.

[16] Consequently, a member-State which receives a request to admit a person to a profession to which access, under national law, depends upon the possession of a diploma or a professional qualification must take into consideration the diplomas, certificates and other evidence of qualifications which the person concerned has acquired in order to exercise the same profession in another member-State by making a comparison between the specialised knowledge and abilities certified by those diplomas and the knowledge and qualifications required by the national rules.

 Alert

[17] That examination procedure must enable the authorities of the host member-State to assure themselves, on an objective basis, that the foreign diploma certifies that its holder has knowledge and qualifications which are, if not identical, at least equivalent to those certified by the national diploma. That assessment of the equivalence of the foreign diploma must be carried out exclusively in the light of the level of knowledge and qualifications which its holder can be assumed to possess in the light of that diploma, having regard to the nature and duration of the studies and practical training to which the diploma relates: see Case 222/86, *UNECTEF v Heylens*, cited above.

[18] In the course of that examination, a member-State may, however, take into consideration objective differences relating to both the legal framework of the profession in question in the member-State of origin and to its field of activity. In the case of the profession of lawyer, a member-State may therefore carry out a comparative examination of diplomas, taking account of the differences identified between the national legal systems concerned.

[19] If that comparative examination of diplomas results in the finding that the knowledge and qualifications certified by the foreign diploma correspond to those required by the national provisions, the member-State must recognise that diploma as fulfilling the requirements laid down by its national provisions. If, on the other hand, the comparison reveals that the knowledge and qualifications certified by the foreign diploma and those required by the national provisions correspond only partially, the host member-State is entitled to require the person concerned to show that he has acquired the knowledge and qualifications which are lacking.

 Alert

[20] In this regard, the competent national authorities must assess whether the knowledge acquired in the host member-State, either during a course of study or by way of practical experience, is sufficient in order to prove possession of the knowledge which is lacking.

[21] If completion of a period of preparation or training for entry into the profession is required by the rules applying in the host member-State, those national authorities must determine whether professional experience acquired in the member-State of origin or in the host member-State may be regarded as satisfying that requirement in full or in part.

[22]... It follows that any decision taken must be capable of being made the subject of judicial proceedings in which its legality under Community law can be reviewed and

that the person concerned must be able to ascertain the reasons for the decision taken in his regard: see Case 222/86, *UNECTEF v. Heylens*, cited above.

[23] Consequently, the answer to the question submitted by the Bundesgerichtshof must be that Article 52 of the EEC Treaty must be interpreted as requiring the national authorities of a member-State to which an application for admission to the profession of lawyer is made by a Community subject who is already admitted to practise as a lawyer in his country of origin and who practises as a legal adviser in the first-mentioned member-State to examine to what extent the knowledge and qualifications attested by the diploma obtained by the person concerned in his country of origin correspond to those required by the rules of the host State; if those diplomas correspond only partially, the national authorities in question are entitled to require the person concerned to prove that he has acquired the knowledge and qualifications which are lacking.

Vlassopoulou set out in one case all of the requirements that ought to be followed by a Member State when it is assessing whether a migrant professional claiming the right of establishment under Article 49 TFEU possesses the appropriate skill and knowledge (in the absence of harmonising legislation). It is the basic formula in this case which was to be subsequently followed by the mutual recognition legislation itself.

Even today where there is no appropriate directive the case law will be used to require the State to take both the qualifications and appropriate experience into account. Of course where there is appropriate legislation then a Member State must follow this and ignore its own national standards.

The process of creating legislation began by attempting to harmonise the differing national standards across the EU but this was abandoned in the face of the endless problems involved. The solution was to be found by resolving the problem by a short progression of mutual recognition directives beginning with Directive 89/48 [1989] OJ L19/16. A 'residual directive' this was meant to cover all regulated professions requiring university level education of at least three years and not covered by a specific directive. It embraced the mutual recognition principle of *Vlassopoulou*: a professional in one Member State ought to be recognised as such in another.

Directive 89/48 was then supplemented by Directive 92/51 [1992] OJ L208/25 which covered courses other than three year higher education courses before both being amended by Directive 2001/19 [2001] OJ L206/1 (The SLIM directive) and then replaced by Directive 2005/36 OJ L255/22 covering both Establishment and Services.

4.2.4 Non-EU Qualifications

All of the cases considered thus far concerned the recognition of qualifications awarded in other Member States. This raised the question of whether or not the principles governing the recognition of qualifications also applied to qualifications obtained outside of the EU by the nationals of Member States. This was considered in:

Abdullah Tawil-Albertini v Ministre des Affaires Sociales (Case C-154/93) [1995] 1 CMLR 612

Panel: Due CJ, Díez de Velasco and Edward (rapporteur) PPC, Kakouris, Joliet, Schockweiler and Zuleeg JJ. M. Marco Darmon, Advocate-General

Legislation: Directives 78/686 and 78/687

Facts: Abdullah Tawil-Albertini, was a French national who had qualified as a dentist in the Lebanon. After Belgium recognised his Lebanese qualification as equivalent to their own, he was authorised to practise in Belgium. He was also authorised to practise in the UK and Ireland. However the French authorities refused to allow him to practise in France and upon his appeal the national court referred the question of whether qualifications obtained by virtue of equivalence and which have not been acquired in one of the Member States of the EU could be covered by the mutual recognition principle.

JUDGMENT

[11] It should be noted that Article 2 of Directive 78/686 provides for the mutual recognition by Member States of qualifications in dentistry exhaustively listed in Article 3 and awarded by those States. That recognition has been automatic since the implementation of the directive because, concurrently, Directive 78/687 defined the minimum criteria which dental training in the various States of the Community must satisfy. The mutual recognition of qualifications in dentistry awarded by the Member States, mentioned in Directive 78/686, is based on the guarantees provided by the application of minimum criteria for training imposed by Directive 78/687.

[12] In relations with non-member States, such co-ordination of legislation on training can be established only by agreements concluded between the States concerned. Thus, by virtue of Article 1(4) of Directive 78/687, Member States remain free, in accordance with their own rules in respect of their own territory, to authorise holders of qualifications obtained in non-Community States to take up and pursue the activities of a dental practitioner.

[13] Accordingly, recognition by a Member State of qualifications awarded by non-member States does not bind the other Member States.

[14] Article 7 concerns only qualifications awarded by the Member States.

[15] The answer to the question referred to the Court for a preliminary ruling should therefore be that Article 7 of Directive 78/686 does not require Member States to recognise diplomas, certificates and other evidence of formal qualifications which do not testify to dental training acquired in one of the Member States of the Community.

Note that in this case, Tawil-Albertini was a Union citizen by reason of his French nationality. This case could not have been brought otherwise.

This case was decided after the implementation of EU legislation. The legislation in question was Directive 78/686 which allowed for the mutual recognition of dental qualifications across the EU. This case sought a more detailed answer as to what was meant by mutual recognition and how far mutual recognition could be taken. If one Member State has acknowledged a qualification awarded outside the EU as equivalent to its own national standard then must other Member States do likewise?

In answering this question the court pointed out that the only reason mutual recognition works is because the EU directives guarantee minimum standards of professional competence across the EU. Individual Member States were free to establish similar arrangements with non-EU states but only on an individual basis. This could not oblige other Member States to do likewise. However, if such a state were to grant recognition to the qualification, they would have to take any period of professional experience gained in another Member State into account when assessing any shortfall in professional competence.

This question was further considered by the Court of Justice in:

Salomone Haim v Kassenzahnärztliche Vereinigung Nordrhein (Case C-319/92) [1994] 2 CMLR 169 ('Haim I')

Panel: Due C.J.; Díez de Velasco and Edward PP.C.; Kakouris, Joliet, Schockweiler and Zuleeg JJ.

Legislation: Article 52 EEC (now Article 49 TFEU) and Directives 78/686 and 78/787

Facts: Haim was an Italian national holding a diploma in dentistry awarded in 1946 by the University of Istanbul in Turkey. The qualification was recognised by the Belgian Ministry for National Education and French Culture as being the equivalent to the Belgian legal diploma in dental science. By virtue of this, Haim practiced for 8 years in Belgium as a dental practitioner of a social security scheme. He subsequently applied to the Association of Dental Practitioners of Social Security Schemes in Nordrhein (the 'KVN') in Germany to be entered on the register of dental practitioners in order to be able to practice a dental practitioner of a social security scheme. The KVN refused to register him as he had not completed the two year training period required by German law.

The German court referred three questions to the Court of Justice for a preliminary ruling. The first two asked about the effect of Article 20 of Directive 78/686. The response of the Court of Justice to these questions echoed that in *Tawil-Albertini*:

JUDGMENT

[17] ...the scope of Article 20 [of Directive 78/686] is the same as that of the directive of which it is a part and that it refers only to holders of a qualification conferred in the Member States.

[18] The reply to the first question should therefore be that Article 20 does not prohibit a Member State from requiring a national of another Member State who has none of the qualifications listed in Article 3 of the directive to complete a preparatory training period in order to be eligible for appointment as a dental practitioner of a social security scheme even though he is authorised to practise his profession in the territory of the first State.

...

[21] ...as the Court indicated in paragraph [13] of its judgment in Case C-154/93, *Tawil-Albertini* recognition by a Member State of qualifications awarded by non-Member States, even if they have been recognised as equivalent in one or more Member States, does not bind the other Member States.

[22] The reply to the second question should therefore be that Article 20 of Directive 78/686 does not exempt from the preparatory training period a national of a Member State who holds a qualification awarded by a non-Member State, where that qualification has been recognised by another Member State as equivalent to one mentioned in Article 3 of the directive.

The third question referred by the German court asked the Court of Justice about the effect of Article 52 EEC (now Article 49 TFEU). The Court's response here was different:

[23] The third question seeks to ascertain whether it is permissible under Article 52 of the Treaty for the competent authorities of a Member State to refuse appointment as a dental practitioner of a social security scheme to a national of another Member State who has none of the qualifications mentioned in Article 3 of Directive 78/686 but who has been authorised to practise, and who has been practising, his profession both in the first and in another Member State, on the ground that he has not completed the preparatory training period required by the legislation of the first State without examining whether that condition may be regarded as having been fulfilled in whole or in part in view of the professional experience he has acquired.

[24] The purpose of Article 52 of the Treaty is to abolish restrictions on the freedom of establishment of nationals of a Member State in the territory of another Member State.

[25] A case such as this, where a Community national makes use of the freedom conferred upon him by the Treaty to establish himself in a Member State other than that of his nationality, falls within the scope of that provision.

[26] As the Court has already indicated in the judgment in Case C-340/89, *Vlassopoulou*, even if applied without any discrimination on the basis of nationality, national requirements concerning qualifications may have the effect of hindering nationals of the other Member States in the exercise of their right of establishment guaranteed to them by Article 52 EEC. That could be the case if the national rules in question took no account of the knowledge and qualifications already acquired by the person concerned in another Member State.

 Alert

[27] In the same judgment, the Court also held that a Member State which receives a request to admit a person to a profession to which access, under national law, depends upon the possession of a diploma or a professional qualification must take into consideration the diplomas, certificates and other evidence of qualifications which the person concerned has acquired in order to exercise the same profession in another Member State by making a comparison between the specialised knowledge and abilities certified by those diplomas and the knowledge and qualifications required by the national rules.

[28] By application of that same principle, it should be considered in the present case that the competent national authority, in order to verify whether the training period requirement prescribed by the national rules is met, must take into account the professional experience of the plaintiff in the main proceedings, including that which he has acquired during his appointment as a dental practitioner of a social security scheme in another Member State.

[29] The reply to the third question should therefore be that it is not permissible under Article 52 of the Treaty for the competent authorities of a Member State to refuse appointment as a dental practitioner of a social security scheme to a national of another Member State who has none of the qualifications mentioned in Article 3 of Directive 78/686, but who has been authorised to practise, and has been practising, his profession both in the first and in another Member State, on the ground that he has not completed the preparatory training period required by the legislation of the first State, without examining whether and, if so, to what extent, the experience already established by the person concerned corresponds to that required by that provision.

Thus, the principles established in *Vlassopoulou* also apply to qualifications obtained by national of Member States outside of the EU.

4.2.5 Internal Situations

All of the above cases involved nationals of one Member State who were seeking to rely upon Article 49 of TFEU (as it is now) in another Member State. They were not dealing with internal situations in which a national of a Member State was seeking to rely on the right to freedom of establishment under the Treaty and secondary legislation in their own home Member State. That issue was addressed in:

Ministère Public v Vincent Auer (Case 136/78) [1979] 2 CMLR 373

Panel: Kutscher C.J., Mertens de Wilmars and Lord Mackenzie Stuart PP.C, Donner , Pescatore, Sørensen, O'Keeffe, Bosco and Touffait JJ.

Legislation: Article 52 EEC (now Article 49 TFEU); Directives 78/1026 and 78/1027

In the excerpt: Article 3 and 63 EEC have since been repealed. Articles 7, 54 and 57 EEC are now Articles 18, 50 and 53 TFEU (although references to the transitional period have been removed).

Facts: Auer was originally of Austrian nationality. He had studied veterinary medicine in Austria and France before qualifying as a Doctor of Veterinary Medicine in Italy where he was granted a provisional certificate to practice as a veterinary surgeon in accordance with Italian law. Auer subsequently moved to France and acquired French nationality. He applied on several occasions to the French Ministry of Agriculture for authorisation to undertake the medical and surgical treatment of animals but each application was rejected on the basis that his veterinary qualification was not the equivalent to a French degree. Nevertheless, he practised veterinary medical in France and was prosecuted for doing so on several occasions.

JUDGMENT

[10] The situation referred to by the national court is that of a natural person who is a national of the member-State in which he actually resides, and who is invoking the provisions of the Treaty relating to freedom of establishment with a view to being authorised to practise the profession of veterinary surgeon there, whereas he does not possess the degrees required of nationals for that purpose but possesses degrees and qualifications acquired in another member-State which allow him to practise that profession in that other member-State.

...

[14] Consideration must therefore be given to the question whether, and if so to what extent, nationals of the member-State in which they were established were entitled, at the time in question, to rely on the provisions of Articles 52 to 57 of the Treaty in situations such as those described above.

[15] These provisions must be interpreted in the light of their place in the general structure of the Treaty and its objectives.

[16] Under Article 3 of the Treaty the activities of the Community with a view to the establishment of the Common Market include, *inter alia*, the abolition of obstacles to freedom of movement for persons and services.

[17] In the words of Article 7 of the Treaty, within the scope of its application, any discrimination on grounds of nationality is prohibited.

[18] Thus freedom of movement for persons is intended to contribute to the establishment of a common market, in which nationals of the member-States have the opportunity to carry on their economic activities by establishing themselves or by providing services in any place within the territory of the Community.

[19] As regards freedom of establishment, the realisation of this objective is in the first place brought about by Article 52 of the Treaty which provides, first, that 'restrictions on the freedom of establishment of nationals of a member-State in the territory of another member-State shall be abolished by progressive stages in the course of the transitional period' and, secondly, that such freedom of establishment shall include the right to take up and pursue activities as self-employed persons, 'under the conditions laid down for its own nationals by the law of the country where such establishment is effected'.

[20] In so far as it is intended to ensure, within the transitional period, with direct effect, the benefit of national treatment, Article 52 concerns only—and can concern only—in each member-State the nationals of other member-States, those of the host member-State coming already, by definition, under the rules in question.

 Alert

This made it clear that Article 52 EEC (now Article 49 TFEU) could not be relied upon by a national of a Member State within their own Member State. That could have been enough to have disposed of the question referred by the French national court. However, the Court of Justice had already observed in paragraphs 11 to 13 that the mutual recognition of diplomas, certificates and other qualifications in veterinary medicine had been provided for by Council Directives 78/1026 and 78/1027. In the light of this, it went on to consider whether a national of a Member State could rely upon such Directives in their own Member State:

JUDGMENT

[21] However, it may be seen from the provisions of Articles 54 and 57 of the Treaty that freedom of establishment is not completely ensured by the mere application of the rule of national treatment, as such application retains all obstacles other than those resulting from the non-possession of the nationality of the host State and, in particular, those resulting from the disparity of the conditions laid down by the different national laws for the acquisition of an appropriate professional qualification.

[22] With a view to ensuring complete freedom of establishment, Article 54 of the Treaty provides that the Council shall draw up a general programme for the abolition of existing restrictions on such freedom and Article 57 provides that the Council shall issue directives for the mutual recognition of diplomas, certificates and other evidence of qualifications.

[23] It follows from the general structure both of the General Programmes of 18 December 1961, drawn up in implementation of Articles 54 and 63 of the Treaty, and of the directives issued in implementation of those programmes, that the field of application, *ratione personae*, of the measures for securing freedom of establishment and freedom to provide services is to be determined on each occasion without distinction based on the nationality of those concerned.

[24] This idea, in particular to the extent to which it relates to the effects of mutual recognition of diplomas, certificates and other qualifications, is in conformity with the general rule set out in Article 7 of the Treaty according to which, within the scope of application of the Treaty, any discrimination on grounds of nationality is prohibited.

[25] Moreover, in so far as the practice of the profession of veterinary surgeon is concerned, this idea was fully confirmed by a declaration concerning the definition of the persons covered by the directives, which was recorded in the minutes of the meeting of the Council during which the directives relating to the mutual recognition of diplomas and the co-ordination of provisions laid down by law, regulation or administrative action in respect of the activities of veterinary surgeons were adopted.

[26] That declaration states that: 'The Council reaffirms that it is to be understood that freedom of establishment, particularly for the holders of certificates obtained in other member-States, must be accorded on the same terms to nationals of other member-States and to nationals of the member-State concerned, as is the case with other directives.'

Thus, whilst a national of a Member State could not rely upon Article 52 EEC (now Article 49 TFEU) itself in his or her own Member State, he or she would be able to rely in his or her own Member State upon a Directive made under Articles 54 EEC or Article 57 EEC (now 50 and 53 TFEU respectively). On the facts, though, this did not assist Dr Auer because, as the Court of Justice had pointed out in paragraphs 11 to 13 of its judgment, Directive 78/1026 and 78/1027 had both been enacted after the events which were the subject of the preliminary reference and each of the Directives had provided the Member States with a two period in which to implement them. Therefore, the Court of Justice concluded that:

[30] It follows from the considerations set out above that Article 52 of the Treaty must be interpreted as meaning that for the period prior to the date on which the member-States are required to have taken the measures necessary to comply with Council Directives 78/1026 and 78/1027 of 18 December 1978, the nationals of a member-State cannot rely on that provision with a view to practising the profession of veterinary surgeon in that member-State on any conditions other than those laid down by national legislation.

[31] This answer in no way prejudges the effects of the above-mentioned directives from the time at which the member-States are required to have complied with them.

Auer was not the only case concerning an internal situation which this particular panel of the Court of Justice had been called upon to decide at that time. The panel's decision in a second case was also announced on the same day as its decision in *Auer*. In contrast to *Auer*, this case had involved a directive which had not only been enacted at the relevant time but which also had a deadline for implementation that had long expired:

J. Knoors v Secretary of State for Economic Affairs (Case 115/78) [1979] 2 CMLR 357

Panel: Kutscher CJ, Mertens de Wilmars and Lord Mackenzie Stuart PPC, Donner, Pescatore, Sørensen, O'Keeffe, Bosco and Touffait JJ, Herr Gerhard Reischl, Advocate-General

Legislation: Articles 52 EEC (now Article 49 TFEU) and Directive 64/427

In the excerpt : Articles 3(c) EEC has been repealed. Articles 48 and 59 EEC are now Articles 45 and 56 TFEU.

Facts: The plaintiff was a Dutch national who had trained in the Netherlands as an engine fitter but in 1963 married a Belgian national and settled with her at Dilsen in Belgium. He was employed at his father-in-law's plumbing and heating business before becoming an independent plumber in his own right in 1970. In 1976 he applied for requisite authority to work as a plumber in the Netherlands but was refused on the grounds that he lacked the requisite Dutch qualifications. He argued that he had worked as a plumber for 15 years in Belgium and that, consequently, in accordance with Directive 64/427, he ought to be granted authorisation to work as a plumber in the Netherlands. Article 3 of the Directive required the Member State to accept as sufficient evidence of knowledge and ability the fact that the activity in question had been pursued in another Member State for certain specified periods. The deadline for implementing the Directive had long passed.

The Dutch authorities argued two points:

i) That to allow him to do this would circumvent their national training requirements and create a precedent whereby tradesmen would simply train abroad to avoid the Dutch training requirements; and

ii) As a Dutch national he could not invoke the Treaty in his own state. He could not be a beneficiary of Treaty rights in such a situation.

ADVOCATE-GENERAL REISCHL

... It is simply absurd for the plaintiff to be treated differently from a Belgian or national of another member-State in the same situation solely because of his Dutch nationality. Such a procedure would be clear discrimination against the plaintiff exclusively on the ground of his nationality, which would be absolutely incompatible with the principles laid down in the EEC Treaty.

... He was and is therefore in the same situation as a Belgian national with the same background. The Commission correctly refers to the fact that if the interpretation put forward by the Dutch Government were followed the freedom of movement for all persons who have exercised their right to freedom of movement and have learned or carried on another occupation in the member-State in which they established themselves would in practice be restricted in so far as they would be unable to return to their home State without having to expect difficulties with regard to the exercise of their new occupation

JUDGMENT

[14] The persons to whom the directive [Directive 64/427] applies are essentially defined by Article 1(1) [of the Directive], under which 'member-States, acting in accordance with the provisions hereinafter laid down, shall adopt the following transitional measures in respect of establishment or provision of services in their territories by natural persons or companies or firms covered by Title I of the General Programmes (hereinafter called "beneficiaries") wishing to engage in activities as self-employed persons in manufacturing and processing industries'

[15] The General Programme for the abolition of restrictions on freedom to provide services, in the first indent of Title I, defines as beneficiaries the 'nationals of member-States who are established within the Community,' without making any distinction as to the nationality or residence of the persons concerned.

[16] The same idea is expressed by Title I of the General Programme for the abolition of restrictions on freedom of establishment, which designates as beneficiaries, in the first and third indents, the 'nationals of member-States' without any distinction as regards nationality or residence.

[17] It may therefore be stated that Directive 64/427 is based on a broad definition of the 'beneficiaries' of its provisions, in the sense that the nationals of all member-States must be able to avail themselves of the liberalising measures which it lays down, provided that they come objectively within one of the situations provided for by the

directive, and no differentiation of treatment on the basis of their residence or nationality is permitted.

[18] Thus the provisions of the directive may be relied upon by the nationals of all the member-States who are in the situations which the directive defines for its application, even in respect of the State whose nationality they possess.

 Alert

[19] This interpretation is justified by the requirements flowing from freedom of movement for persons, freedom of establishment and freedom to provide services, which are guaranteed by Articles 3(c), 48, 52 and 59 of the Treaty.

[20] In fact, these liberties, which are fundamental in the Community system, could not be fully realised if the member-States were in a position to refuse to grant the benefit of the provisions of Community law to those of their nationals who have taken advantage of the facilities existing in the matter of freedom of movement and who have acquired, by virtue of such facilities, the trade qualifications referred to by the directive in a member-State other than that whose nationality they possess

[21] In contesting this solution the Dutch Government states, first, that the first paragraph of Article 52 provides for the abolition of 'restrictions on the freedom of establishment of nationals of a member-State in the territory of another member-State' and, secondly, that according to the second paragraph of the same Article, freedom of establishment is to include the right to take up activities as self-employed persons under the conditions laid down by the law of the country where such establishment is effected 'for its own nationals'.

[22] It is claimed that those provisions of the Treaty show that the nationals of the host State are not regarded by the Treaty as being beneficiaries of the liberalisation measures for which provision is made and that they therefore remain entirely subject to the provisions of their national legislation.

[23] Moreover, the Dutch Government draws attention to the risk that the nationals of a member-State might evade the application of their national provisions in the matter of training for a trade if they were authorised to avail themselves, as against their own national authorities, of the facilities created by the directive.

[24] Although it is true that the provisions of the Treaty relating to establishment and the provision of services cannot be applied to situations which are purely internal to a member-State, the position nevertheless remains that the reference in Article 52 to 'nationals of a member-State' who wish to establish themselves 'in the territory of another member-State' cannot be interpreted in such a way as to exclude from the benefit of Community law a given member-State's own nationals when the latter, owing to the fact that they have lawfully resided on the territory of another member-State and have there acquired a trade qualification which is recognised by the provisions of Community law, are, with regard to their State of origin, in a situation which may be assimilated to that of any other persons enjoying the rights and liberties guaranteed by the Treaty.

 Alert

[25] However, it is not possible to disregard the legitimate interest which a member-State may have in preventing certain of its nationals, by means of facilities created

under the Treaty, from attempting wrongly to evade the application of their national legislation as regards training for a trade.

[26] In this case, however, it should be borne in mind that, having regard to the nature of the trades in question, the precise conditions set out in Article 3 of Directive 64/427, as regards the length of periods during which the activity in question must have been pursued, have the effect of excluding, in the fields in question, the risk of abuse referred to by the Dutch Government.

[27] Moreover, it should be emphasised that it is always possible for the Council, by virtue of the powers conferred upon it by Article 57 of the Treaty, to remove the causes of any abuses of the law by arranging for the harmonisation of the conditions of training for a trade in the various member-States.

[28] The answer to be given to the question referred to the Court should therefore be that Council Directive 64/427 of 7 July 1964 laying down detailed provisions concerning transitional measures in respect of activities of self-employed persons in manufacturing and processing industries falling within ISIC Major Groups 23–40 (Industry and small craft industries) must be understood to mean that persons who possess the nationality of the host member-State are also 'beneficiaries' within the meaning of Article 1 (1) of the directive.

The Court's approach in *Knoors* broadly echoed that in its parallel judgment in *Auer*. In both cases, it had denied that Article 52 EEC (now Article 49 TFEU) could apply to purely internal situations. But it had also accepted in both cases that this would not prevent a national of a Member State from benefitting from a directive within his or her own home Member state where it provided for the mutual recognition of qualifications obtained in another Member State. Yet this still depended on the directive in question having been enacted at the time of the events complained of and on the deadline for its implementation having passed so that it could have direct effect. These two basic requirements had been fulfilled in *Knoors*. They had not in *Auer*. This was to change a few years later when Dr Auer was prosecuted yet again for continuing to practise as a veterinary surgeon in France without authorisation from the French Ministry of Agriculture. By this time, the deadline for implementing Directives 78/1026 and 78/1027 had passed but France had failed to implement them. In *Vincent Auer v Ministere Public (No. 2)* (Case 271/82) [1985] 1 CMLR 123, the Court of Justice held that the Directives had direct effect and provided him with a right to practice as a veterinary surgeon in France so long as the requirements of the Directive were satisfied.

4.2.6 Companies and Firms

Article 49 TFEU is unusual amongst some of the other Free Movement provisions in that it also applies to companies as well as natural persons. However the basic principles which have been seen to apply in earlier case law are equally relevant here. Article 54 TFEU in fact specifies that companies or firms '... be treated in the same way as natural persons who are nationals of Member States.' For example:

Centros Ltd v Erhvervs- og Selskabsstyrelsen (Case C-212/97) [1999] 2 CMLR 551

Panel: Rodríguez Iglesias P, Kapteyn, Puissochet, Hirsch and Jann PPC, Mancini, Moitinho de Almeid, Gulmann, Murray, Edward, Ragnemalm, Sevón, Wathelet (Rapporteur), Schintgen and Ioannou JJ. Mr Antonio La Pergola, Advocate-General

Legislation: Article 52, 56 and 58 EC (now Articles 49, 52 and 58 TFEU)

In the excerpt: Article 54(3)(g) EC is now Article 50(2)(g) TFEU.

Facts: Centros was a private limited company registered in England and Wales. Mr and Mrs Bryde were business partners with Mrs Bryde being the sole registered director of Centros Ltd. They were both Danish nationals residing in Denmark. They bought Centros Ltd intending it to be a wine import and export business. Its company address was that of a personal friend in the UK. They applied to the Danish authorities to register a branch of Centros in Denmark. Danish law did not impose any requirement as to minimum capital for companies from other EU countries seeking to establish a branch in Danish territory. However Danish law did require a substantial minimum paid up share capital to incorporate a company in Denmark. This sum was intended to be used as a reserve to pay creditors in the event of a bankruptcy. By only registering a branch in Denmark the Brydes hoped to avoid this sum. For this reason the Danish authorities turned down their application arguing that they were protecting creditors by preventing fraudulent insolvencies.

The national court referred to the Court of Justice the question whether it was compatible with Article 52 EC (now Article 49 TFEU) to refuse registration of a branch of a company which had its registered office in another Member State yet intended to carry out its entire business in the country in which the branch was established in order to avoid paying company capital?

JUDGMENT

[24] It is true that according to the case law of the Court a Member State is entitled to take measures designed to prevent certain of its nationals from attempting, under cover of the rights created by the Treaty, improperly to circumvent their national legislation or to prevent individuals from improperly or fraudulently taking advantage of provisions of Community law.

[25] However, although, in such circumstances, the national courts may, case by case, take account—on the basis of objective evidence—of abuse or fraudulent conduct on the part of the persons concerned in order, where appropriate, to deny them the benefit of the provisions of Community law on which they seek to rely, they must nevertheless assess such conduct in the light of the objectives pursued by those provisions.

[26] In the present case, the provisions of national law, application of which the parties concerned have sought to avoid, are rules governing the formation of companies and not rules concerning the carrying on of certain trades, professions or businesses. The provisions of the Treaty on freedom of establishment are intended specifically to enable companies formed in accordance with the law of a Member State and having their

121

registered office, central administration or principal place of business within the Community to pursue activities in other Member States though an agency, branch or subsidiary.

[27] That being so, the fact that a national of a Member State who wishes to set up a company chooses to form it in the Member State whose rules of company law seem to him the least restrictive and to set up branches in other Member States cannot, in itself, constitute an abuse of the right of establishment. The right to form a company in accordance with the law of a Member State and to set up branches in other Member States is inherent in the exercise, in a single market, of the freedom of establishment guaranteed by the Treaty.

 Alert

[28] In this connection, the fact that company law is not completely harmonised in the Community is of little consequence. Moreover, it is always open to the Council, on the basis of the powers conferred upon it by Article 54(3)(g) EC, to achieve complete harmonisation.

[29] In addition, it is clear from paragraph [16] of *Segers* that the fact that a company does not conduct any business in the Member State in which it has its registered office and pursues its activities only in the Member State where its branch is established is not sufficient to prove the existence of abuse or fraudulent conduct which would entitle the latter Member State to deny that company the benefit of the provisions of Community law relating to the right of establishment.

[30] Accordingly, the refusal of a Member State to register a branch of a company formed in accordance with the law of another Member State in which it has its registered office on the grounds that the branch is intended to enable the company to carry on all its economic activity in the host State, with the result that the secondary establishment escapes national rules on the provision for and the paying-up of a minimum capital, is incompatible with Articles 52 and 58, in so far as it prevents any exercise of the right freely to set up a secondary establishment which Articles 52 and 58 are specifically intended to guarantee.

4.3 Freedom to Provide Services

Procureur du Roi v Marc Debauve and Others (Case 52/79) [1981] 2 CMLR 362

Panel: Kutscher CJ, O'Keeffe and Touffait PPC, Mertens de Wilmars, Pescatore, Lord Mackenzie Stuart, Bosco, Koopmans and Due JJ. Mr. Jean-Pierre Warner, Advocate-General

Legislation: Articles 59 and 60 EEC (now Articles 56 and 57 TFEU)

Facts: Cable broadcasting companies operating within Belgium were prosecuted by the Belgian authorities for allowing the broadcasting of advertisements during their programmes contrary to Belgian law of that time. The main company that we are concerned with in this case would receive aerial television signals that had been broadcast over the air and then distribute these by cable to the television sets of their subscribers; such cable diffusion had a number of advantages for the subscribers to this service. Such subscribers received all TV programmes through the cable including both Belgian and foreign but it was the foreign broadcasts which contained the advertisements and which breached Belgian law. The effect of Belgian law upon the cable companies was to require them to blot out any advertisements in foreign programmes that they relayed. The principle question addressed by way of preliminary reference to the Court of Justice was whether the Belgian law prohibiting the transmission of adverts interfered with the right to receive a broadcasting service even though it was possible to receive these adverts in those parts of Belgium within the natural zone of broadcasting from the foreign stations? While the Belgian measure was only indirectly discriminatory did it have a disproportionate effect?

In its findings the court very quickly arrived at the main issue of this case:

JUDGMENT

... [9] However, it should be observed that the provisions of the Treaty on freedom to provide services cannot apply to activities whose relevant elements are confined within a single member-State. Whether that is the case depends on findings of fact which are for the national court to establish. Since the Tribunal Correctionnel has concluded that in the given circumstances of this case the services out of which the prosecutions brought before it arose are such as to come under provisions of the Treaty relating to services, the questions referred to the Court should be examined from the same point of view.

[10] The central question raised by the national court is whether Articles 59 and 60 of the Treaty must be interpreted as prohibiting all national rules against the transmission of advertisements by cable television to the extent to which such rules do not make any distinction based on the origin of the advertisements, the nationality of the person providing the services or his place of establishment.

[11] According to the first paragraph of Article 59 of the Treaty restrictions on freedom to provide services within the Community shall be progressively abolished during the transitional period in respect of nationals of member-States of the Community. The strict requirements of that provision involve the abolition of all discrimination against a provider of services on the grounds of his nationality or of the fact that he is established in a member-State other than that where the service is to be provided.

[12] In view of the particular nature of certain services such as the broadcasting and transmission of television signals, specific requirements imposed upon providers of services which are founded upon the application of rules regulating certain types of activity and which are justified by the general interest and apply to all persons and

undertakings established within the territory of the said member-State cannot be said to be incompatible with the Treaty to the extent to which a provider of services established in another member-State is not subject to similar regulations there.

[13] From information given to the Court during these proceedings it appears that the television broadcasting of advertisements is subject to widely divergent systems of law in the various member-States, passing from almost total prohibition, as in Belgium, by way of rules comprising more or less strict restrictions, to systems affording broad

commercial freedom. In the absence of any approximation of national laws and taking into account the considerations of general interest underlying the restrictive rules in this area, the application of the laws in question cannot be regarded as a restriction upon freedom to provide services so long as those laws treat all such services identically whatever their origin or the nationality or place of establishment of the persons providing them.

[14] A prohibition of the type contained in the Belgian legislation referred to by the national court should be judged in the light of those considerations. It must be stressed that the prohibition on the transmission of advertisements by cable television contained in the Royal Decree referred to above cannot be examined in isolation. A review of all the Belgian legislation on broadcasting shows that that prohibition is the corollary of the ban on the broadcasting of commercial advertisements imposed on the Belgian broadcasting organisations. This is also the way in which the judgment making the reference sets out the relevant legislation, indicating that the Royal Decree prohibits the transmission of advertisements in order to maintain conformity with the scheme imposed on the national broadcasting organisations.

[15] In the absence of any harmonization of the relevant rules, a prohibition of this type falls within the residual power of each member-State to regulate, restrict or even totally prohibit television advertising on its territory on grounds of general interest. The position is not altered by the fact that such restrictions or prohibitions extend to television advertising originating in other member-States in so far as they are actually applied on the same terms to national television organisations.

[16] The answer must therefore be that Articles 59 and 60 of the Treaty do not preclude national rules prohibiting the transmission of advertisements by cable television—as they prohibit the broadcasting of advertisements by television—if those rules are applied without distinction as regards the origin, whether national or foreign, of those advertisements, the nationality of the person providing the service, or the place where he is established.

[17] In view of that answer the question concerning the consequences which may arise from the direct applicability of Articles 59 and 60 of the Treaty where there is conflict between those provisions and national legislation has become devoid of object.

Graziana Luisi and Giuseppe Carbone v Ministero del Tesoro (Cases 286/82 & 26/83) [1985] 3 CMLR 52

Panel: Presiding, Mertens de Wilmars CJ, Koopmans, Bahlmann and Galmot PPC, Pescatore, Lord Mackenzie Stuart, Bosco, Everling and Kakouris JJ. Sig. Federico Mancini, Advocate-General

Legislation: Articles 59 and 60 EEC (now Articles 56 and 57 TFEU)

Case Facts: Two Italian residents, Mrs Graziana Luisi and Mr Giuseppe Carbone, were each fined by the Italian Minister for the Treasury for exceeding the limits on Italian currency which could be taken abroad at that time. The plaintiffs contested this decision on the basis that it was in breach of EU law. Mrs Luisi stated that she had used the money for reasons of tourism and medical treatment. Mr Carbone stated that he had used the money for tourism. Both plaintiffs argued that the restrictions on export of the means of payment for tourism or medical treatment were contrary to the provisions of the EU Treaty relating to current payments and the movement of capital. The main question for our purpose was whether the Italian limits on currency export were an impediment to the provision of services abroad.

ADVOCATE GENERAL FEDERICO MANCINI

Let us begin with tourism ... A State which is free to limit or prohibit the export of foreign currency by its own residents is also free to deny them tourist services available in other member countries and thereby adversely to affect the business of whoever offers such services. ... Among the values embodied in the Treaty, the free movement of services stands in the forefront. To remove from it an extremely important economic sector such as tourism would be to curtail its scope drastically, ...

And the same may be said of health or educational facilities. To ask that the person moving from one country to another should be the doctor, who relies upon

sophisticated instruments close at hand or operates only in a clinic where he has the necessary equipment and expert helpers, or to ask that it should be the school which goes to the place where the pupils reside, is unreasonable. ...

JUDGMENT

[9] According to Article 60 of the Treaty, services are deemed to be 'services' within the meaning of the Treaty where they are normally provided for remuneration, in so far as they are not governed by the provisions relating to freedom of movement for goods, capital and persons...

[10] By virtue of Article 59 of the Treaty, restrictions on freedom to provide such services are to be abolished in respect of nationals of member-States who are established in a member-State other than that of the person for whom the service is intended. In order to enable services to be provided, the person providing the service may go to the member-State where the person for whom it is provided is established or else the latter may go to the State in which the person providing the service is established. Whilst the former case is expressly mentioned in the third paragraph of Article 60, which permits the person providing the service to pursue his activity temporarily in the member-State where the service is provided, the latter case is the necessary corollary thereof, which fulfils the objective of liberalising all gainful activity not covered by the free movement of goods, persons and capital.

 Alert

... 16] It follows that the freedom to provide services includes the freedom, for the recipients of services, to go to another member-State in order to receive a service there, without being obstructed by restrictions, even in relation to payments, and that tourists, persons receiving medical treatment and persons travelling for the purpose of education or business are to be regarded as recipients of services.

Article 56 TFEU specifically covers the removal of 'restrictions on freedom to provide services within the Community'. This case is seminal in establishing the breadth of application of that article beyond the literal interpretation of its wording.

In extending the provision of services to the recipient *Luisi and Carbone* set a precedent that would lead logically enough to additional rights being acquired by the service recipient including education, health care and other public services. As in so many other areas the case law developed an approach which would essentially be followed by legislation (e.g. Directive 2006/123/EC (the Services Directive)).

Society for the Protection of Unborn Children Ireland Ltd. (S.P.U.C.) v Stephen Grogan and Others (Case C-159/90) [1991] 3 CMLR 849

Panel: Presiding, Due CJ, Mancini, O'Higgins, Moitinho de Almeida, Rodríguez Iglesias and Díez de Velasco PPC, Slynn, Kakouris Joliet, Schockweiler, Grévisse, Zuleeg and Kapteyn JJ. Mr. Walter Van Gerven, Advocate-General

Legislation: Articles 59 and 60 EEC (now Articles 56 and 57 TFEU)

In the excerpt: Articles 30 and 36 EEC are now 34 and 36 TFEU. Article 31 EEC has since been repealed.

Facts: Abortions were prohibited in Eire both by the constitution and by criminal law. The Society for the Protection of Unborn Children Ireland Ltd. ('SPUC') was a company incorporated in Eire to prevent the decriminalisation of abortion in that country. It brought a case in the Irish High Court seeking an injunction against Stephen Grogan and fourteen other officers of students associations to prevent their distributing information to students concerning the location of clinics in the UK where abortions were carried out. The student organisations concerned had no links with the particular clinics mentioned.

The three questions referred to the Court of Justice by the High Court for a preliminary ruling asked:

(a)   Does carrying out an abortion come within the definition of 'services' provided for in Article 60 EEC?

(b)   Can a Member State prohibit the distribution of specific information about the identity, location and means of communication with a specified clinic or clinics in another Member State where abortions are performed?

(c)   Is there a right for a person in one Member State, where the provision of abortion is prohibited under both the Constitution and the criminal law, to distribute specific information about the identity, location and means of communication with clinics in another Member State where abortions are lawful under certain conditions?

JUDGMENT

First Question

[16] In its first question, the national court essentially seeks to establish whether medical termination of pregnancy, performed in accordance with the law of the State where it is carried out, constitutes a service within the meaning of Article 60 EEC.

[17] According to the first paragraph of that provision, services are to be considered to be 'services' within the meaning of the Treaty where they are normally provided for

remuneration, in so far as they are not governed by the provisions relating to freedom of movement for goods, capital or persons. Indent (d) of the second paragraph of Article 60 expressly states that activities of the professions fall within the definition of services.

[18] It must be held that termination of pregnancy, as lawfully practised in several member-States, is a medical activity which is normally provided for remuneration and may be carried out as part of a professional activity. In any event, the Court has already held in *Luisi and Carbone* that medical activities fall within the scope of Article 60 EEC.

[19] SPUC, however, maintains that the provision of abortion cannot be regarded as being a service, on the grounds that it is grossly immoral and involves the destruction of the life of a human being, namely the unborn child.

[20] Whatever the merits of those arguments on the moral plane, they cannot influence the answer to the national court's first question. It is not for the Court to substitute its assessment for that of the legislature in those member-States where the activities in question are practised legally.

[21] Consequently, the answer to the national court's first question must be that medical termination of pregnancy, performed in accordance with the law of the State in which it is carried out, constitutes a service within the meaning of Article 60 EEC.

 Alert

Second and third questions

[22] Having regard to the facts of the case, it must be considered that, in its second and third questions, the national court seeks essentially to establish whether it is contrary to Community law for a member-State in which medical termination of pregnancy is forbidden to prohibit students associations from distributing information about the identity and location of clinics in another member-State where voluntary termination of pregnancy is lawfully carried out and the means of communicating with those clinics, where the clinics in question have no involvement in the distribution of the said information.

[23] Although the national court's questions refer to Community law in general, the Court takes the view that its attention should be focused on the provisions of Article 59 *et seq*. EEC, which deal with the freedom to provide services, and the argument concerning human rights, which has been treated extensively in the observations submitted to the Court.

[24] As regards, first, the provisions of Article 59 EEC, which prohibit any restriction on the freedom to supply services, it is apparent from the facts of the case that the link between the activity of the students associations of which Mr. Grogan and the other defendants are officers and medical terminations of pregnancies carried out in clinics in another member-State is too tenuous for the prohibition on the distribution of information to be capable of being regarded as a restriction within the meaning of Article 59.

[25] The situation in which students associations distributing the information at issue in the main proceedings are not in co-operation with the clinics whose addresses they publish can be distinguished from the situation which gave rise to the judgment in *GB-INNO-BM*, in which the Court held that a prohibition on the distribution of advertising

was capable of constituting a barrier to the free movement of goods and therefore had to be examined in the light of Articles 30, 31 and 36 EEC.

[26] The information to which the national court's questions refer is not distributed on behalf of an economic operator established in another member-State. On the contrary, the information constitutes a manifestation of freedom of expression and of the freedom to impart and receive information which is independent of the economic activity carried on by clinics established in another member-State.

[27] It follows that, in any event, a prohibition on the distribution of information in circumstances such as those which are the subject of the main proceedings cannot be regarded as a restriction within the meaning of Article 59 EEC.

...

[32] The reply to the national court's second and third questions must therefore be that it is not contrary to Community law for a member-State in which medical termination of pregnancy is forbidden to prohibit students associations from distributing information about the identity and location of clinics in another member-State where voluntary termination of pregnancy is lawfully carried out and the means of communicating with those clinics, where the clinics in question have no involvement in the distribution of the said information.

 Alert

Grogan was a seminal case in revealing the extent of what could be seen as a service and hence fall under Article 56 TFEU (as it is now). At the time of this case, a great many Irish women travelled to the UK to obtain abortions. The arguments made by the parties before the Court of Justice had been presented not only in terms of the provision of services but also on the basis of wider issues of human rights. The Court confronted the thorny issue of abortion and held that it was a medical service provided for remuneration within the meaning of Article 60 EEC (now Article 57 TFEU). But it distinguished the distribution of information about abortion clinics operating in other Member States which was not being provided on behalf of the operators of the clinics. Had such information been provided on behalf of the clinics, it may well have been held to have been a service and fallen under the protection of Article 56 TFEU.

Christelle Deliège v Ligue Francophone de Judo et Disciplines Associees ASBL and Others (Joined Cases 51/96 and 191/97) [2002] 2 CMLR 65

Panel: Rodríguez Iglesias, P.; Moitinho de Almeida, Edward and Sevón PP.C; Kapteyn, Puissochet, Hirsch, Jann and Ragnemalm (Rapporteur), JJ.

Legislation: Articles 59, 60 and 66 EC (now Articles 56, 57 and 62 TFEU respectively)

In the excerpt: Article 2 EC has since been repealed.

Facts: Deliège had been Belgian judo champion on several occasions in the under 52kg category, European champion once and under-19 world champion once. She had also won and been highly placed in international tournaments. She complained that the Belgian Judo Federation (the 'LBJ') and her regional judo league (the 'LFJ') had improperly frustrated her career. She had not been selected for two Olympic games and for other international championships. The event which directly gave rise to the proceedings was a decision by the LBJ not to select Deliège for an international tournament in Paris and to select instead two other athletes who, in her view, had achieved less outstanding results than her own. In the course of the proceedings against the LBJ and the LFJ, Deliège sought to challenge the rules of the European Judo Union governing the selection of competitors for international competitions.

JUDGMENT

[41] It is to be remembered at the outset that, having regard to the objectives of the Community, sport is subject to Community law only in so far as it constitutes an economic activity within the meaning of Article 2 of the Treaty. The Court has also recognised that sporting activities are of considerable social importance in the Community.

[42] That case law is also supported by the Declaration on Sport (Declaration 29) annexed to the final act of the Conference which adopted the text of the Amsterdam Treaty, which emphasises the social significance of sport and calls on the bodies of the European Union to give special consideration to the particular characteristics of amateur sport. In particular, that declaration is consistent with the abovementioned case law in so far as it relates to situations in which sport constitutes an economic activity.

[43] It must be recalled that the Treaty provisions concerning freedom of movement for persons do not prevent the adoption of rules or practices excluding foreign players from certain matches for reasons which are not of an economic nature, which relate to the particular nature and context of such matches and are thus of sporting interest only, such as, for example, matches between national teams from different countries. The Court stressed, however, that that restriction on the scope of the provisions in question must remain limited to its proper objective and cannot be relief upon to exclude the whole of a sporting activity.

[44] The selection rules at issue in the main proceedings do not relate to events between teams or selected competitors from different countries comprising only nationals of the State of which the Federation which selected them is a member, such as the Olympic Games or certain world or European championships, but reserve participation, by the national federation, in certain other international events of a high level to athletes who are affiliated to the federation in question, regardless of their nationality. The mere circumstance that the placings achieved by athletes in those competitions are taken into account in determining which countries may enter representatives for the Olympic Games cannot justify treating those competitions as events between national teams which might fall outside the scope of Community law.

[45] The LFJ submits in particular that sports associations and federations are entitled freely to determine the conditions governing access to competitions which concern only amateur sportsmen.

[46] In that regard, it is important to note that the mere fact that a sports association or federation unilaterally classifies its members as amateur athletes does not in itself mean that those members do not engage in economic activities within the meaning of Article 2 of the Treaty.

[47] As regards the nature of the rules at issue, it is clear from the judgments in *Walrave and Koch* and *Bosman*, cited above, that the Community provisions on the free movement of persons and services not only apply to the action of public authorities but extend also to rules of any other nature aimed at regulating gainful employment and the provision of services in a collective manner. The abolition as between Member States of obstacles to freedom of movement for persons and to freedom to provide services would be compromised if the abolition of State barriers could be neutralised by obstacles resulting from the exercise, by associations or organisations not governed by public law, of their legal autonomy.

[48] It follows that the Treaty, and in particular Articles 59, 60 and 66 thereof, may apply to sporting activities and to the rules laid down by sports associations of the kind at issue in the main proceedings.

 Alert

[49] In view of the foregoing considerations and the conflicting views expressed before the Court, it is important to verify whether an activity of the kind engaged in by Ms Deliège is capable of constituting an economic activity within the meaning of Article 2 of the Treaty and more particularly, the provision of services within the meaning of Article 59 of that Treaty.

[50] In the context of judicial cooperation between national courts and the Court of Justice, it is for national courts to establish and to evaluate the facts of the case and for the Court of Justice to provide the national court with such guidance on interpretation as may be necessary to enable it to decide the dispute.

[51] In that connection, it is important to note first that the judgment making the reference in Case C-191/97 refers among other things to grants awarded on the basis of earlier sporting results and to sponsorship contracts directly linked to the results achieved by the athlete. Moreover, Ms Deliège stated to the Court—and produced supporting documents—that she had received, by reason of her sporting achievements, grants from the Belgian French-speaking Community and from the Belgian Inter-Federal and Olympic Committee and that she has been sponsored by a banking institution and a motor-car manufacturer.

[52] As regards, next, the concepts of economic activities and the provision of services within the meaning of Articles 2 and 59 of the Treaty respectively, it must be pointed out that those concepts define the field of application of one of the fundamental freedoms guaranteed by the Treaty and, as such, may not be interpreted restrictively.

[53] As regards more particularly the first of those concepts, according to settled case law, the pursuit of an activity as an employed person or the provision of services for remuneration must be regarded as an economic activity within the meaning of Article 2 of the Treaty.

[54] However, as the Court held in particular in *Levin* and *Steymann*, the work performed must be genuine and effective and not such as to be regarded as purely marginal and ancillary.

 Alert

[55] As regards the provision of services, under the first paragraph of Article 60 services are considered to be "services" within the meaning of the Treaty where they

are normally provided for remuneration, in so far as they are not governed by the provisions relating to freedom of movement for goods, capital and persons.

[56] In that connection, it must be stated that sporting activities and, in particular, a high-ranking athlete's participation in an international competition are capable of involving the provision of a number of separate, but closely related, services which may fall within the scope of Article 59 of the Treaty even if some of those services are not paid for by those for whom they are performed.

[57] For example, an organiser of such a competition may offer athletes an opportunity of engaging in their sporting activity in competition with others and, at the same time, the athletes, by participating in the competition, enable the organiser to put on a sports event which the public may attend, which television broadcasters may retransmit and which may be of interest to advertisers and sponsors. Moreover, the athletes provide their sponsors with publicity the basis for which is the sporting activity itself.

[58] Finally, as regards the objections expressed in the observations submitted to the Court according to which, first, the main proceedings concern a purely internal situation and, second, certain international events fall outside the territorial scope of the Treaty, it must be remembered that the Treaty provisions on the freedom to provide services are not applicable to activities which are confined in all respects within a single Member State. However, a degree of extraneity may derive in particular from the fact that an athlete participates in a competition in a Member State other than that in which he is established.

[59] It is for the national court to determine, on the basis of those criteria of interpretation, whether Ms Deliège's sporting activities, and in particular her participation in international tournaments, constitutes an economic activity within the meaning of Article 2 of the Treaty and, more particularly, the provision of services within the meaning of Article 59 of the Treaty.

The Court of Justice went on to hold that, were Deliège's activity to be classified as a service, the selection rules would not constitute a restriction on the freedom to provide services. This was because international high-level sports events necessarily involve certain selection rules or criteria being adopted. In any event, the adoption of one system for selecting participants for an international tournament rather than another system had to be based on a large number of considerations unconnected with the personal situation of any athlete, such as the nature, the organisation and the financing of the sport concerned.

Conclusion

The case law developing Freedom of Establishment and Provision of Services has followed the well worn path shared with the other Freedom provisions. The process normally begins with the removal of direct discrimination, then indirect discrimination before going on to delineate the extent of that particular freedom. The essential problem in all of these situations is the balancing of State and EU interests. While in this Chapter this has specifically been concerned with achieving a balance between the Member States legitimate concerns about the maintenance of professional standards and the EU need to establish a Europe wide availability for the services provided by professionals, common solutions with the other Freedoms will have been observed.

EU legislation however now plays a dominating part in achieving a broad measure of harmonisation and it is the interplay between legislation and case law that represents the most significant recent development.

Further Reading

Cabral, Pedro: 'The Internal Market and the Right to Cross Border Medical Care' (2004) 29 ELR 673

Fairhurst, John: *The Law of the European Union* 7th ed Longman/Peason, Chapter 13

Horspool and Humphreys: *European Union Law* 4TH ed, OUP, Chapters 7 and 8

Siemms, Mathias: 'Convergance, Competition, Centros and Conflicts of law' (2002) 27 ELR 47

Steiner, Woods and Twigg-Flesner: *EU Law* 10th ed OUP Chapters 22,23 and 24

5

Article 101: Collusion

Introduction

Competition law plays an important role in maintaining the proper function of the common market. The aim of the legislation is to prevent companies acting in a collusive manner or abusing a dominant position to the detriment of other businesses and consumers.

The legislative framework in the UK is as follows: Article 101 and Article 102 TFEU set out the law applicable on an EU wide basis and any purported breach with a cross border element will be investigated under this legislation. The UK has enacted the Competition Act 1998, the Enterprise Act 2002 and the Enterprise and Regulatory Reform Act 2013. A purported breach within the UK will be investigated under this legislation. The provisions of Articles 101 and 102 are mirrored in the Competition Act 1998.

Since the introduction of the Modernisation Regulation (Regulation 1/2003) the majority of investigations that do not have a cross-border element will fall to be investigated by the National Competition Authorities ('NCAs'). Therefore, investigations by the Commission under Articles 101 and 102 are now the exception rather than the rule.

The NCA in the United Kingdom is currently the Office of Fair Trading. However, this is scheduled to be abolished under the Enterprise and Regulatory Reform Act 2013 and to be replaced by a new Competition and Markets Authority.

Appeals of decisions of the NCAs are heard in national courts of the Member States. In the United Kingdom, this will be the Competition Appeal Tribunal, the Court of Appeal and the Supreme Court in the UK. However, all such decisions must be compatible with the decisions of the Court of First Instance and the Court of Justice as well as EU legislation.

The Commission and NCAs in each Member State enjoy extensive powers to investigate and issue penalties to undertakings. Appeals by parties of the decisions of the Commission have led to a detailed examination of all parts of Articles 101 and 102 over the years. On the whole this examination has taken place within the Court of First Instance (now the General Court) and Court of Justice, which hear appeals from undertakings on decisions of the Commission.

Jurisprudence relating to Article 101 is considered in this chapter. The next chapter will deal with jurisprudence relating to Article 102.

All the judgments contained within this chapter result from appeals of decisions of the Commission and the majority were heard before the introduction of the Modernisation Regulation. Accordingly, they are all judgments of the Court of First Instance and the Court of Justice. The case law of the national courts is not considered in this text and is outside the scope of this course.

5.1 Agreements, Decisions and Concerted Practices

By its nature anti-competitive behaviour is often established in an informal fashion. However, there are also many circumstances in which undertakings do formally document their intentions. Article 101 TFEU was drafted in a way that tried to ensure that all forms of collusive behaviour between undertakings which could distort competition, whether formally or informally documented, were prohibited. For this reason Article 101 identifies three different types of collusion: agreement between undertakings, decisions by associations of undertakings and concerted practices.

Commission v ANIC Partecipazioni SpA (Case 49/92P) [2001] 4 CMLR 17

Panel: Kapteyn PC, Hirsc, Mancini (Rapporteur), Murray and Ragnemalm JJ, Georgios Cosmas, Advocate-General

Legislation: Article 85 EC (now Article 101 TFEU)

Facts: The Commission made an initial decision that a number of undertakings in the polypropylene market had for some time met regularly in secret meetings and put in place a number of measures to control prices and allocate market share over a long period of time.

JUDGMENT

102. By its fourth plea in law, ANIC criticises the Court of First Instance for having wrongly rejected its complaint that the infringement had not been legally characterised as either an agreement or a concerted practice within the meaning of Article 85 of the Treaty.

103. First, the Court of First Instance has not clearly indicated the actual criteria for characterising the type of infringement. Moreover, its classification does not correspond to the distinction made by the Commission in its decision, which uses the concept of concerted practice as a catch-all device for preventing suspected infringements from going unpunished, in the absence of proof of common intention between the producers. According to ANIC, the distinction between an agreement and a concerted practice has consequences for the level of proof required of the Commission and therefore for the rights of defence of the parties. The Commission's line of argument would lead to the conclusion that the reference to agreements in Article 85 of the Treaty is superfluous. If a concerted practice could consist in the mental element alone, with no need for any physical element, the two concepts would become redundant and would differ only as to the degree of manifestation of intention, joint intention in the case of an agreement and the manifestation of unilateral intention in the case of a concerted practice. ...

105. Thirdly, ANIC states that the characterisation of the alleged cartel as a single infringement, treated as an agreement and concerted practice, may have dangerous legal consequences. In particular it led in this case to the grouping

together, as a 'single' infringement, of the various lines of conduct followed by 15 undertakings over a period of approximately five years and prevented infringements which could actually be ascribed to an individual undertaking from being distinguished from those alleged.

106. Fourthly, ANIC complains that the Court of First Instance accepted the Commission's dual characterisation of the infringement as an agreement and concerted practice. ANIC considers that such a characterisation alters the burden of proof for the Commission and, consequently, the thrust of the defence mounted by the undertaking concerned...

107. The Commission states that this plea is based on a supposed difference in the burden of proof according to whether the infringement is a concerted practice or an agreement. That supposed difference is wrongly based on a literal construction of the term 'concerted practice', according to which 'practice' refers to conduct on the market and, consequently, to an objectively observable element. Such a construction is contrary to the *ratio legis* which bolsters the prohibition by widening it to cover concerting arrangements that are less elaborate than a real agreement, so as to prevent the rule being too easily circumvented. ANIC's argument would paradoxically weaken the prohibition, by requiring more exacting proof for a concerted practice than for an agreement. Article 85 of the Treaty would thus be disarmed in relation to concerted practices since, contrary to what counts for agreements, only the anti-competitive effect would count, not the object.

108. The list in Article 85(1) of the Treaty is intended to apply to all collusion between undertakings, whatever the form it takes. There is continuity between the cases listed. The only essential thing is the distinction between independent conduct, which is allowed, and collusion, which is not, regardless of any distinction between types of collusion. ANIC's argument would break down the unity and generality of the prohibited phenomenon and would remove from the ambit of the prohibition, without any reason, certain types of collusion which are no less dangerous than others. The Court of First Instance rightly rejected that argument at paragraph 199 of the judgment when it referred to the mental element without requiring an observable physical element.

109. The Court observes first of all that, at paragraphs 198 and 202 of the contested judgment, the Court of First Instance held that the Commission was entitled to categorise as agreements certain types of conduct on the part of the undertakings concerned, and, in the alternative, as concerted practices certain other forms of conduct on the part of the same undertakings. At paragraph 204, the Court of First Instance held that ANIC had taken part in an integrated set of schemes constituting a single infringement which progressively manifested itself in both unlawful agreements and unlawful concerted practices. ...

111. At paragraph 205, the Court of First Instance held that the Commission was entitled to characterise that single infringement as 'an agreement and a concerted practice', since the infringement involved at one and the same time factual elements to be characterised as 'agreements' and factual elements to be characterised as 'concerted practices' within the meaning of Article 85(1) of the Treaty. According to the Court of First Instance, given such a complex infringement, the dual characterisation by the Commission in Art. 1 of the Polypropylene Decision had to be understood not as requiring, simultaneously and cumulatively, proof that each of those factual elements presented the constituent elements both of an agreement and of a concerted practice, but rather as referring to a complex whole comprising a number of factual elements some of which were characterised as agreements and others as concerted practices for the purposes of Article 85(1) of the Treaty, which lays down no specific category for a complex infringement of this type.

112. Secondly, it must be observed that, if Article 85 of the Treaty distinguishes between 'concerted practices', 'agreements between undertakings' and 'decisions by associations of undertakings', the aim is to have the prohibitions of that Article catch different forms of coordination and collusion between undertakings (see, to that effect, in particular, *Imperial Chemical Industries Ltd. v Commission of the European Communities* (Case 48/69).

 Alert

113. It does not, however, follow that patterns of conduct having the same anti-competitive object, each of which, taken in isolation, would fall within the meaning of 'agreement', 'concerted practice' or 'a decision by an association of undertakings', cannot constitute different manifestations of a single infringement of Article 85(1) of the Treaty.

114. The Court of First Instance was therefore entitled to consider that patterns of conduct by several undertakings were a manifestation of a single and complex infringement, corresponding partly to an agreement and partly to a concerted practice.

115. Thirdly, it must be borne in mind that a concerted practice, within the meaning of Article 85(1) of the Treaty, refers to a form of coordination between undertakings which, without having been taken to a stage where an agreement properly so called has been concluded, knowingly substitutes for the risks of competition practical cooperation between them...

116. The Court of Justice has further explained that criteria of coordination and cooperation must be understood in the light of the concept inherent in the provisions of the Treaty relating to competition, according to which each economic operator must determine independently the policy which he intends to adopt on the market (see (Case 40/73) *Suiker Unie v Commission*).

117. According to that case-law, although that requirement of independence does not deprive economic operators of the right to adapt themselves intelligently to the existing and anticipated conduct of their competitors, it does however strictly

preclude any direct or indirect contact between such operators, the object or effect whereof is either to influence the conduct on the market of an actual or potential competitor or to disclose to such a competitor the course of conduct which they themselves have decided to adopt or contemplate adopting on the market, where the object or effect of such contact is to create conditions of competition which do not correspond to the normal conditions of the market in question, regard being had to the nature of the products or services offered, the size and number of the undertakings and the volume of the said market.

118. It follows that, as is clear from the very terms of Article 85(1) of the Treaty, a concerted practice implies, besides undertakings' concerting together, conduct on the market pursuant to those collusive practices, and a relationship of cause and effect between the two. ...

132. It follows that, whilst the concepts of an agreement and of a concerted practice have partially different elements, they are not mutually incompatible. Contrary to ANIC's allegations, the Court of First Instance did not therefore have to require the Commission to categorise either as an agreement or as a concerted practice each form of conduct found but was right to hold that the Commission had been entitled to characterise some of those forms of conduct as principally 'agreements' and others as 'concerted practices'.

 Alert

The Court of Justice has interpreted the terms "agreement" and "decision" widely. Accordingly any agreement whether oral or written and whether imposing legally or only morally binding obligations is likely to be capable of constituting collusion. Equally, any decision of associations of undertaking, even if not binding upon the members of the association, may constitute collusion.

The term "concerted practice" has provided more food for thought than the terms "agreement" and "decision". The reason is simple: the term "concerted practice" is intended to sweep up the forms of collusive behaviour which do not constitute an agreement between undertakings or a decision by an association of undertakings. It is therefore likely to be a less formal type of arrangement. However, because of a lack of certainty as to the form of the collusion where a concerted practice is suspected the Court of Justice has to be careful not to confuse behaviour which is normal in a particular market with collusive behaviour.

The nature of a concerted practice came to be discussed by the Court of Justice in detail in the following case.

Imperial Chemical Industries Ltd. v Commission (Case 48/69) [1972] CMLR 557 ('Dyestuffs')

Panel: R Lecourt P, Mertens de Wilmars, H. Kutscher, A M Donner, A Trabucchi, R Monaco and P Pescatore JJ, Monsieur Henri Mayras, Advocate-General

Legislation: Article 85 EEC (now Article 101 TFEU)

Facts: A subsidiary of Imperial Chemical Industries Ltd ('ICI') within the EU increased the price of a bleaching agent. This led the Commission to investigate allegations of concerted practices within the dyestuffs industry. Investigations found that the remainder of the competitors in the same market increased their respective prices within a short space of time and by the same margin as each other. Similar price increases occurred on three separate occasions in 1964, 1965 and 1967.

JUDGMENT

64. Article 85 draws a distinction between the concept of "concerted practices" and that of "agreements between undertakings" or of "decisions by associations of undertakings"; the object is to bring within the prohibition of that Art. a form of coordination between undertakings which, without having reached the stage where an agreement properly so-called has been concluded, knowingly substitutes practical cooperation between them for the risks of competition.

65. By its very nature, then, a concerted practice does not have all the elements of a contract but may inter alia arise out of coordination which becomes apparent from the behaviour of the participants .

66. Although parallel behaviour may not by itself be identified with a concerted practice, it may however amount to strong evidence of such a practice if it leads to conditions of competition which do not correspond to the normal conditions of the market, having regard to the nature of the products, the size and number of the undertakings, and the volume of the said market. **Alert**

67. This is especially the case if the parallel conduct is such as to enable those concerned to attempt to stabilize prices at a level different from that to which competition would have led, and to consolidate established positions to the detriment of effective freedom of movement of the products in the common market and of the freedom of consumers to choose their suppliers.

68. Therefore the question whether there was a concerted action in this case can only be correctly determined if the evidence upon which the contested decision is based is considered, not in isolation, but as a whole, account being taken of the specific features of the market in the products in question.

The characteristic features of the market in dyestuffs

69. The market in dyestuffs is characterized by the fact that 80 per cent of the market is supplied by about ten producers, very large ones in the main, which often manufacture these products together with other chemical products or pharmaceutical specialities.

70. The production patterns and therefore the cost structures of these manufacturers are very different and this makes it difficult to ascertain competing manufacturers' costs.

71. The total number of dyestuffs is very high, each undertaking producing more than a thousand.

72. The average extent to which these products can be replaced by others, is considered relatively good for standard dyes, but it can be very low or even non-existent for speciality dyes.

73. As regards speciality products, the market tends in certain cases towards an oligopolistic situation.

74. Since the price of dyestuffs forms a relatively small part of the price of the final product of the user undertaking, there is little elasticity of demand for dyestuffs on the market as a whole and this encourages price increases in the short term.

75. Another factor is that the total demand for dyestuffs is constantly increasing, and this tends to induce producers to adopt a policy enabling them to take advantage of this increase.

76. In the territory of the community, the market in dyestuffs in fact consists of five separate national markets with different price levels which cannot be explained by differences in costs and charges affecting producers in those countries.

77. Thus the establishment of the common market would not appear to have had any effect on this situation, since the differences between national price levels have scarcely decreased.

78. On the contrary, it is clear that each of the national markets has the characteristics of an oligopoly and that in most of them price levels are established under the influence of a "priceleader", who in some cases is the largest producer in the country concerned, and in other cases is a producer in another member state or a third state, acting through a subsidiary. ...

88. In 1964 all the undertakings in question announced their increases and immediately put them into effect, the initiative coming from Ciba-Italy which, on 7 January 1964, following instructions from Ciba-Switzerland, announced and immediately introduced an increase of 15 per cent. This initiative was followed by the other producers on the Italian market within two or three days.

89. On 9 January ICI Holland took the initiative in introducing the same increase in the Netherlands, whilst on the same day Bayer took the same initiative on the Belgo-Luxembourg market.

   [The Court went on to consider two further rounds of price increases in 1965 and 1967].

   ...

99. Viewed as a whole, the three consecutive increases reveal progressive cooperation between the undertakings concerned.

100. In fact, after the experience of 1964, when the announcement of the increases and their application coincided, although with minor differences as regards the range of products affected, the increases of 1965 and 1967 indicate a different mode of operation.

Here, the undertakings taking the initiative, BASF and Geiger respectively, announced their intentions of making an increase some time in advance, which allowed the undertakings to observe each other's reactions on the different markets, and to adapt themselves accordingly.

101. By means of these advance announcements the various undertakings eliminated all uncertainty between them as to their future conduct and, in doing so, also eliminated a large part of the risk usually inherent in any independent change of conduct on one or several markets.

102. This was all the more the case since these announcements, which led to the fixing of general and equal increases in prices for the markets in dyestuffs, rendered the market transparent as regard the percentage rates of increase.

103. Therefore, by the way in which they acted, the undertakings in question temporarily eliminated with respect to prices some of the preconditions for competition on the market which stood in the way of the achievement of parallel uniformity of conduct.

104. The fact that this conduct was not spontaneous is corroborated by an examination of other aspects of the market.

105. In fact, from the number of producers concerned it is not possible to say that the European market in dyestuffs is, in the strict sense, an oligopoly in which price competition could no longer play a substantial role.

106. These producers are sufficiently powerful and numerous to create a considerable risk that in times of rising prices some of them might not follow the general movement but might instead try to increase their share of the market by behaving in an individual way.

107. Furthermore, the dividing-up of the common market into five national markets with different price levels and structures makes it improbable that a spontaneous and equal price increase would occur on all the national markets. ...

109. Therefore, although parallel conduct in respect of prices may well have been an attractive and risk-free objective for the undertakings concerned, it is hardly conceivable that the same action could be taken spontaneously at the same time, on the same national markets and for the same range of products.

110. Nor is it any more plausible that the increases of January 1964, introduced on the Italian market and copied on the Netherlands and Belgo-Luxembourg markets which have little in common with each other either as regards the level of prices or the pattern of competition, could have been brought into effect within a period of two or three days without prior concertation.

111. As regards the increases of 1965 and 1967 concertation took place openly, since all the announcements of the intention to increase prices with effect from a certain date and for a certain range of products made it possible for producers to decide on their conduct regarding the special cases of France and Italy.

112. In proceeding in this way, the undertakings mutually eliminated in advance any uncertainties concerning their reciprocal behaviour on the different markets and thereby also eliminated a large part of the risk inherent in any independent change of conduct on those markets.

113. The general and uniform increase on those different markets can only be explained by a common intention on the part of those undertakings, first, to adjust the level of prices and the situation resulting from competition in the form of discounts, and secondly, to avoid the risk, which is inherent in any price increase, of changing the conditions of competition.

The decision of the Court of Justice in *Dyestuffs* can be contrasted with the decision of the Court of Justice in the next case in which it found that the pricing decisions were found to be a normal feature of the market.

A. Ahlström Osakeyhtiö and others v Commission (Cases 89,104,114,116-117 & 125-129/85) [1988] 4 CMLR 901 (the 'Wood Pulp Cartel' case)

Panel: Lord Mackenzie Stuart CJ; Bosco, Due, Moitinho de Almeida and Rodriguez Iglesias PPC; Koopmans, Everling, Bahlmann, Galmot, Kakouris, Joliet, O'Higgins and Schockweiler JJ. M. Marco Darmon, Advocate General

Legislation: Article 85 EEC (now Article 101 TFEU)

Facts: The Commission investigated allegations of concerted practices by a large number of wood pulp producers suspecting that the producers were colluding to co-ordinate price changes.

JUDGMENT

126. ...[In] this case, concertation is not the only plausible explanation for the parallel conduct. To begin with, the system of price announcements may be regarded as constituting a rational response to the fact that the pulp market constituted a long-term market and to the need felt by both buyers and sellers to limit commercial risks. Further, the similarity in the dates of price announcements may be regarded as a direct result of the high degree of market transparency, which does not have to be described as artificial. Finally, the parallelism of prices and the price trends may be satisfactorily explained by the oligopolistic tendencies of the market and by the specific circumstances prevailing in certain periods. Accordingly, the parallel conduct established by the Commission does not constitute evidence of concertation.

127. In the absence of a firm, precise and consistent body of evidence, it must be held that concertation regarding announced prices has not been established by the Commission. Article 1(1) of the contested decision must therefore be annulled.

5.2 Effect on Trade between Member States

Collusive behaviour will fall within the prohibition contained in Article 101 TFEU if it may affect trade between member states. As the Court of Justice set out in *Société*

Technique Minière v Maschinenbau Ulm GmbH (Case 32/65) [1966] CMLR 357 (the 'STM' case) the mere potential to affect trade is sufficient.

The decision of the Court of Justice in *Brasserie de Haecht SA v Wilkin-Janssen* (Case 3/67) [1968] CMLR 26 provided that the cumulative effect of a number of small agreements within even one single Member State could have the potential to effect trade between Member States. However, it is important when analysing any agreement between undertakings which have less than 10-15% share of the relevant market may be considered *de minimus* under the 'Notice on Agreements of Minor Importance' [2001] OJ C368/13.

5.2.1 The object or effect of prevention, restriction or distortion of competition

Collusive behaviour, which has, as its object or effect the prevention, restriction or distortion of competition is capable of falling within the prohibition contained within Article 101 TFEU. Both horizontal and vertical agreements are capable of having as their object or effect the prevention, restriction or distortion of competition.

The terms "object" and "effect" are provided in the alternative and it is only necessary to show one or the other. As a result, the mere intention to distort competition may be enough even if an undertaking is not successful in its aims. The Court of Justice discussed this point in:

Société Technique Minière v Maschinenbau Ulm GmbH (Case 32/65) [1966] CMLR 357 (the 'STM' case),

Panel: L. Hammes CJ, L. Delvaux, A. M. Donner, A. Trabucchi, R. Lecourt JJ. Herr Karl Roemer, Advocate-General

Legislation: Article 85 EEC (now Article 101 TFEU)

Facts: Société Technique Minière ('STM') held an exclusive supply contract with an exclusive right to sell in France equipment produced by Maschinenbau Ulm GmbH ('MBU'). The contract contained an agreement by STM not to sell their competing equipment in France and MBU also agreed not to compete with STM in France. However, as MBU's contract with STM and its contract with other distributors did not prevent the selling of MBU equipment into other countries the companies did not have protection within their territory against another MBU distributor selling into that country. As a result STM was unhappy about the contract and so argued that it was invalid under Article 85 EEC.

JUDGMENT

Finally, for the agreement at issue to be caught by the prohibition contained in Article 85(1) it must have as its 'object or effect the prevention, restriction or distortion of competition within the common market'.

The fact that these are not cumulative but alternative requirements, indicated by the conjunction 'or', leads first to the need to consider the precise purpose of the agreement, in the economic context in which it is to be applied. This interference with competition referred to in Article 85(1) must result from all or some of the clauses of the agreement itself. Where, however, an analysis of the said clauses does not reveal the effect on competition to be sufficiently deleterious, the consequences of the agreement should then be considered and for it to be caught by the prohibition it is then necessary to find that those factors are present which show that competition has in fact been prevented or restricted or distorted to an appreciable extent.

If matters are not clear from the object of an agreement, the NCA's must apply a logical methodology in deciding whether the effect of an agreement is in fact to prevent, restrict or distort competition. The Court of Justice discussed the requirements of this methodology in the following case:

European Night Services and others v Commission (Cases T-374, 375, 384, 388/94) [1998] 5 CMLR 718

Panel: Kalogeropoulos P, Bellamy, and Pirrung JJ

Legislation: Article 85 EC (now Article 101 TFEU)

Facts: Four rail companies, including British Rail, established European Night Services ('ENS') to operate overnight rail services through the channel tunnel from the UK and into continental Europe. The agreement was found by the Commission to breach Article 85 EC unless stringent conditions were adhered to. ENS argued that the Commission has failed to give sufficient reasons as to why the agreement breached Article 85 EC and so the case was referred to the Court of First Instance.

JUDGMENT

136. Before any examination of the parties' arguments as to whether the Commission's analysis as regards restrictions of competition was correct, it must be borne in mind that in assessing an agreement under Article 85(1) of the Treaty, account should be taken of the actual conditions in which it functions, in particular the economic context in which the undertakings operate, the products or services covered by the agreement and the actual structure of the market concerned ...

137. It must also be stressed that the examination of conditions of competition is based not only on existing competition between undertakings already present on the relevant market but also on potential competition, in order to ascertain whether, in the light of the structure of the market and the economic and legal context within which it functions, there are real concrete possibilities for the undertakings concerned to compete among themselves or for a new competitor to penetrate the relevant market and compete with the undertakings already established.... .

Therefore the methodology of the NCAs should be to undertake an analysis of the relevant product and geographical market in which the behaviour operates together with any other relevant features of the particular market in question to establish whether the collusive behaviour has in fact had an anti-competitive effect.

5.2.2 The Prevention, Restriction or Distortion of Competition

Article 101(1) TFEU sets out at paragraphs (a) to (e) a non-exhaustive list of agreements, decisions and concerted practices which are prohibited. The list is illustrative only and any type of collusive behaviour is generally likely to be capable of falling within the prohibition of Article 101(1) if the pattern of competition within the relevant market differs as a result of the collusive behaviour.

5.3 Defences

5.3.1 The Article 101(3) TFEU Defence

In some cases it will be clear that collusive behaviour is made up only of anti-competitive elements. For instance, an agreement between two undertakings to fix a tender process is unlikely to be viewed as anything other than a blatant distortion of competition. However, the NCAs and the courts face more difficulties where arrangements between undertakings contain both competitive and anti-competitive elements. Such agreements can in certain circumstances not threaten competition within the common market and they may actually assist competition. This is recognised in Article 101(3) TFEU which disapplies the prohibition contained within Article 101(1) in respect of such agreements.

Since the introduction of Regulation 1/2003, an undertaking may decide that an agreement falls within Article 101(3) by looking at the individual circumstances in which that agreement operates. Alternatively an undertaking may decide that the agreement is exempt as it falls within a block exemption issued by the Commission. However, if the view of that undertaking is challenged by the NCAs it is necessary for the court to apply a methodology in deciding whether the agreement does properly fall within Article 101(3).

5.3.2 The Rule of Reason Defence?

It has already been noted above that an agreement or other form of collusive behaviour will be contrary to Article 101(1) TFEU if it as their object or effect the prevention, restriction or distortion of competition within the internal market. The approach of the Court of Justice initially seemed to indicate that the collusive behaviour may not be deemed to have such an effect if its anti-competitive effects were outweighed by any pro-competitive effects. This has become known as the Rule of Reason defence. The development of this approach can be seen in:

Société Technique Minière v Maschinenbau Ulm GmbH (Case 39/65) [1966] CMLR 357

Facts: See earlier for the facts of this case.

JUDGMENT

The competition in question must be understood within the actual context in which it would occur in the absence of the agreement in dispute. In particular it may be doubted whether there is an interference with competition if the said agreement seems really necessary for the penetration of a new area by an undertaking. Therefore, in order to decide whether an agreement containing a clause 'granting an exclusive right of sale' is to be considered as prohibited by reason of its object or of its effect, it is appropriate to take into account in particular the nature and quantity, limited or otherwise, of the products covered by the agreement, the position and importance of the grantor and the concessionaire on the market for the products concerned, the isolated nature of the disputed agreement or, alternatively, its position in a series of agreements, the severity of the clauses intended to protect the exclusive dealership or, alternatively, the opportunities allowed for other commercial competitors in the same products by way of parallel re-exportation and importation.

Pronuptia de Paris GmbH v Pronuptia de Paris Irmgard Schillgallis (Case 161/84) [1986] 1 CMLR 414

Panel: Lord Mackenzie Stuart CJ, Everling, Bahlmann and Joliet PPC, Koopmans, Due and Galmot JJ, Mr Pieter Verloren Van Themaat, Advocate-General

Legislation: Article 85 EEC (Article 101 TFEU)

Facts: A dispute arose in the German courts between a franchisor and franchisee concerning their agreement for the distribution of wedding dresses and other articles sold under the Pronuptia de Paris trademark. The German court asked the Court of Justice whether the franchise agreement infringed Article 85 EEC.

JUDGMENT

27.   In view of the foregoing, the answer to the first question must be that:

(1)   The compatibility of franchise agreements for the distribution of goods with Article 85(1) depends on the provisions contained therein and on their economic context.

(2)   Provisions which are strictly necessary in order to ensure that the know-how and assistance provided by the franchisor do not benefit competitors do not constitute restrictions of competition for the purposes of Article 85(1).

(3)   Provisions which establish the control strictly necessary for maintaining the identity and reputation of the network identified by the common name or symbol do not constitute restrictions of competition for the purposes of Article 85(1).

(4)   Provisions which share markets between the franchisor and the franchisees or between franchisees constitute restrictions of competition for the purposes of Article 85(1).

(5)   The fact that the franchisor makes price recommendations to the franchisee does not constitute a restriction of competition, so long as there is no concerted practice between the franchisor and the franchisees or between the franchisees themselves for the actual application of such prices.

(6)   Franchise agreements for the distribution of goods which contain provisions sharing markets between the franchisor and the franchisees or between franchisees are capable of affecting trade between member states.

However, the Court of First Instance has since denied the existence of a rule of reason defence in:

Métropole Télévision (M6) and others v Commission (Case T-112/99) [2001] ECR II-02459

Legislation: Article 85 EC (now Article 101 TFEU)

Facts: Six French broadcasting and telecommunications companies had entered into an agreement to establish Télévision par Satellite with objective of devising, developing and broadcasting a range of television programmes and services by satellite to French speaking viewers in European for payment. At the time, this market was dominated by Canal+ and its subsidiary, CanalSatellite. Certain clauses in the agreement were either cleared by the Commission or granted an exemption by it, but only for a period of three years. One of the grounds for challenging the Commission's decision was that it had failed to apply the rule of reason.

JUDGMENT

72.   According to the applicants, as a consequence of the existence of a rule of reason in Community competition law, when Article 85(1) of the Treaty is applied it is necessary to weigh the pro and anti-competitive effects of an agreement in order to determine whether it is caught by the prohibition laid down in that article. It should, however, be observed, first of all, that contrary to the applicants' assertions the existence of such a rule has not, as such, been confirmed by the Community courts. Quite to the contrary, in various judgments the Court of Justice and the Court of First Instance have been at pains to indicate that the existence of a rule of reason in Community competition law is doubtful (see Case C-235/92 P *Montecatini v Commission* [1999] ECR I-4539, paragraph 133 ('... even if the rule of reason did have a place in the context of Article [101](1) of the Treaty'), and Case T-14/89 *Montedipe v Commission* [1992] ECR II-1155, paragraph 265, and in Case T-148/89 *Tréfilunion v Commission* [1995] ECR II-1063, paragraph 109).

73.   Next, it must be observed that an interpretation of Article 85(1) of the Treaty, in the form suggested by the applicants, is difficult to reconcile with the rules prescribed by that provision.

74.   Article 85 of the Treaty expressly provides, in its third paragraph, for the possibility of exempting agreements that restrict competition where they satisfy a

number of conditions, in particular where they are indispensable to the attainment of certain objectives and do not afford undertakings the possibility of eliminating competition in respect of a substantial part of the products in question. It is only in the precise framework of that provision that the pro and anti-competitive aspects of a restriction may be weighed (see, to that effect, Case 161/84 *Pronuptia* [1986] ECR 353, paragraph 24, and Case T-17/93 *Matra Hachette v Commission* [1994] ECR II-595, paragraph 48, and *European Night Services and Others v Commission*, cited in paragraph 34 above, paragraph 136). Article 85(3) of the Treaty would lose much of its effectiveness if such an examination had to be carried out already under Article 85(1) of the Treaty.

75. It is true that in a number of judgments the Court of Justice and the Court of First Instance have favoured a more flexible interpretation of the prohibition laid down in Article 85(1) of the Treaty (see, in particular, *Société technique minière and Oude Luttikhuis and Others*, cited in paragraph 70 above, *Nungesser and Eisele v Commission and Coditel and Others*, cited in paragraph 68 above, *Pronuptia*, cited in paragraph 74 above, and *European Night Services and Others v Commission*, cited in paragraph 34 above, as well as the judgment in Case C-250/92 *DLG* [1994] ECR I-5641, paragraphs 31 to 35).

76. Those judgments cannot, however, be interpreted as establishing the existence of a rule of reason in Community competition law. They are, rather, part of a broader trend in the case-law acording to which it is not necessary to hold, wholly abstractly and without drawing any distinction, that any agreement restricting the freedom of action of one or more of the parties is necessarily caught by the prohibition laid down in Article 85(1) of the Treaty. In assessing the applicability of Article 85(1) to an agreement, account should be taken of the actual conditions in which it functions, in particular the economic context in which the undertakings operate, the products or services covered by the agreement and the actual structure of the market concerned (see, in particular, *European Night Services and Others v Commission*, cited in paragraph 34 above, paragraph 136, *Oude Luttikhuis*, cited in paragraph 70 above, paragraph 10, and *VGB and Others v Commission*, cited in paragraph 70 above, paragraph 140, as well as the judgment in Case C-234/89 *Delimitis* [1991] ECR I-935, paragraph 31).

77. That interpretation, while observing the substantive scheme of Article 85 of the Treaty and, in particular, preserving the effectiveness of Article 85(3), makes it possible to prevent the prohibition in Article 85(1) from extending wholly abstractly and without distinction to all agreements whose effect is to restrict the freedom of action of one or more of the parties. It must, however, be emphasised that such an approach does not mean that it is necessary to weigh the pro and anti-competitive effects of an agreement when determining whether the prohibition laid down in Article 85(1) of the Treaty applies.

78. In the light of the foregoing, it must be held that, contrary to the applicants' submission, in the contested decision the Commission correctly applied Article 85(1) of the Treaty to the exclusivity clause and the clause relating to the special-

interest channels inasmuch as it was not obliged to weigh the pro and anti-competitive aspects of those agreements outside the specific framework of Article 85(3) of the Treaty.

79. It did, however, assess the restrictive nature of those clauses in their economic and legal context in accordance with the case-law. Thus, it rightly found that the general-interest channels presented programmes that were attractive for subscribers to a pay-TV company and that the effect of the exclusivity clause was to deny TPS' competitors access to such programmes (points 102 to 107 of the contested decision). As regards the clause relating to the special-interest channels, the Commission found that it resulted in a limitation of the supply of such channels on that market for a period of 10 years (point 101 of the contested decision).

80. This objection must therefore be rejected.

5.3.3 The *De Minimis* Defence

An undertaking may also be able to able to avoid the prohibition contained within Article 101(1) if it can demonstrate that the agreement does not have an appreciable effect on either competition or inter-state trade (the *de minimis* defence). The defence was introduced in the judgment of the Court of Justice in:

Völk v S.P.R.L. Etablissements J. Vervaecke (Case 5/69) [1969] CMLR 273

Panel: R. Lecourt P, A. Trabucchi, Mertens de Wilmars, A. M. Donner, W. Strauss, R. Monaco and P. Pescatore JJ. M. Joseph Gand, Advocate-General

Legislation: Article 85 EEC (now Article 101 TFEU)

Facts: Mr Völk was the owner of Erd & Co which manufactured washing machines and of Vervaecke which manufactured electrical appliances. Both were small companies. Vervaecke held exclusive rights to sell Völk's products in Belgium and Luxemburg. The German court asked the Court of Justice whether the agreement breached Article 101 considering the small market shares of the parties.

JUDGMENT

...The question is thus reduced to whether, in deciding whether such agreements fall within the prohibition set out in Article 85(1) of the treaty, regard must be had to the proportion of the market which the grantor controls or endeavours to obtain in the territory ceded.

If an agreement is to be capable of affecting trade between member states it must be possible to foresee with a sufficient degree of probability on the basis of a set of objective factors of law or of fact that the agreement in question may have an influence, direct or indirect, actual or potential, on the pattern of trade between member states in such a way that it might hinder the attainment of the objectives of a single market between states. Moreover, the prohibition in Article 85(1) is applicable only if the agreement in question also has as its object or effect, the prevention, restriction or distortion of competition within the common market. Those conditions must be understood by reference to the actual circumstances of the agreement. Consequently an agreement falls outside the prohibition in Article 85 when it has only an insignificant effect on the markets, taking into account the weak position which, the persons concerned have on the market of the product in question. Thus an exclusive dealing agreement, even with absolute territorial protection, may, having regard to the weak position of the persons concerned on the market in the products in question in the area covered by the absolute protection, escape the prohibition laid down in Article 85(1).

The principle developed in *Völk* is now enshrined in the 'Notice on Agreements of Minor Importance' [2001] OJ C368/13. However, it should be noted that this Notice contains a prohibition on certain hardcore restrictions so that, no matter what the market share of the undertakings certain agreements, such as fixing prices, are not exempted by the Notice.

Further reading

van Gerven, G and Varona, E: 'The *Wood Pulp* Case and the Future of Concerted Practices' (1994) 31 CMLRev 575

Robertson, B: 'What is a restriction of competition? The implications of the CFIs judgment in O2 Germany and the rule of reason' [2007] ECLR 59

6

Article 102: Abuse of a Dominant Position

Topic List

Introduction

The previous chapter reviewed how the Court of Justice and Court of First Instance (now the General Court) have applied Article 101 TFEU, which seeks to deal with the threat to competition posed by collusive behaviour. This Chapter contains a review of the treatment by the Court of Justice and Court of First Instance of those cases involving a breach of Article 102 TFEU, which seeks to deal with the abuse by an undertaking of a dominant position.

It is important to remember that dominance in itself is not prohibited as this dominance may be a reflection of a successful and efficient company. For instance most people would suspect that Microsoft Corporation is dominant in several markets such as the market for home PC operating systems. The Commission has indeed found that Microsoft is dominant in certain markets. However, it is only when the Commission has found that Microsoft has abused that dominance that it has faced penalties under the EU competition law regime.

As with Article 101, Regulation 1/2003 (the Modernisation Regulation) provided for the transfer of much of the responsibility for enforcement of Article 102 to NCAs. However, as with Article 101, the analysis of the fundamental elements of Article 102 took place before the introduction of the modernisation regulation. Therefore, the decisions are those of the Court of Justice and Court of First Instance.

In deciding whether a breach has occurred, the Commission, NCAs and courts must identify the following:

(a)   The undertaking(s) which are suspected of being dominant and are accused of abuse of that dominance;

(b)   Whether the undertaking(s) enjoy a dominant position in the relevant market;

(c)   If the undertaking(s) do enjoy a dominant position – are they abusing it?

(d)   Does the abuse affect trade between Member States?

This chapter will examine points (b) and (c).

6.1 The Relevant Market

Before being able to assess whether an undertaking is dominant in a particular market, it is first necessary to establish what that market is. The Commission and the courts do this by identifying the products or services which form the market and by determining the market's geographical area. These two dimensions are known respectively as the Relevant Product Market ('RPM') and the Relevant Geographic Market ('RGM'). It may also be necessary to examine the time dimensions of the market. This is known as the Relevant Temporal Market ('RTM').

The cases involving RPM, RGM and RTM demonstrate that the Commission and the accused undertaking will often be locked in a complex battle to define the market in a manner which suits their position. As a result cases can involve very sophisticated economic arguments and often make use of evidence from economic analysts.

6.1.1 Relevant Product Market

The RPM refers to the products or services which form the relevant market. The Commission will usually want to show that the range of products or services comprising the RPM is narrow as this is more likely to result in an undertaking holding a dominant position. Conversely, the accused undertaking will usually want to show that the RPM is wide.

The RPM is determined by ascertaining which products or services are interchangeable or substitutable. This can be analysed from two different perspectives:

6.1.1.1 Demand substitution

In the analysing the RPM, the Commission and courts will often look at how likely a consumer of a particular product or service is to switch to an alternative product and in what circumstances it will do so. This is known as demand side substitutionality, interchangeability or product substitution. If a consumer is likely to switch between particular products or services easily it is likely that those products or services form part of the same RPM.

The Court of Justice provided a useful analysis of elements to be taken into account when considering demand side substitutionality in:

United Brands Company and United Brands Continentaal BV v Commission (Case 27/76) [1978] 1 CMLR 429

Panel: Kutscher CJ, Sørensen and Bosco PPC, Donner, Mertens de Wilmars, Lord Mackenzie Stuart and Touffait JJ, M Henri Mayras, Advocate-General

Legislation: Article 86 EEC Treaty (now Article 102 TFEU)

Facts: United Brands produced bananas and supplied them to a number of distributors in several EU countries. The Commission accused the company of a number of abusive practices. United Brands contested the decision of the Commission in the Court of Justice. Before reviewing the alleged abusive practices the Court of Justice reviewed the RPM into which bananas fall. The Commission argued that they formed a distinct market of their own. United Brands argued that they formed part of the wider fresh fruit market.

JUDGMENT

22. For the banana to be regarded as forming a market which is sufficiently differentiated from other fruit markets it must be possible for it to be singled out by such special features distinguishing it from other fruits that it is only to a limited extent interchangeable with them and is only exposed to their competition in a way that is hardly perceptible.

23. The ripening of bananas takes place the whole year round without any season having to be taken into account.

24. Throughout the year production exceeds demand and can satisfy it at any time.

25. Owing to this particular feature the banana is a privileged fruit and its production and marketing can be adapted to the seasonal fluctuations of other fresh fruit which are known and can be computed.

26. There is no unavoidable seasonal substitution since the consumer can obtain this fruit all the year round.

27. Since the banana is a fruit which is always available in sufficient quantities the question whether it can be replaced by other fruits must be determined over the whole of the year for the purpose of ascertaining the degree of competition between it and other fresh fruit.

28. The studies of the banana market on the court's file show that on the latter market there is no significant long term cross-elasticity any more than - as has been mentioned - there is any seasonal substitutability in general between the banana and all the seasonal fruits, as this only exists between the banana and two fruits (peaches and table grapes) in one of the countries (West Germany) of the relevant geographic market.

29. As far as concerns the two fruits available throughout the year (oranges and apples) the first are not interchangeable and in the case of the second there is only a relative degree of substitutability.

30. This small degree of substitutability is accounted for by the specific features of the banana and all the factors which influence consumer choice.

31. The banana has certain characteristics, appearance, taste, softness, seedlessness, easy handling, a constant level of production which enable it to satisfy the constant needs of an important section of the population consisting of the very young, the old and the sick.

32. As far as prices are concerned two FAO studies show that the banana is only affected by the prices - falling prices - of other fruits (and only of peaches and table grapes) during the summer months and mainly in July and then by an amount not exceeding 20%.

 Decipher
The FAO is the Food and Agriculture Organisation of the UN.

33. Although it cannot be denied that during these months and some weeks at the end of the year this product is exposed to competition from other fruits, the flexible way in which the volume of imports and their marketing on the relevant geographic market is adjusted means that the conditions of competition are extremely limited and that its price adapts without any serious difficulties to this situation where supplies of fruit are plentiful.

34. It follows from all these considerations that a very large number of consumers having a constant need for bananas are not noticeably or even appreciably enticed away from the consumption of this product by the arrival of other fresh fruit on the market and that even the personal peak periods only affect it for a limited period of time and to a very limited extent from the point of view of substitutability.

 Alert

35. Consequently the banana market is a market which is sufficiently distinct from the other fresh fruit markets.

When determining the likelihood of demand side substitution, the Commission may employ the Small but Significant and Non-transitory Increase in Price ('SSNIP') test. This asks whether "the parties' customers would switch to readily available substitutes or to suppliers located elsewhere in response to a hypothetical small (in the range 5 % to 10 %) but permanent relative price increase in the products and areas being considered" ('Notice on the Definition of the Relevant Market for the Purposes of Community Competition Law' [1997] OJ C372/5, para 17).

6.1.1.2 Supply Substitution

In addition to considering how easily consumers will switch between different products, the Commission and the courts will also consider whether another undertaking could easily start offering the product in question. This is known as supply side substitutionality. The Commission has defined this as meaning "that suppliers are able to switch production to the relevant products and market them in the short term without incurring significant additional costs or risks in response to small and permanent changes in relative prices." ('Notice on the Definition of the Relevant Market for the Purposes of Community Competition Law' [1997] OJ C372/5, para 20).

The Court of Justice considered supply side substitution in the following cases:

Nederlandsche Banden – Industrie Michelin NV v Commission (Case 322/81) [1985] 1 CMLR 282

Panel: Mertens de Wilmars CJ, Koopmans , Bahlmann and Galmot PPC, Pescatore, Lord Mackenzie Stuart, O'Keeffe, Due and Everling JJ, Mr Pieter Verloren Van Themaat Advocate-General

Legislation: Article 86 EEC (now 102 TFEU)

Facts: Michelin produced tyres for a number of types of vehicles. The Commission found Michelin to be dominant in the market for replacement tyres for lorries, buses and similar vehicles and found that Michelin offered discounts to customers based on arbitrary grounds to tie customers in, rather than on the basis of justifiable grounds such as the quantity of tyres ordered. As part of its appeal Michelin questioned the Commission's assessment of the RPM.

JUDGMENT

37. As the court has repeatedly emphasized, most recently in its judgment of 11 December 1980 in case 31/80 *NV L 'Oreal and SA L 'Oreal v PVBA de Nieuwe Amck* (1980) ECR 3775, for the purposes of investigating the possibly dominant position of an undertaking on a given market, the possibilities of competition must be judged in the context of the market comprising the totality of the products which, with respect to their characteristics, are particularly suitable for satisfying constant needs and are only to a limited extent interchangeable with other products. However, it must be noted that the determination of the relevant market

is useful in assessing whether the undertaking concerned is in a position to prevent effective competition from being maintained and behave to an appreciable extent independently of its competitors and customers and consumers. For this purpose, therefore, an examination limited to the objective characteristics only of the relevant products cannot be sufficient: the competitive conditions and the structure of supply and demand on the market must also be taken into consideration.

38. Moreover, it was for that reason that the Commission and Michelin NV agreed that new, original-equipment tyres should not be taken into consideration in the assessment of market shares. Owing to the particular structure of demand for such tyres characterized by direct orders from car manufacturers, competition in this sphere is in fact governed by completely different factors and rules.

39. As far as replacement tyres are concerned, the first point which must be made is that at the user level there is no interchangeability between car and van tyres on the one hand and heavy-vehicle tyres on the other. Car and van tyres therefore have no influence at all on competition on the market in heavy-vehicle tyres.

40. Furthermore, the structure of demand for each of those groups of products is different. Most buyers of heavy-vehicle tyres are trade users, particularly haulage undertakings, for whom, as the Commission explained, the purchase of replacement tyres represents an item of considerable expenditure and who constantly ask their tyre dealers for advice and long-term specialized services adapted to their specific needs. On the other hand, for the average buyer of car or van tyres the purchase of tyres is an occasional event and even if the buyer operates a business he does not expect such specialized advice and service adapted to specific needs. Hence the sale of heavy-vehicle tyres requires a particularly specialized distribution network which is not the case with the distribution of car and van tyres.

41. The final point which must be made is that there is no elasticity of supply between tyres for heavy vehicles and car tyres owing to significant differences in production techniques and in the plant and tools needed for their manufacture. The fact that time and considerable investment are required in order to modify production plant for the manufacture of light-vehicle tyres instead of heavy-vehicle tyres or vice versa means that there is no discernible relationship between the two categories of tyre enabling production to be adapted to demand on the market. Moreover, that was why in 1977, when the supply of tyres for heavy vehicles was insufficient, Michelin NV decided to grant an extra bonus instead of using surplus production capacity for car tyres to meet demand.

 Alert

42. The Commission rightly examined the structure of the market and demand primarily at the level of dealers to whom Michelin NV applied the practice in question. Michelin NV has itself stated, although in another context, that it was compelled to change its discount system to take account of the tendency towards specialization amongst its dealers, some of whom, such as garage owners, no longer sold tyres for heavy vehicles and vans. This confirms the differences existing in the structure of demand between different groups of dealers. Nor has Michelin NV disputed that the distinction drawn between tyres for heavy vehicles, vans and cars is also applied by all its competitors, especially as regards discount terms, even if in the case of certain types of tyre the distinctions drawn by different manufacturers may vary in detail.

43. Nevertheless, it cannot be deduced from the fact that the conduct to which exception is taken in this case affects dealers that Michelin NV's position ought to be assessed on the basis of the proportion of Michelin heavy-vehicle tyres in the dealers' total turnover. Since it is a question of investigating whether Michelin NV holds a dominant position in the case of certain products, it is unimportant that the dealers also deal in other products if there is no competition between those products and the products in question.

44. On the other hand, in deciding whether a dominant position exists, neither the absence of elasticity of supply between different types and dimensions of tyres for heavy vehicles, which is due to differences in the conditions of production, nor the absence of interchangeability and elasticity of demand between those types and dimensions of tyre from the point of view of the specific needs of the user allow a number of smaller markets, reflecting those types and dimensions, to be distinguished, as Michelin NV suggests. Those differences between different types and dimensions of tyre are not vitally important for dealers, who must meet demand from customers for the whole range of heavy-vehicle tyres. Furthermore, in the absence of any specialization on the part of the undertakings concerned, such differences in the type and dimensions of a product are not a crucial factor in the assessment of an undertaking's market position because in view of their similarity and the manner in which they complement one another at the technical level, the conditions of competition on the market are the same for all the types and dimensions of the product.

45. In establishing that Michelin NV has a dominant position the Commission was therefore right to assess its market share with reference to replacement tyres for lorries, buses and similar vehicles and to exclude consideration of car and van tyres.

Europemballage Corporation and Continental Can Company Inc. v Commission (Case 6/72) [1973] 1 CMLR 199

Panel: Mertens de Wilmars CJ, Monaco and O'Keeffe JJ. Herr Gerhard Reischl, Advocate-General

Legislation: Article 86 EEC (now Article 102 TFEU)

Facts: Continental Can Co. Inc. was an American company which manufactured metal packages and packaging materials of paper and plastic, and machines for manufacturing and using those packaging materials. In 1969, it acquired an 85.5% share of Schmalbach-Lubeca-Werke AG, a German company which manufactured containers and sealing machines. In the following year, Continental Can entered into an agreement with Thomassen & Drijver-Verblijfa N.V., a Dutch company which manufactured of metal containers and other packaging. In accordance with the agreement, Continental Can set up Europemballage Corporation, transferred its holding in Schmalbach to Europemballage and then arranged for Europemballage to make an offer to the shareholders of Thomassen to buy their shares which was supported by the management of Thomassen. It succeeded in acquiring 91.07% of Thomassen. The Commission found that Continental Can, through Schmalbach-Lubeca-Werke AG, occupied a dominant position in the markets in light containers for preserved meat and for preserved fish and in the market for metal closures for glass containers. It found that Continental Can had abused its dominant position in these markets by acquiring Thomassen and thereby almost eliminating competition.

JUDGMENT

32. In considering the dominant position of Schmalbach-Lubeca-Werke and the consequences of the merger in question, the delimination of the market concerned is of crucial importance, for the possibilities of competition can only be considered in the light of the characteristics of the products in question, which reveal them to be particularly suited to satisfying a constant demand and interchangeable with other products only to a small extent.

33. In this respect the grounds of the decision deal successively, in Sections 5 to 7 of the second part, with a "market for light containers for preserved meat" , a "market for light containers for preserved fish" and a "market for metal closures for the canning industry, apart from crown corks" , all three of which are alleged to be dominated by Schmalbach-Lubeca-Werke and in which the merger in question is alleged to threaten to eliminate competition. Nevertheless, the decision does not state in detail the peculiarities which distinguish these three markets from one another and therefore necessitate their separate treatment. Nor is it stated by what peculiarities these three markets are distinguished from the general market for light metal containers, especially the market for metal containers for canned fruit and vegetables, condensed milk, olive oil, fruit juices and toilet preparations. However, it can be assumed that the products in question have a special market only if they can be individualised not only by the mere fact that they are used for packaging certain products but also by special production characteristics which give them a specific suitability for this purpose. Accordingly, a dominant position on the market for light metal containers for meat and fish cannot be decisive in so far as it is not proved that competitors in other fields in the market for light metal containers cannot, by a mere adaptation, enter this market with sufficient strength to form a serious counterweight.

 Alert

34. Moreover, the decision itself contains grounds that give reason to doubt whether the three markets must be regarded separately from other markets for light metal containers but on the contrary point to the conclusion that they are parts of a larger market. In the first part of the motivation where the decision deals, in Section J, with the most important competitors of Schmalbach-Lubeca-Werke in Germany and of Thomassen & Drijver-Verblifa in the Benelux states, it mentions a German undertaking which has a bigger share in the production of light metal containers for canned fruit and vegetables than Schmalbach-Lubeca-Werke, and another undertaking which meets 38 to 40 per cent. of the German demand for crown corks. This seems to confirm that the output for metal cans for tinned meat and fish cannot be considered separately from the metal can output for other purposes and that when considering the output of metal closures crown corks cannot be ignored. Furthermore, in dealing with the possibilities for substitution competition in Section 16 of part II, the decision is not confined to the three "markets" in question but also deals with the market in light metal containers for other purposes. In this respect it states that these containers can be replaced by containers made of other materials only to a limited extent. The fact that the Commission was unable to persist with this contention in view of the facts submitted by the applicant companies in the proceedings in itself shows how necessary it is to define sufficiently accurately the market to be considered, so that the relative strength of the undertakings in such a market can be assessed.

35. Since the decision does not contain any data with regard to the special characteristics whereby metal containers for canned meat and fish and metal closures for the canning industry, apart from crown corks, are alleged to have their own markets, which can be dominated by the manufacturer with the largest share of this market, the decision is tainted by a fundamental uncertainty which affects the other findings from which the decision deduces the absence of actual or potential competition in the relevant market...

The Court of Justice then provided examples of contradictions in the Commission's reasoning before concluding that:

37. It follows from all these considerations that the decision has not sufficiently explained the facts and appraisals on which it is based. It must therefore be annulled.

6.1.2 Relevant Geographic Market

Alongside the RPM, it is also necessary to establish the geographical area of the relevant market. Under Article 102 TFEU, the relevant market must be "...within the common market or a substantial part of it." The requirements for determining the RGM were considered by the Court of Justice in:

United Brands Company and United Brands Continentaal BV v Commission (Case 27/76) [1978] 1 CMLR 429

Facts: Having decided the RPM as discussed above the Court of Justice moved on to discuss the RGM.

Legislation: Article 86 EEC Treaty (now Article 102 TFEU)

JUDGMENT

36. The Commission has taken the Federal Republic of Germany, Denmark, Ireland, the Netherlands and the BLEU [the Belgium-Luxembourg Economic Union] as the geographic market and it is in respect of this market that it is necessary to consider whether UBC has the power to hinder effective competition.

37. It takes the view that the economic conditions in this part of the community allow importer/distributors of bananas to market their products there in the ordinary course without there being any significant economic barriers for UBC to overcome compared with other importer/distributors.

38. The other member states of the Community (France, Italy, the United Kingdom) must however be excluded from this geographic definition of the market notwithstanding the significant presence of UBC in these states, because of the special circumstances relating to import arrangements and trading conditions and the fact that bananas of various types and origin are sold there.

39. The applicant points out that the geographic market where an undertaking's economic and commercial power is taken into consideration should only comprise areas where the conditions of competition are homogeneous.

40. Although the commission had good reason to exclude France, Italy and the United Kingdom from the said market it failed to take account of the differences in the conditions of competition in the other member states which should have led it to come to the same conclusions with regard to the latter as it came to in the case of the three countries referred to above.

41. In fact three substantially different systems of customs duty apply in the member states concerned: a zero tariff in Germany covering a banana quota which meets most of this country's requirements, a transitional tariff in Ireland and Denmark and the common Customs Tariff of 20% for imports into Benelux.

42. The Commission has not either taken account of the consumer habits of the member states concerned (the annual consumption of fresh fruits *per capita* in Germany is equal to 2.5 times that of Ireland and twice that of Denmark), differing commercial patterns, concentrations and monetary points of view.

43. The applicant draws the conclusion from all these findings that the geographic market taken by the Commission includes areas in which the conditions of competition are so different that they cannot be considered as constituting a single market.

44. The conditions for the application of Article 86 to an undertaking in a dominant position presuppose the clear delimitation of the substantial part of the common market in which it may be able to engage in abuses which hinder effective competition and this is an area where the objective conditions of competition applying to the product in question must be the same for all traders. Alert

45. The community has not established a common organization of the agricultural market in bananas.

46. Consequently import arrangements vary considerably from one member state to another and reflect a specific commercial policy peculiar to the states concerned.

47. This explains why for example the French market owing to its national organization is restricted upstream by a particular import arrangement and obstructed downstream by a retail price monitored by the administration.

48. This market, in addition to adopting certain measures relating to a "target price" ("prix objectif") fixed each year and to packaging and grading standards and the minimum qualities required, reserves about two thirds of the market for the production of the overseas departments and one third to that of certain countries enjoying preferential relations with France (Ivory Coast, Madagascar, Cameroon) the bananas whereof are imported duty- free, and it includes a system the running of which is entrusted to the "comite interprofessionnel bananier" ("C.I.B.").

49. The United Kingdom market enjoys "commonwealth preferences", a system of which the main feature is the maintenance of a level of production favouring the developing countries of the commonwealth and of a price paid to the associations of producers directly linked to the selling price of the green banana charged in the united kingdom.

50. On the Italian market, since the abolition in 1965 of the state monopoly responsible for marketing bananas, a national system of quota restrictions has been introduced, the ministry for shipping and the exchange control office supervising the imports and the charter parties relating to the foreign ships which carry the bananas.

51. The effect of the national organization of these three markets is that the applicant's bananas do not compete on equal terms with the other bananas sold in these states which benefit from a preferential system and the Commission was right to exclude these three national markets from the geographic market under consideration.

52. On the other hand the six other states are markets which are completely free, although the applicable tariff provisions and transport costs are of necessity different but not discriminatory, and in which the conditions of competition are the same for all.

53. From the standpoint of being able to engage in free competition these six states form an area which is sufficiently homogeneous to be considered in its entirety. Alert

54. UBC has arranged for its subsidiary in Rotterdam - UBCBV - to market its products. UBCBV is for this purpose a single centre for the whole of this part of the community.

55. Transport costs do not in fact stand in the way of the distribution policy chosen by UBC which consists in selling F.O.R. Rotterdam and Bremerhaven, the two ports where the bananas are unloaded.

56. These are factors which go to make relevant market a single market.

57. It follows from all these considerations that the geographic market as determined by the Commission which constitutes a substantial part of the common market must be regarded as the relevant market for the purpose of determining whether the applicant may be in a dominant position.

Thus, the Court of Justice accepted in *United Brands* that the RGM must be an area in which the conditions of competition are sufficiently homogenous when considered in its entirely. This is also found in the definition of the RGM provided by the Commission in its 'Notice on the Definition of Relevant Market for the Purposes of Community Competition Law' (para 8). The Commission's assessment may involve a form of the SSNIP test which focuses on whether the parties would switch their orders to companies located elsewhere in the short term and at a negligible cost in response to relative changes in prices (see para 29).

Whether or not the RGM is a substantial part of the common market may not necessarily be simply a question of the size of the surface area. It will depend on the context of the RPM:

Sealink/B & I Holyhead: Interim Measures ('Sealink I') [1992] 5 CMLR 255

Legislation: Article 86 EEC (now Article 102 TFEU)

Facts: Sealink Harbours Ltd ('SHL') was the owner and operator of the port of Holyhead in the United Kingdom. Sealink Steana Line Ltd ('SSL') operated two ferries from Holyhead. Both SHL and SSL were part of the Stena Group controlled by Stena Line AB. The other ferry operator at Holyhead was B&I Line Plc which operated one ferry. It had a berth in the outer harbour. Each of SSL's ferries had to sail past this berth to reach their own berths in the inner harbour. If either of these ferries was to pass the berth whilst B&I's ferry was moored there, the turbulence caused to the water would make it necessary for the B&I ferry to disengage its linkspan, thereby causing delay and disruption to the process of loading and unloading passengers and vehicles from that ferry. B&I complained that SSL intended to introduce a new timetable, with the approval of SHL, which would seriously disrupt B&I's ferry service by causing SSL's ferries to pass by twice while the B&I ferry was moored at its berth. It asked the Commission to adopt interim measures to prevent the implementation of the timetable on the ground that SSL and SHL were jointly abusing a dominant position. SSL and SHL are jointly referred to in the Commission's decision as 'Sealink'.

DECISION

36. To determine whether an undertaking is dominant, it is necessary to identify the "relevant market", i.e., the relevant product, geographical and service markets in which to assess the market power or the allegedly dominant undertaking.

37. The essence of the complaint concerns, the use of the port of Holyhead, and discrimination in the provision of port services at that port which will lead to the strengthening of Sealink's position on the market for the provision of maritime transport services on the short sea routes between Great Britain and Ireland.

38. The short sea routes tor multi-purpose ferries between Great Britain and Ireland are as follows:

    a) the "northern corridor", between the ports of Androssan, Stranraer, Heysham, and Fleetwood in Great Britain and Larne, Belfast and Warrenpoint in Northern Ireland.

    b) the "central corridor" route between Liverpool and Holyhead in England and Wales respectively, and Dublin and Dun Laoghaire in Ireland; and

    c) the "Southern corridor" routes between Fishguard, Pembroke and Swansea in Wales and Rosslare and Cork in Ireland.

39. The relevant market in this case is the market for the provision of port facilities for passenger and vehicle ferry services on the central corridor routes between the United Kingdom and Ireland. The port of Holyhead is the only port now serving this market on the British side, giving Sealink, in its capacity as port authority, a dominant position. The abuse alleged is discriminatory provision of port services by Sealink as port authority in allowing schedule changes of its ferry services which will result in disruption to B&I's services, thus imposing a competitive disadvantage on that company. Although freight is part of the operations of multi-purpose ferry services, the disruption alleged by B&I does not relate so much to this part of the service as to the passenger and the vehicle ferry services. Therefore it is not relevant that Liverpool, the nearest alternative port to Holyhead, although it presently does not have any passenger ferry services operating from it, is a competitor on the roll-on/roll-off ferry market. Potential competition from Liverpool does not constrain the market power of Sealink at Holyhead.

40. Further, even if there were passenger ferry services operating from Liverpool, the sea journey from Dublin to Liverpool is about four hours longer than the Dublin-Holyhead route, and thus the Liverpool port is not substitutable for vehicle and passenger ferry services. B&I itself operated a passenger ferry service on the Liverpool route in the past but was forced to abandon it due to the small number of customers using the route. Hence, in the present circumstances, B&I could not, if they wished to run multi-purpose ferry services on the central corridor at a port other than Holyhead, do so without increasing the time of the crossing or building a new port themselves.

The port of Holyhead constitutes a substantial part of the common market because it is a port providing one of the main links between two Member States, more especially it provides the direct link between Great Britain and the capital city of Ireland. It should also be noted that this is, at least for passenger and cars, the most popular ferry route between Ireland and Great Britain.

The Commission granted the interim measure sought on the ground that a *prima facie* case had been made out that Sealink had abused this dominant position. Sealink not only owned the port (as SHL) but it also used it (as SSL). The port was a facility which competitors had to have access to in order to be able to provide their ferry services. It was an abuse for Sealink, in these circumstances, to change the schedules in a manner which suited its own commercial interests but which put B&I, its competitor, at a competitive disadvantage by disrupting its operations without any relevant objective justification.

The approach taken by the Commission in *Sealink* was echoed, albeit in much more succinct terms, by Advocate General Van Gerven and the Court of Justice in:

Merci Convenzionali Porto di Genova SpA v Siderurgica Gabrielli SpA (Case C-179/90) [1991] ECR I-5889

Legislation: Articles 48, 86 and 90(1) EEC (now Articles 45, 102 and 106(1) TFEU respectively)

Facts: Italian law reserved all dock work within Italian sea ports, including the loading, unloading, transhipment, storage and general movement of goods or material of any kind within the ports, to dock-work companies and dock workers affiliated to them. It also granted to dock-work undertakings the exclusive right to organise dock work on behalf of third persons in Italian ports. Merci Convenzionali Porto di Genova SpA was the dock-work undertaking in the port of Genoa. It was asked by Siderurgica Gabrielli SpA to organise the unloading of a consignment of steel. Merci sought to do so by arranging for the Compagnia Unica Lavoratori Merci Varie del Porto di Genova, the dock-work company for the port of Genoa, to unload the steel. However, Compagnia was prevented from performing this task for some months by a long series of strikes by its workforce. Siderurgica brought an action before the Italian courts for delivery of the consignment, compensation and the reimbursement of charges it had paid. The Italian court made a preliminary reference to the Court of Justice concerning the effect of Article 90(1) EEC (now Article 106(1) TFEU), which prohibits Member States from enacting or maintaining in force any measure contrary to the rules contained in the Treaty. One such rule raised in the reference was Article 86 EEC (now Article 102 TFEU).

ADVOCATE GENERAL VAN GERVEN

17.   Under Article 86 of the EEC Treaty, any abuse by one or more undertaking of a dominant position within the common market or in a substantial part of it is prohibited as incompatible with the common market in so far as it may affect trade between Member States. In this case, as far as Merci is concerned, the market in question is the market of organizing for third parties dock work with

regard to ordinary freight in the Port of Genoa, whilst for Compagnia the market in question is that of the actual performance of such dock work.

Of course it is for the national court to decide whether these markets may be regarded as constituting a substantial part of the common market. However, it is clear from the documents before the Court that, in view of the scale of dock work with regard to ordinary freight organized on behalf of third parties and performed there, the Port of Genoa is amongst the most important in the Community and is the most important in Italy and that, in view of its situation and infrastructure, users of the port often have no other choice than to use the Port of Genoa. These are, in my view, serious indications that the two markets referred to, which are, moreover, closely linked together since they relate to the same dock work, are sufficiently important to be regarded as a substantial part of the common market.

JUDGMENT

14. In the second place, as to the existence of exclusive rights, it should be stated first that with regard to the interpretation of Article 86 of the Treaty the Court has consistently held that an undertaking having a statutory monopoly over a substantial part of the common market may be regarded as having a dominant position within the meaning of Article 86 of the Treaty (see the judgments in Case C-41/90 *Hoefner and Elser v Macrotron* [1991] ECR I-1979, paragraph 28; Case C-260/89 *ERT v DEP* [1991] ECR I-2925, paragraph 31).

15. As regards the definition of the market in question, it may be seen from the order for reference that it is that of the organization on behalf of third persons of dock work relating to ordinary freight in the Port of Genoa and the performance of such work. Regard being had in particular to the volume of traffic in that port and its importance in relation to maritime import and export operations as a whole in the Member State concerned, that market may be regarded as constituting a substantial part of the common market.

 Alert

This left the Court of Justice to address the question of abuse. It held that the Italian law had created a situation in which the dock-work undertakings and dock-work companies were liable to be induced to commit certain abuses of that dominant position. This was contrary to Article 86 EEC (now Article 102 TFEU).

6.1.3 Relevant Temporal Market

The temporal market embodies the relevant market's time dimensions. These are often treated as part of the RPM and RGM. For example, the Commission did not treat time as a distinct dimension of the relevant market in its 'Notice on the Definition of Relevant Market for the Purposes of Community Competition Law' [1997] OJ C372/5. Nevertheless, time can be significant. Some examples of this have been provided by the United Kingdom's Office of Fair Trading which has been responsible for enforcing Article 102 TFEU in the United Kingdom in its capacity as the National Competition Authority:

Office of Fair Trading, *Market Definition — Understanding Competition Law* (2004) OFT403

Temporal Markets

5.1.　A third possible dimension to market definition is time. Examples of how the timing of production and purchasing can affect markets include:

- peak and off peak services. This can be a factor in transport services or utilities such as electricity supply

- seasonal variations, such as summer versus winter months, and

- innovation/inter-generational products. Customers may defer expenditure on present products because they believe innovation will soon produce better products or because they own an earlier version of the product, which they consider to be a close substitute for the current generation.

5.2.　A time dimension might be appropriate where:

- it is not possible for customers to substitute between time periods. For example, peak customers might not view peak and off peak train tickets as substitutes, and

- suppliers cannot substitute between time periods. For example, capacity to produce fruit may vary between time periods and it may not be possible to store fruit from one period to another.

5.3.　To some extent, the time dimension is simply an extension of the product dimension: i.e. the product can be defined as the supply of train services at a certain time of day.

One particularly good example of how the temporal dimensions of a market can be significant in their own right for shaping that market is the following case which concerned the effect of the OPEC oil crisis on the market in petrol in the Netherlands over the four months in which the crisis lasted:

***ABG Oil Companies Operating in the Netherlands* (Decision 77/327/EEC) [1977] OJ L 117/1**

Legislation: Article 86 EEC (now Article 102 TFEU)

Facts: Benzine en Petroleum Handelsmaatschappij BV ('BP') was engaged in the production of petrol in the Netherlands. Aardolie Belangen Gemeenschap BV ('ABG') was a purchasing co-operative of 19 members of the AVIA group in the Netherlands. BP had supplied petrol to ABG under a contract until 1972 when BP had exercised a clause entitling it to cancel the contract with six months' notice. However, BP continued to act as ABG's principal supplier whilst the two parties sought to reach an agreement under which BP would make refining capacity available to ABG. At that time, BP held 26% of the refinery capacity in the Netherlands. In November 1973, the OPEC oil crisis began and continued until March 1974. The crisis was caused by members of the Organization of Petroleum Exporting Countries ('OPEC') increasing the price of crude oil whilst reducing production. Meanwhile, the Arab members of OPEC had imposed an embargo on shipments to states which had supported Israel during the Yom Kippur war in the previous month. One of the states targeted by the embargo was the Netherlands. By December, shipments of crude oil had dropped to 50% of their October level. BP responded by reducing deliveries of petrol to its customers. ABG complained to the Commission that BP had reduced its deliveries to ABG to a substantially greater extent than it had to other companies.

The Commission found that the market in petrol ('motor spirit') had been transformed during the OPEC oil crisis to the extent that it placed BP and other companies in a dominant position for that period in relation to their customers:

DECISION

The market under consideration is that of motor spirit.

The general economic scene was set towards 1 November 1973 with the outbreak of the oil crisis, which was caused by a simultaneous reduction in the supply of oil offered on the world market combined with a substantial increase in the price demanded for it.

In this situation, the only people who still had access to oil supplies at economically viable prices were the large international oil companies refining or having oil refined in the Netherlands. This was because of their special relationships with the oil-producing countries of the Middle East, their integrated structures and the multinational nature of their installations and organizations.

Such a sudden shortage, especially one that was not brought about by economic considerations, led to a restriction of both actual and potential competition among the small group of companies concerned, a restriction that was particularly marked at the level of distribution.

The general fear of shortage, the sudden reduction in supplies of oil offered and the fact that the maximum prices for motor spirit fixed by the Dutch government were below international prices meant that the independent firms in the Netherlands could only obtain supplies from the world market at prices giving rise to losses; hence they could no longer import petroleum products in large quantities without endangering their longer-term survival. Imports were no longer available on the Dutch market and the independent buyers could only obtain their supplies from companies with refineries in the Netherlands. Thus the relevant market for this case is the Netherlands, which constitutes a substantial part of the common market.

Economic restrictions such as existed in the Netherlands during the oil crisis can substantially alter existing commercial relations between suppliers who have a substantial share of the market and quantities available and their customers. For reasons completely outside the control of the normal suppliers, their customers can become completely dependent on them for the supply of scare products. Thus, while the situation continues, the suppliers are placed in a dominant position in respect of their normal customers.

With the general shortage of supplies all the oil companies were faced with the same problem, that of maintaining supplies to their regular customers. Thus they were not able to make up the deficiencies of the other companies with substantial market shares and they were in no way in competition with each other to supply each others customers.

In the prevailing circumstances each of these companies found itself in a dominant position relative to its customers.

The Commission moved on to conclude that BP had abused this dominant position in relation to ABG by cutting back supplies to ABG far more sharply than it had to other customers. This difference in the treatment of a regular, long-standing and substantial customer was not objectively based and was clearly discrimination.

BP applied to the Court of Justice for the decision to be annulled in:

Benzine en Petroleum Handelsmaatschappij BV v Commission (Case 77/77) [1978] ECR 1513 ('*ABG Oil*')

Legislation: Article 86 EEC (now Article 102 TFEU)

Facts: See above

Advocate General Warner severely criticised the Commission's analysis. However, the Court of Justice chose to proceed on the supposition that BP did hold a dominant position during the crisis:

JUDGMENT

16. The contested decision states that in this matter there existed a dominant position not only on the part of BP relative to its customers but also on that of each of the large international oil companies refining or having refining done for them in the Netherlands relative each to its own customers.

17. The reasons given for this conclusion are based essentially on considerations of a general nature relating to the conditions of the whole of the Netherlands market during the crisis as regards the supply of petroleum products and the state of commercial relations, which, in a market such as this one, inevitably arise between "suppliers who have a substantial share of the market and quantities available and their customers".

18. The first question to be examined is whether, on the supposition that special market conditions such as those in this case did in fact ensure a dominant position in the Netherlands for the large oil companies established there as against their respective customers, the factual and legal circumstances on which the commission relies to characterize in particular the individual conduct of BP during the crisis make it possible to consider that conduct as an abuse within the meaning of article 86 of the treaty.

 Alert

The Court chose to annul the Commission's decision on the ground that BP had not abused its position. ABG had ceased to be a contractual customer of BP in 1972 and had become an occasional customer. The Commission should not have compared ABG to a traditional customer of BP and thereby accused BP of treating ABG less favourably than its other traditional customers.

6.1.4 Establishing Dominance

The Court of Justice defined dominance in:

***United Brands Company and United Brands Continentaal BV v Commission* (Case 27/76) [1978] CMLR 429**

Facts: see earlier.

Legislation: Article 86 EEC (now Article 102 TFEU)

In the excerpt: Article 3(f) EEC is the predecessor of Article 3(1)(b) TFEU.

JUDGMENT

63. Article 86 is an application of the general objective of the activities of the community laid down by article 3(f) of the treaty: the institution of a system ensuring that competition in the common market is not distorted.

64. This article prohibits any abuse by an undertaking of a dominant position in a substantial part of the common market in so far as it may affect trade between member states.

65. The dominant position referred to in this article relates to a position of economic strength enjoyed by an undertaking which enables it to prevent effective competition being maintained on the relevant market by giving it the power to behave to an appreciable extent independently of its competitors, customers and ultimately of its consumers.

 Alert

66. In general a dominant position derives from a combination of several factors which, taken separately, are not necessarily determinative.

67. In order to find out whether UBC is an undertaking in a dominant position on the relevant market it is necessary first of all to examine its structure and then the situation on the said market as far as competition is concerned.

68. In doing so it may be advisable to take account if need be of the facts put forward as acts amounting to abuses without necessarily having to acknowledge that they are abuses.

The Court of Justice subsequently added to this definition in the following case.

Hoffman-La-Roche & Co v Commission (Case 85/76) [1979] 3 CMLR 211

Panel: Kutscher CJ; Mertens de Wilmars and Lord Mackenzie Stuart PPC; Donner, Pescatore, Sørensen, O'Keeffe, Bosco and Touffait JJ, Herr Gerhard Reischl, Advocate-General

Legislation: Article 86 EEC (now Article 102 TFEU)

In the excerpt: Article 3(f) EEC is the predecessor of Article 3(1)(b) TFEU

Facts: Hoffmann-La-Roche produced vitamins. The Commission found that Hoffman-La-Roche held a dominant position in the markets for certain vitamins and accused the company of abusing that position by entering into exclusive agreements or agreements which provided discounts on arbitrary grounds rather than justifiable grounds such as the quantity of goods ordered.

JUDGMENT

38. Article 86 is an application of the general objective of the activities of the community laid down by Article 3(f) of the treaty namely, the institution of a system ensuring that competition in the common market is not distorted.

Article 86 prohibits any abuse by an undertaking of a dominant position in a substantial part of the common market in so far as it may affect trade between member states.

The dominant position thus referred to relates to a position of economic strength enjoyed by an undertaking which enables it to prevent effective competition being maintained on the relevant market by affording it the power to behave to an appreciable extent independently of its competitors, its customers and ultimately of the consumers.

 Alert

39. Such a position does not preclude some competition, which it does where there is a monopoly or a quasi-monopoly, but enables the undertaking which profits by it, if not to determine, at least to have an appreciable influence on the conditions under which that competition will develop, and in any case to act largely in disregard of it so long as such conduct does not operate to its detriment.

A dominant position must also be distinguished from parallel courses of conduct which are peculiar to oligopolies in that in an oligopoly the courses of conduct interact, while in the case of an undertaking occupying a dominant position the conduct of the undertaking which derives profits from that position is to a great extent determined unilaterally.

The existence of a dominant position may derive from several factors which, taken separately, are not necessarily determinative but among these factors a highly important one is the existence of very large market shares.

40. A substantial market share as evidence of the existence of a dominant position is not a constant factor and its importance varies from market to market according to the structure of these markets, especially as far as production, supply and demand are concerned.

Even though each group of vitamins constitutes a separate market, these different markets, as has emerged from the examination of their structure, nevertheless have a sufficient number of features in common to make it possible for the same criteria to be applied to them as far as concerns the importance of the market shares for the purpose of determining whether there is a dominant position or not.

41. Furthermore although the importance of the market shares may vary from one market to another the view may legitimately be taken that very large shares are in themselves, and save in exceptional circumstances, evidence of the existence of a dominant position.

> An undertaking which has a very large market share and holds it for some time, by means of the volume of production and the scale of the supply which it stands for – without those having much smaller market shares being able to meet rapidly the demand from those who would like to break away from the undertaking which has the largest market share - is by virtue of that share in a position of strength which makes it an unavoidable trading partner and which, already because of this secures for it, at the very least during relatively long periods, that freedom of action which is the special feature of a dominant position.

Dominance is often evident therefore either from the substantial market share of an undertaking or from the barriers to entry into that market faced by potential competitors.

6.2 Abuse of Dominance

Dominant undertakings are deemed to have a special responsibility not to distort genuine competition. The Court of Justice emphasised this in:

Nederlandsche Banden – Industrie Michelin NV v Commission (Case 322/81) [1985] 1 CMLR 282

Facts: See earlier. Michelin NV challenged the Commission's decision that it had a dominant position in the market for replacement tyres for lorries, buses and similar vehicles which it was abusing. One of Michelin NV's objections maintained that the lead which the Michelin group had over its competitors in investment and research and the special extent of its range of products should not have been taken into account in determining whether or not Michelin NV had a dominant position as this effectively penalised it for the quality of its products and services. The Court of Justice rejected this objection:

JUDGMENT

57. It is not possible to uphold the objections made against those arguments by Michelin NV, supported on this point by the French government, that Michelin NV is thus penalized for the quality of its products and services. A finding that an undertaking has a dominant position is not in itself a recrimination but simply means that, irrespective of the reasons for which it has such a dominant position, the undertaking concerned has a special responsibility not to allow its conduct to impair genuine undistorted competition on the common market.

Article 102 TFEU itself provides a list of forms of abuse. However, this list is not exhaustive. The Court of Justice has found particular types of behaviour to constitute abuse.

6.2.1 Refusal to Supply

United Brands Company and United Brands Continentaal BV v Commission (Case 27/76) [1978] CMLR 429

Facts: see earlier.

Legislation: Article 86 EEC Treaty (now Article 102 TFEU)

JUDGMENT

151. The court's examination must be limited to the clause relating to the prohibition of the resale of green bananas in the form in which it was notified to the Commission on 15 November 1968 without it being necessary to consider the clause as drawn up by UBC on 31 January 1976, that is to say at a date subsequent to the Commission's decision.

152. The clause applied in Belgium, Denmark and the Netherlands, in so far as it has been drawn up in writing, prohibited the resale of bananas while still green whether branded or unbranded and even between ripeners of chiquita bananas.

153. Since UBC thought it should state in the circular letter of 31 January 1976, which it sent to all ripener/distributors including those established in Germany, that the clause had not been put in writing for Germany, it thereby impliedly acknowledges that the said clause was in force on the German market, since it had clearly been implied or mentioned orally.

154. Under the terms of the clause UBC required their customers to ensure forthwith that the bananas in their possession are not resold to foreign dealers; it had imposed the same requirement on its foreign customers as far as the Netherlands are concerned. It would not hesitate to take such steps as it deems to be necessary if the foregoing is not complied with in some way or other '.

155. This wording implies that UBC, far from rejecting the idea of imposing sanctions on duly appointed ripener/distributors which do not comply with its directions, held out this possibility as a threat.

156. Moreover Olesen unquestionably experienced the harsh effects of this clause after UBC refused to supply it and it wanted to obtain supplies of chiquita bananas from Scipio and the duly appointed Danish distributors.

157. To impose on the ripener the obligation not to resell bananas so long as he has not had them ripened and to cut down the operations of such a ripener to contacts only with retailers is a restriction of competition.

158. Although it is commendable and lawful to pursue a policy of quality, especially by choosing sellers according to objective criteria relating to the qualifications of the seller, his staff and his facilities, such a practice can only be justified if it does not raise obstacles, the effect of which goes beyond the objective to be attained.

159. In this case, although these conditions for selection have been laid down in a way which is objective and not discriminatory, the prohibition on resale imposed upon duly appointed chiquita ripeners and the prohibition of the resale of unbranded bananas - even if the perishable nature of the banana in practice restricted the opportunities of reselling to the duration of a specific period of time – when without any doubt an abuse of the dominant position since they limit markets to the prejudice of consumers and affects trade between member states, in particular by partitioning national markets.

 Alert

160. Thus UBC's organization of the market confined the ripeners to the role of suppliers of the local market and prevented them from developing their capacity to trade vis-à-vis UBC, which moreover tightened its economic hold on them by supplying less goods than they ordered.

161. It follows from all these considerations that the clause at issue forbidding the sale of green bananas infringes Article 86 of the treaty.

162. On this point the contested decision is therefore justified.

Microsoft v Commission (Case T-201/04) [2005] 4 CMLR 5

Panel: Vesterdorf P, Jaeger, Pirrung, García-Valdecasas, Tiili, Azizi, Cooke, AWH Meij, Norwood, Martins Ribeiro, Wiszniewska-Białecka, Vadapalas and Labucka, JJ

Legislation: Article 82 EC (now Article 102 TFEU)

Facts: In this case the Court of First Instance reviewed the Decision of the Commission in relation to refusal to supply interoperability information and also abuse of dominance in the market for media players. The Court of First Instance went on to uphold the decision of the Commission in respect of all but one element, which is not relevant to matters set out below. The summary of the Court of First Instance provides a useful overview of the potential abuse caused by refusal to supply and "tying", increasingly relevant matters with the growth of digital technology where one undertaking may need to make its software "plug in" to the software or hardware of a competitor.

JUDGMENT

III Abuse of a dominant position

A – Refusal to supply and authorise the use of interoperability information

 its refusal to supply its competitors with 'interoperability information' and to authorise the use of that information for the purpose of developing and distributing products competing with Microsoft's own products on the work group server operating systems market, between October 1998 and the date of notification of the contested decision (Article 2(a) of the contested decision). That conduct is described at recitals 546 to 791 to the contested decision.

37. For the purposes of the contested decision, 'interoperability information' is the 'complete and accurate specifications for all the protocols [implemented] in Windows work group server operating systems and ... used by Windows work group servers to deliver file and print services and group and user administrative services, including the Windows domain controller services, Active Directory services and "group Policy" services to Windows work group networks' (Article 1(1) of the contested decision).

38. 'Windows work group network' is defined as 'any group of Windows client PCs and Windows work group servers linked together via a computer network' (Article 1(7) of the contested decision).

39. A 'protocol' is defined as 'a set of rules of interconnection and interaction between various instances of Windows work group server operating systems and Windows client PC operating systems running on different computers in a Windows work group network' (Article 1(2) of the contested decision).

40. In the contested decision, the Commission emphasises that the refusal in question does not relate to Microsoft's 'source code', but only to specifications of the protocols concerned, that is to say, to a detailed description of what the software in question must achieve, in contrast to the implementations, consisting in the implementation of the code on the computer (recitals 24 and 569 to the contested decision). It states, in particular, that it 'does not contemplate ordering Microsoft to allow copying of Windows by third parties' (recital 572 to the contested decision).

41. The Commission further considers that Microsoft's refusal to Sun is part of a general pattern of conduct (recitals 573 to 577 to the contested decision). It also asserts that Microsoft's conduct involves a disruption of previous, higher levels of supply (recitals 578 to 584 to the contested decision), causes a risk of elimination of competition on the work group server operating systems (recitals 585 to 692 to the contested decision) and has a negative effect on technical development and on consumer welfare (recitals 693 to 708 to the contested decision).42   Last, the Commission rejects Microsoft's arguments that its refusal is objectively justified (recitals 709 to 778 to the contested decision)

B – Tying of the Windows client PC operating system and Windows Media Player

43. The second abusive conduct in which Microsoft is found to have engaged consists in the fact that from May 1999 to the date of notification of the contested decision Microsoft made the availability of the Windows client PC operating system conditional on the simultaneous acquisition of the Windows Media Player software (Article 2(b) of the contested decision). That conduct is described at recitals 792 to 989 to the contested decision.

44. In the contested decision, the Commission considers that that conduct satisfies the conditions for a finding of a tying abuse for the purposes of Article 82 EC (recitals 794 to 954 to the contested decision). First, it reiterates that Microsoft has a dominant position on the client PC operating systems market (recital 799 to the contested decision). Second, it considers that streaming media players and client PC operating systems constitute separate products (recitals 800 to 825 to the contested decision). Third, it asserts that Microsoft does not give consumers the opportunity to buy Windows without Windows Media Player (recitals 826 to 834 to the contested decision). Fourth, it contends that the tying in question restricts competition on the media players market (recitals 835 to 954 to the contested decision).

45. Last, the Commission rejects Microsoft's arguments to the effect that, first, the tying in question produces efficiency gains capable of offsetting the anti-competitive effects identified in the contested decision (recitals 955 to 970 to the

177

contested decision) and, second, Microsoft had no interest in 'anti-competitive' tying (recitals 971 to 977 to the contested decision).

Later in the decision the Court of First Instance reviewed the approach of the Commission in its interpretation of Article 82 EC (now Article 102 TFEU):

228. In the second place, the Court observes that the Commission assessed the degree of interoperability by reference to what, in its view, was necessary in order to enable developers of non-Microsoft work group server operating systems to remain viably on the market (see, in particular, footnote 712 and recital 779 to the contested decision).

229. The correctness of that approach is not open to dispute. Article 82 EC deals with the conduct of one or more economic operators involving the abuse of a position of economic strength which enables the operator concerned to hinder the maintenance of effective competition on the relevant market by allowing it to behave to an appreciable extent independently of its competitors, its customers and, ultimately, consumers (Joined Cases C-359/96 P and C-396/96 P *Compagnie maritime belge transports and Others v Commission* [2000] ECR I-1365, paragraph 34). Furthermore, whilst the finding of a dominant position does not in itself imply any criticism of the undertaking concerned, that undertaking has a special responsibility, irrespective of the causes of that position, not to allow its conduct to impair genuine undistorted competition on the common market (Case 322/81 *Michelin v Commission* [1983] ECR 3461, paragraph 57, and Case T-228/97 *Irish Sugar v Commission* [1999] ECR II-2969, paragraph 112). Should it be established in the present case that the existing degree of interoperability does not enable developers of non-Microsoft work group server operating systems to remain viably on the market for those operating systems, it follows that the maintenance of effective competition on that market is being hindered

6.2.2 Directly or Indirectly Imposing Unfair Prices

Hoffman-La-Roche & Co v Commission (Case 85/76) [1979] 3 CMLR 211

Facts: Having found Hoffman-La Roche to be dominant in the relevant market the Court of Justice considered whether the company had abused that dominance through exclusivity agreements and fidelity rebates.

Legislation: Article 86 EEC (now Article 102 TFEU)

JUDGMENT

80. According to the contested decision the applicant has abused its dominant position by concluding with 22 large purchasers of vitamins contracts of sale - about 30 (some of them moreover were renewals with or without amendments of a previous contract) - under which these purchasers undertook to obtain all or most of their requirements of vitamins or certain vitamins expressly mentioned

therein exclusively from Roche or which gave them an incentive to do so by including a promise of a discount which the Commission classifies as a fidelity rebate.

According to the Commission (recitals 22 to 24 of the contested decision) the exclusivity agreements and the fidelity rebates complained of are an abuse within the meaning of Article 86 of the treaty, on the one hand, because they distort competition between producers by depriving customers of the undertaking in a dominant position of the opportunity to choose their sources of supply and, on the other hand, because their effect was to apply dissimilar conditions to equivalent transactions with other trading partners, thereby placing them at a competitive disadvantage, in that Roche offers two purchasers two different prices for an identical quantity of the same product depending on whether these two buyers agree or not to forego obtaining their supplies from Roche's competitors.

81. The contracts at issue are for the sale of vitamins which belong to one or more of the groups in respect of which a dominant position has been found to exist to purchasers owning within the common market undertakings for which part or all of these vitamins are intended.

...

89. An undertaking which is in a dominant position on a market and ties purchasers - even if it does so at their request - by an obligation or promise on their part to obtain all or most of their requirements exclusively from the said undertaking abuses its dominant position within the meaning of article 86 of the treaty, whether the obligation in question is stipulated without further qualification or whether it is undertaken in consideration of the grant of a rebate.

 Alert

The same applies if the said undertaking, without tying the purchasers by a formal obligation, applies, either under the terms of agreements concluded with these purchasers or unilaterally, a system of fidelity rebates, that is to say discounts conditional on the customer's obtaining all or most of its requirements - whether the quantity of its purchases be large or small - from the undertaking in a dominant position.

90. Obligations of this kind to obtain supplies exclusively from a particular undertaking, whether or not they are in consideration of rebates or of the granting of fidelity rebates intended to give the purchaser an incentive to obtain his supplies exclusively from the undertaking in a dominant position, are incompatible with the objective of undistorted competition within the common market, because - unless there are exceptional circumstances which may make an agreement between undertakings in the context of article 81 and in particular of paragraph (3) of that article, permissible - they are not based on an economic transaction which justifies this burden or benefit but are designed to deprive the purchaser of or restrict his possible choices of sources of supply and to deny other producers access to the market.

The fidelity rebate, unlike quantity rebates exclusively linked with the volume of purchases from the producer concerned, is designed through the grant of a financial advantage to prevent customers from obtaining their supplies from competing producers.

Furthermore the effect of fidelity rebates is to apply dissimilar conditions to equivalent transactions with other trading parties in that two purchasers pay a different price for the same quantity of the same product depending on whether they obtain their supplies exclusively from the undertaking in a dominant position or have several sources of supply.

Finally these practices by an undertaking in a dominant position and especially on an expanding market tend to consolidate this position by means of a form of competition which is not based on the transactions effected and is therefore distorted.

The Court of Justice then went on to consider specific clauses in contracts with customers. Hoffman-La-Roche sought to argue that they merely allowed for rebates based on the quantity of purchases and so could be permissible. The Commission argued that the rebates were disguised fidelity rebates.

98. Although the contracts at issue contain elements which appear at first sight to be of a quantitative nature as far as concerns their connexion with the granting of a rebate on aggregate purchases, an examination of them however shows that they are in fact a specially worked out form of fidelity rebate.

99. In the first place it is noticeable that this particular form of rebate is incorporated in those very contracts in which the undertaking by the purchaser to obtain supplies was drawn up in the form which placed him under the least constraint, namely that the purchaser was to obtain 'most of his requirements', so that the purchaser concerned was left with considerable freedom of action.

The indeterminate nature of the undertaking thus worded is to a great extent offset by an estimate of annual requirements and by the granting of a rebate increasing in accordance with the percentage of the requirements which are met and this progressive rate is clearly a powerful incentive to obtain the maximum percentage of the said requirements from Roche.

100. This method of calculating the rebates differs from the granting of quantitative rebates, linked solely to the volume of purchases from the producers concerned in that the rebates at issue are not dependent on quantities fixed objectively and applicable to all possible purchasers but on estimates made, from case to case, for each customer according to the latter's presumed capacity of absorption, the objective which it is sought to attain being not the maximum quantity but the maximum requirements.

 Alert

101. Consequently the Commission was also right to regard the said contracts containing fidelity rebates as an abuse of a dominant position.

6.3 May Affect Inter-state Trade

All that is required is to show that the behaviour might affect interstate trade – the test is the same as for Article 101 TFEU.

Further Reading

Fuller, B: 'Economic Analysis of the Existence of a Dominant Position' [1979] 4 ELR 423

Turnbull, S: 'Barriers to Entry, Article 86 EC and the Abuse of a Dominant Position: An Economic Critique of European Community Competition Law' [1996] ECLR 96

Notes

Notes

Notes

Notes

Notes

Notes

Notes

Notes

Notes

Notes

Notes